Apple Confidential:

The Real Story of Apple Computer, Inc.

Apple Confidential:

The Real Story of Apple Computer, Inc.

Owen W. Linzmayer

No Starch Press
San Francisco, California

Publisher: William Pollock
Project Editor: Karol Jurado
Copy Editor: Carol Lombardi
Editor: Alane M. Bowling
Proofreader: Christine Sabooni
Page Layout: Owen W. Linzmayer
Cover Designer: Derek Yee
Indexer: Nancy Humphreys

Printed in the USA on recycled paper.
2 3 4 5 6 7 8 9 10-01 00 99

Apple Confidential: The Real Story of Apple Computer, Inc.
Copyright © 1999 by Owen W. Linzmayer

Distributed to the book trade in the North America by Publishers Group West, 1700 4th Street, Berekeley, CA 94710, (800) 788-3123 or (510) 528-1444.

For information on translations or book distributors outside the United States, please contact No Starch Press, 555 De Haro Street, Suite 250, San Francisco, CA 94107, (415) 863-9900, fax (415) 863-9950, info@nostarch.com, http://www.nostarch.com.

Library of Congress Cataloging-in-Publication Data
Linzmayer, Owen W.
      Apple confidential : the real story of Apple Computer, Inc. / Owen W. Linzmayer.
            p.   cm.
      Includes index.
      ISBN 1-886411-28-X (pbk. : alk. paper)
      1. Apple Computer, Inc.--History. 2. Computer industry--United States--History. I. Title.
HD9696.2.U64A674 1999
338.7'6100465--dc21   98-49132

Dedication

Dedicated to my wife, Alane, for her unwavering confidence in me and this book.

Acknowledgments

While the cover of this book bears my name alone, I could not have written it without the contributions of many others to whom I am deeply indebted: Jeff Alnwick, Gil Amelio, Ed Archer, Erik J. Barzeski, Peter Baum, Sandy Benett, Ken Bousquet, Alane M. Bowling, Richard L. Brandt, Christopher Breen, John Bukovinsky, Steve Capps, Sylvia Chevrier, Michael Collopy, Wayne Cooper, Greg Cornelison, David Thomas Craig, Marie D'Amico, Bruno Delessard, Karla Delgado, Donn Denman, Joel Dibble, Carol Elfstrom, Cheryl England, Rick English, Chris Espinosa, Daniel Fanton, Jonathan Fitch, Robert Frankston, Gordon Garb, Adele Goldberg, Joseph Graziano, John Greenleigh, Bill Griffis, Trevor Griffiths, Galen Gruman, Martin P. Haeberli, Rhona Hamilton, Mark Harlan, Trip Hawkins, Steve Hayden, Terry Hefferman, April Hill, Joe Holmes, Fred Huxham, Russ Ito, Michael Jamison, Camille Johnson, Sandy Jones, Raymond Kam, Cathy King, Cal Klepper, Daniel G. Kottke, Kathie Lentz, Marianne Lettieri, Steven Levy, Steve Lipson, Donna Loughlin, Alex Louie, John Lund, Alfred J. Mandel, Clifford T. Matthews, Doug McKenna, Joan Moreton, William Mosgrove, Dan Muse, Ike Nassi, Jai Nelson, Richard O'Neil, Tom Neumayr, Jeffery Newbury, Jane Oros, Carol Parcels, Ben Pang, Eric Perret, Audrey Pobre, Jef Raskin, David Reynolds, Gregory M. Robbins, Heidi Roizen, David Roots, Josh Rothleder, Ken Rothmuller, Sue Runfola, Steve Sakoman, Kevin Schoedel, Michael M. Scott, Andrew Shalit, Linda Siegel, Mark Simmons, Erica Stearns, Robert Stone, Kimberly Strop, Jeff Sullivan, Michael Swaine, Sylvia Tam, Marcio Luis Teixeira, Gordon Thygeson, Jeff Valvano, Charles West, Fabian West, and Steve Wozniak. Those are just the individuals who agreed to speak on the record. To everyone whose name I forgot to jot down or was asked not to publish, thank you, too.

Finally, thanks to everyone who has ever worked at Apple or any of the many fine third-party developers and manufacturers. Without you there would be no Macintosh, and the world of computing wouldn't be nearly as enjoyable.

Contents

Introduction

If you read only one book about Apple, make it *Apple Confidential*.

As a journalist covering Apple Computer since the early 1980s, I have read nearly everything ever written about the company. Rather than rehash old myths and repeat conventional wisdom, I've uncovered the truth about Apple by rummaging through forgotten archives, interviewing key players, and never taking anything at face value.

Apple Confidential chronicles the best and worst of the company's first two decades. Follow Apple as it grows from upstart media darling, becomes an industry-leading powerhouse, falters under a series of disastrous executive decisions, takes its licks as technology whipping boy, and rebounds to profitability after the return of legendary founder Steve Jobs.

No boring business case study, *Apple Confidential* is the only book* that tells the complete history of Apple through revealing stories, illustrations, and quotes, all backed by meticulous research and presented in an engaging format. I'm confident that you will find *Apple Confidential* as fascinating as it is factual.

Owen W. Linzmayer
San Francisco, California
OWL@Bigfoot.com
http://www.netcom.com/~owenink

*Some material in *Apple Confidential* originally appeared in my previous book, *The Mac Bathroom Reader,* but has been significantly revised and completely updated with an entirely new layout.

The Forgotten Founder

Thanks to a never-ending campaign by Apple's powerful public relations machine to protect the myths surrounding the company's origin, almost everyone believes that Apple was started in a garage by "the two Steves," Stephen Gary Wozniak, 25, and Steven Paul Jobs, 21. Actually, the operation began in a *bedroom* at 11161 Crist Drive in Los Altos (the house number changed to 2066 when the land was annexed from the county to the city in late 1983), where Jobs—after having dropped out of Reed College in Portland, Oregon—was living with his adoptive parents, Paul R. (a machinist at Spectra Physics) and Clara (a payroll clerk at Varian). That mere semantic distinction can be forgiven. When the bedroom became too crowded, the operation did indeed move to the garage.

When they adopted Steve (born February 24, 1955), Paul and Clara Jobs lived at 1758 45th Avenue in San Francisco's Sunset district. After five months, the family moved to South San Francisco and then Mountain View before settling in Los Altos. It wasn't until Steve was in his 30s that he met his birth mother. At that time he also learned he had a half-sister, writer Mona Simpson, who subsequently used Steve as a model for the main character in one of her recent books, *A Regular Guy*.

After moving out of Jobs' garage, Apple Computer rented suite B3 at 20833 Stevens Creek Boulevard in Cupertino, then built 10260 Bandley Drive, which became known as Bandley One when occupied on January 28, 1978.

Apple started life in "the garage" of Steve Jobs' parents on Crist Drive in Los Altos, California (inset: the exterior of the house as it is today).

When Apple was founded, Steve Wozniak lived at 1618 Edmonton Ave. in Sunnyvale and Ron Wayne lived at 1900 California St. in Mountain View.

The bigger story here is that the two Steves weren't alone in forming Apple. Just as Soviet propagandists doctored photos to remove party members who had fallen out of favor, Apple suffers from a convenient case of institutional amnesia by routinely ignoring the fact that when Apple was originally founded as a partnership on April Fools' Day 1976, there were three founders: Woz, Jobs, and a fellow by the name of Ronald Gerald Wayne, 41.

Courtesy of Ron Wayne

Ronald Gerald Wayne, Apple's forgotten founder, seen here in a passport photo from 1975 (imprint of USA Department of State seal still evident).

Jobs was freelancing at Atari in the early 1970s when founder Nolan Kay Bushnell hired Wayne as chief draftsman (badge #395) for the video game maker. Despite the difference in their ages, Jobs and Wayne became casual friends and would often have philosophical discussions on the ethics of making money. Desiring a tie-breaker in any potential conflicts with Woz, Jobs enticed Wayne to become a partner in Apple by offering him 10 percent interest in the company.

"Either I was going to be bankrupt or the richest man in the cemetery," Wayne recalls thinking. Since Apple was far from a sure thing, Wayne retained his day job at Atari and worked nights on the original Apple logo and documentation for the Apple I. Meanwhile, Jobs was hustling up customers. At a Homebrew Computer Club meeting (the club met monthly at the Stanford Linear Accelerator Center auditorium in Palo Alto), Jobs gave a demonstration of the Apple I to Paul Jay Terrell, who operated the Byte Shop—arguably the first retail computer store chain in the country, which opened its doors on December 8, 1975 (Terrell's birthday). Terrell was intrigued and asked Jobs to keep in touch.

The original Apple I (shown here in a custom-built wooden case) was little more than a circuit board to which customers were expected to add a case, power supply, monitor, and keyboard.

The next day, a barefooted Jobs dropped in on Terrell at his store in Mountain View and exclaimed, "I'm keeping in touch." To Jobs' utter amazement, Terrell agreed to buy 50 computers for $500 each, cash on delivery. There was only one catch to the $25,000 order: Terrell wanted fully assembled computers.

"[The Byte Shop order] was the biggest single episode in the company's history. Nothing in subsequent years was so great and so unexpected. It was not what we had intended to do."
Steve Wozniak

The Byte Shop at 1063 El Camino Real West in Mountain View, California, was the first retail computer store chain in the world and Apple's first big customer.

The trio had originally planned to produce bare circuit boards for $25 each and sell them for $50 to hobbyists who would populate them with the necessary chips and other parts. They didn't have the money necessary to buy all of the parts required to build 50 complete computers, but Jobs was undaunted. On April 6, he obtained a three-month $5,000 loan from Elmer and Allen J. Baum (one of Woz's co-workers at Hewlett-Packard), then convinced suppliers to extend 30 days' credit on $15,000 worth of parts.

The young, ambitious Jobs had no qualms about going into debt to fulfill the Byte Shop order, but the seasoned Wayne was anxious. He wasn't convinced Terrell would pay for the computers, and the partnership agreement meant that he had unlimited personal liability for any debts incurred by Apple. Just four years prior, Wayne underwent the emotionally painful experience of folding Siand, his own Las Vegas-based engineering firm. Wayne didn't want to risk another financial failure, so on April 12—less than two weeks after Apple's founding—he renounced his 10 percent interest for a one-time payment of $800. "I had already learned what gave me indigestion," explained Wayne years later. "If Apple had failed, I would have had bruises on top of bruises. Steve Jobs was an absolute whirlwind and I had lost the energy you need to ride whirlwinds."

Steve Wozniak (left) and Steve Jobs, showing off the Apple I motherboard that started it all.

Freed from the financial liabilities of the partnership agreement, Wayne spent his free time consulting on projects such as designing an enclosure for the Apple I. Meanwhile, Woz and Jobs got part-time assembly help from Bill Fernandez, who had originally introduced Jobs to Woz in 1968, as well as from Daniel G. Kottke, who had met Jobs at Reed College and had made a spiritual journey to India with him in 1974.

"Steve Wozniak looks like a Steiff Teddy bear on a maintenance dose of marshmallows."
Time *reporter* **Jay Cocks**

Paul Terrell went on to found Romox, Software Emporium, and Sorcerer Computer.

Everyone worked furiously to build the computers by hand. Terrell was a bit dismayed when Jobs showed up on the 29th day to deliver a batch of motherboards stuffed with components. When Terrell asked for "fully assembled" computers, he meant the whole works: a case, power supply, monitor, and keyboard. Nonetheless, Terrell kept his word and handed over the cash, allowing Apple to pay off its parts suppliers in the nick of time.

Jobs was excited. Apple had made roughly $8,000 profit, and he was planning to expand the business by going farther into debt with parts suppliers to build even more computers. Jobs' ambitious plans required more money than the Apple I orders were generating, so in August 1976, he approached his old Atari boss, Nolan Bushnell, who recommended he meet with Don Valentine of the venture capital firm Sequoia Capital. At the time, Valentine wasn't interested, but he in turn referred Jobs to Armas Clifford "Mike" Markkula Jr., 34, who had retired a year prior after making a small fortune on his stock options at chipmakers Fairchild Semiconductor and Intel.

"Why did you send me this renegade from the human race?"

*Venture capitalist **Don Valentine**, complaining about Jobs, then just a kid with ripped jeans and bare feet*

Markkula wrote several early software programs for the Apple II and freely distributed them under the alias Johnny Appleseed.

Courtesy of Michael Swaine

Armas Clifford "Mike" Markkula Jr. stepped in when Ron Wayne bailed out of Apple.

In November 1976, Markkula came out of retirement to help Jobs devise a business plan. With the Apple I computer boards being sold through just ten retail stores in the U.S., Markkula boldly set a goal for sales to grow to $500 million in ten years. Recognizing a chance to hitch a ride on a rocket that was about to take off, Markkula invested $92,000 of his own money and secured a $250,000 line of credit at Bank of America. Now properly funded, the three of them filed for incorporation of Apple Computer on January 3, 1977. To avoid any possible legal complications, in March the corporation purchased the partnership for $5,308.96 and Wayne was sent a check for a third of that amount to make certain he would have no future claim against the company. Wayne, who had walked away voluntarily for $800 less than a year ago, was thrilled to receive this unexpected windfall.

Jobs set the list price of the original 4K Apple I at $666.66 by doubling the cost of manufacturing, allowing dealers a 33.3 percent markup on the wholesale price of $500. Fundamentalist Christians were quick to complain that 666 was the "mark of the beast." Jobs blew these people off with a concocted story about how he had taken 7 (the mystical number seven), subtracted one (another mystical number), and arrived at a perfectly innocent price. Actually, Jobs wanted to charge $777, but Woz insisted that was too much.

Reflecting on the situation, Woz understands Wayne's decision to bail out early. "Steve had no money. I had no money, and the creditors were going to wind up coming to him for the money that was going to be owed. So he decided it was better to get out of it. At the time it was the right decision." To someone who was there to witness the events firsthand, it may have made sense, but in retrospect, it's hard for an outsider to see Wayne's decision as anything but a mistake of colossal proportions.

Granted, Wayne would surely have had to give up some of his interest in Apple as the firm grew. If Jobs' initial 45 percent stake in Apple translated into 7.5 million shares when the company went public in 1980, it's reasonable to assume that Wayne's 10 percent would have equalled more than 1.6 million shares. Following a two-for-one stock split on May 15, 1987, such a holding would have been worth approximately $244 million (not including dividends) when the stock peaked at $73.25 on April 12, 1991, and would still be worth over $42.5 million at $12.75 per share, the lowest price since then. Does Wayne ever regret relinquishing his supporting role in one of the greatest American business success stories ever told? Amazingly enough, 20 years later Wayne convincingly stated, "I have never had the slightest pangs of regret, because I made the best decision with the information available to me at the time. My contribution was not so great that I felt I had been diddled with in any way." A person of lesser character might be paralyzed with bitterness and self-doubt after walking away from such fame and fortune, but not Ron Wayne. He put it behind him and got on with his life.

Although Jobs tried over the years to convince Ron to return to Apple as an employee, Wayne continued working at Atari until 1978, at which point he took a job at Lawrence Livermore Labs. In 1980, Wayne opened a small store on Dempsey Street in Milpitas. Dealing in stamps, coins, and other collectibles, Wayne's Philatelics became so successful in just two months that he quit his job at Lawrence Livermore Labs. Following the collapse of the stamp market and two break-ins, Wayne closed the store in 1982 but continued operating the business out of his home. After a brief stint working on documentation and drafting for Scientific Technology Systems, in 1985 Wayne took a job working on slot machines at Thor Electronics of California. The Salinas-based manufacturer has since shifted its focus from slot machines to military electronics, and Ron Wayne continues to work for Thor as chief engineer from his home in Tucson, Arizona.

Woz and Jobs' first commercial venture was peddling illegal "blue boxes" designed by Woz based on information contained in the October 1971 issue of *Esquire*. These hand-held electronic circuits allowed phone calls to be made free of charge by emulating signals used by the phone company. Jobs supplied $40 in parts and sold the boxes door-to-door in UC Berkeley dorm rooms for $150, splitting the profits with Woz. In keeping with the spirit of "phone phreaking," Woz assumed the name Berkeley Blue and Jobs, Oaf Tobark. During one demonstration, Woz called the Vatican posing as Henry Kissinger and asked to speak to the pope. Informed that the pope was sleeping but would be awakened, Woz lost his nerve and hung up.

Who would have dreamed that these two would go from making pontifical prank calls to actually meeting world leaders? But that's exactly what happened. In February 1985, Woz and Jobs received the National Technology Medal from President Reagan at the White House. On May 19, 1993, Woz presented a PowerBook to Poland's President Lech Walesa, the former leader of the Solidarity movement. During the Clinton administration, Jobs slept in the White House's Lincoln Bedroom after making a $100,000 donation to the Democratic National Committee.

Woz met his first girlfriend through a popular Dial-a-Joke operation he was running from a bank of phones in his apartment. Normally his answering machine played a Polish joke that he had recorded earlier, but Woz happened to be home when Alice Robertson called, so he picked up the phone, identifying himself as Stanley Zeber Zenskanitsky. The two hit it off and were married soon after their playful start.

The Apple Logo

One of Ron Wayne's first duties after co-founding Apple was to design a logo for the infant company. The logo he created was a pen-and-ink drawing of Sir Isaac Newton leaning against an apple tree with a portion of a William Wordsworth poem (*Prelude, Book III, Residence of Cambridge*) running around the border: "Newton … A mind forever voyaging through strange seas of thought … alone."

> "One of the deep mysteries to me is our logo, the symbol of lust and knowledge, bitten into, all crossed with the colors of the rainbow in the wrong order. You couldn't dream of a more appropriate logo: lust, knowledge, hope, and anarchy."
>
> *President of Apple Products*
> **Jean-Louis Gassée**

In late 1997, interim CEO Jobs decided that future products would be adorned with solid-colored Apple logos. The first Mac to receive this treatment was the revised PowerBook G3 introduced on May 6, 1998. It featured a large, solid "crystal white" Apple logo on its lid.

Apple's original logo was designed by Ron Wayne.

Wayne's logo was used for a short time, but Jobs eventually came to feel that it was too cerebral and not easily reproduced at small sizes, so in April 1977, he instructed Rob Janov, an art director at the Regis McKenna public relations agency, to come up with a better logo. Janov started with a black and white silhouette of an apple, but felt something was missing. "I wanted to simplify the shape of an apple, and by taking a bite—a byte, right?—out of the side, it prevented the apple from looking like a cherry tomato," explains Janov.

For a touch of class, Janov added six colorful, horizontal stripes that paid tribute to the Apple II's impressive color capabilities. Although separating the green, yellow, orange, red, purple, and blue bars with thin black lines would have reduced registration problems during reproduction, Jobs nixed the proposal, resulting in the Apple logo as we know it today, which former president Michael M. Scott calls "the most expensive bloody logo ever designed."

Apple II Timeline

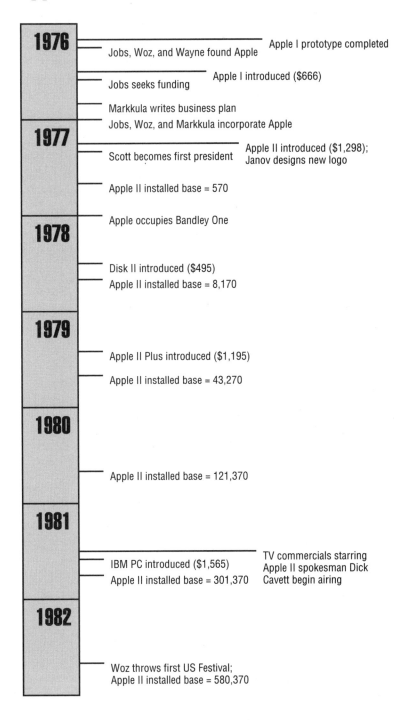

1976
— Apple I prototype completed
— Jobs, Woz, and Wayne found Apple
— Apple I introduced ($666)
— Jobs seeks funding
— Markkula writes business plan
— Jobs, Woz, and Markkula incorporate Apple

1977
— Scott becomes first president
— Apple II introduced ($1,298); Janov designs new logo
— Apple II installed base = 570
— Apple occupies Bandley One

1978
— Disk II introduced ($495)
— Apple II installed base = 8,170

1979
— Apple II Plus introduced ($1,195)
— Apple II installed base = 43,270

1980
— Apple II installed base = 121,370

1981
— IBM PC introduced ($1,565)
— TV commercials starring Apple II spokesman Dick Cavett begin airing
— Apple II installed base = 301,370

1982
— Woz throws first US Festival; Apple II installed base = 580,370

Apple's first president, Michael M. Scott, brought a lot of professional experience when he was hired in May 1977 from National Semiconductor. One of his first attempts at imposing a little organization was to issue numbered identification badges, based roughly on each employee's date of hire. "Scotty" gave himself number seven because that's his lucky number, and he issued badge number one to Wozniak because without his brilliant design of the Apple I, there would be no company. This didn't sit too well with Jobs, who rushed to Scott asking him to reconsider. Scott held his ground. "Jobs would be unbearable if he was number one," felt Scott. Realizing Scott wasn't about to name him employee number one, Jobs suggested a compromise: He'd accept number zero instead. That seemed only fair, so to keep the peace, Jobs got badge number zero, but Apple's official personnel records list him as employee number two because the Bank of America check processing software wouldn't allow zero. To this day, a low employee number is a badge of honor in the corridors of Apple.

Hoping to recreate some Woodstock magic, Woz sponsored the US Festivals, three-day "celebrations of contemporary music and technology." The first was held Labor Day weekend in 1982 at the Glen Helen Regional Park, just north of San Bernardino, California. Over 20 different entertainers performed, and there were exhibits on the impact of technological developments. The event was marred by low paid attendance, 340 arrests, and about 12 drug overdoses. Woz tried again Memorial Day weekend 1983. Woz lost an estimated $20 million on the two US Festivals, but he had fun and still considers them successful.

Apple II Timeline (continued)

The one millionth Apple II was awarded to Ellis Elementary school in Sunnyvale, California, on July 18,1983, as part of the "Kids Can't Wait" program.

Q. What's the difference between PCS (Personal Computer Systems; the Apple II division) and the *Titanic*?
A. The *Titanic* had a dance band.

After resigning from Apple in 1985 over the lack of support for the Apple II, Steve Wozniak eventually returned to college to complete his degree. He enrolled in Berkeley under the name Rocky Raccoon Clark and earned a bachelors degree in electrical engineering in June 1986. Woz's pet dog at the time was named Rocky.

Forever = 6,072 Days
The Apple IIc was introduced on April 24, 1984, in San Francisco's Moscone Center during a celebration called "Apple II Forever." Incidentally, the pre-show setup was interrupted by an earthquake measuring 6.2 on the Richter scale. On November 15, 1993, more than 16 years after the original Apple II was introduced and with over 5 million units shipped, Apple quietly dropped the last of the line, the Apple IIe, from its product list. As a token gesture to the faithful, for a while Apple continued to offer Apple II technology through an expansion card for some early Mac LC and Performa models.

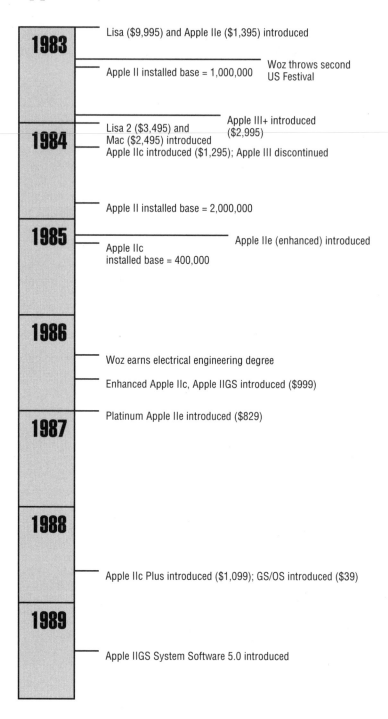

1983
Lisa ($9,995) and Apple IIe ($1,395) introduced

Apple II installed base = 1,000,000 — Woz throws second US Festival

1984
Lisa 2 ($3,495) and Mac ($2,495) introduced — Apple III+ introduced ($2,995)
Apple IIc introduced ($1,295); Apple III discontinued

Apple II installed base = 2,000,000

1985
Apple IIe (enhanced) introduced
Apple IIc installed base = 400,000

1986
Woz earns electrical engineering degree

Enhanced Apple IIc, Apple IIGS introduced ($999)

1987
Platinum Apple IIe introduced ($829)

1988
Apple IIc Plus introduced ($1,099); GS/OS introduced ($39)

1989
Apple IIGS System Software 5.0 introduced

What Were They Thinking?

Looking back over the years, it's interesting (and perhaps even a bit gratifying) to see that many supposedly sophisticated professionals and institutions made outrageously shortsighted decisions at crucial moments during the development of the microcomputer industry. Recounted here are just a few tales of woe guaranteed to leave you slapping your forehead and asking, "What were they thinking?!"

Hewlett-Packard

After creating the prototype of the original Apple I computer in his spare time during March 1976, Steve Wozniak approached his employer, Hewlett-Packard (www.hp.com), and tried to convince the company to consider making microcomputers. "I pitched my boss, the calculator lab manager, and got him all excited, but it was obvious it didn't have a place at HP," recalls Woz.

Although his boss didn't think the Apple I was appropriate for his division, he instructed an HP lawyer to call each division head asking, "You interested in an $800 machine that can run BASIC and hook up to a TV?" Everyone declined, saying "HP doesn't want to be in that kind of market."

Eventually HP would change its mind and produce its own line of personal computers (reaching fourth place in worldwide PC sales in 1997, according to Dataquest), but with a release letter from HP in hand, Woz was free to go off and market the Apple I on his own time. What makes the story all the more ironic is that HP itself had been started by William Hewlett and David Packard in a garage at 367 Addison Avenue in Palo Alto (now a California historical landmark), not far from Steve Jobs' boyhood home in Los Altos.

"It's not like we were all smart enough to see a revolution coming. Back then, I thought there might be a revolution in opening your garage door, balancing your checkbook, keeping your recipes, that sort of thing. There are a million people who study markets and analyze economic trends, people who are more brilliant than I am, people who worked for companies like Digital Equipment and IBM and Hewlett-Packard. None of them foresaw what was going to happen either."

Steve Wozniak

Atari

Steve Wozniak was comfortable pulling down $24,000 annually from his job in the calculator division at Hewlett-Packard, and he wasn't about to quit to sell the bare Apple I circuit board to hobbyists. He didn't share Steve Jobs' vision of a huge personal computer marketplace, nor did he have the ambition to build his own company to exploit it. So after discussing the matter with Jobs, they approached game maker Atari (which is equivalent to the chess term "check" in the ancient Japanese game of Go), where Jobs worked as a technician.

"After we had the Apple I built on a board, we showed it to Al Alcorn of Atari," recalls Woz. "Atari had just come out with their first Home Pong game and it was going to be so big that they had their hands full. They thought the Apple I was a great thing, but they had plenty going themselves."

Home Pong was code-named Darleen, after an Atari employee.

Like Hewlett-Packard before it, Atari decided not to buy out Apple. Of course, Atari went on to dominate the early home video game market, selling 150,000 Home Pongs in its first year. Atari was itself purchased by Warner Communications for $28 million in October 1976, and in 1978 entered the home computer market with the Atari 400 and Atari 800.

Courtesy of Atari Corp.

Although it passed on the Apple I in 1976, by 1978 Atari was selling its own line of computers (shown here, the Atari 800).

"Many people have said that the home computer will be the death of camaraderie at the office ... Following that argument to its logical conclusion, you might just as well say that masturbation should take the market away from sex."

former president of Apple Products
Jean-Louis Gassée

Atari enjoyed moderate success in the home computer market, but when the video game market crashed in 1983, Atari lost $538 million, prompting Warner to split the company into two divisions. The arcade division became an independent company called Atari Games, and the home division was sold to industry legend Jack Tramiel, who had founded computing rival Commodore Business Machines.

At COMDEX 1985, Atari introduced the low-end Atari 520ST, nicknamed the Jackintosh, because its graphical user interface was so similar to Apple's Mac. Still, the company never managed to break out of its niche position and released its last computer, the Falcon030, in December 1992. On July 31, 1996, Atari merged with JTS Corporation, a hard disk drive manufacturer in San Jose, California, and dropped off the radar screen for good.

Commodore Business Machines

Turned down by both of their employers, Woz and Jobs decided to go it alone. To scrape together the $1,350 cost of producing the original Apple I printed circuit board, Woz sold his Hewlett-Packard 65 programmable calculator for $250 and Jobs sold his red and white Volkswagen bus for $1,500. By all accounts, the Apple I was only a moderate success, selling a total of 200 units.

But after building the Apple II prototype, they realized they had a potentially big winner on their hands. Unfortunately, they lacked the funds to turn it into a success. The Apple I was relatively inexpensive to build, and it generated just enough income to sustain itself. In contrast, the Apple II cost several hundred dollars each to produce. "How do you build 1,000 of something that costs a lot of money?" Woz asks rhetorically. "We didn't have any money."

Knowing that calculator maker Commodore Business Machines was anxious to get into the nascent microcomputer market, Jobs invited a couple of representatives to come to his parents' garage and see the Apple II breadboard putting high-resolution color spirals on the screen, an impressive feat in the fall of 1976. Commodore was interested and Jobs offered to sell the company for $100,000 in cash, some stock, and salaries of $36,000 a year for himself and Wozniak.

"I thought it was atrocious. I had put a man-year of work into it, and I thought it was grossly outrageous to ask for so much," Woz naively recalls. Nonetheless, he would have gladly taken the deal because his passion was building computers, not companies. His father, Jerry (a Lockheed engineer), was also appalled by Jobs' demands, but not for the same reasons. He felt that Jobs was taking advantage of his son.

To his credit, Jobs did investigate their suitor. "The more I looked into Commodore, the sleazier they were. I couldn't find one person who had made a deal with them and was happy. Everyone felt they had been cheated," said Jobs.

"We were real small-time operators, kind of like somebody who sold arts and crafts on the side."
Steve Wozniak, *describing Apple's early days*

"You didn't do shit."
Jerry Wozniak *to Steve Jobs, when told that Jobs expected an even split with his son*

Fortunately for Apple, Commodore founder Jack Tramiel thought it was ridiculous to acquire two guys working out of a garage. Instead, in October 1976, Commodore bought MOS Technology, the firm that developed the inexpensive ($25) 6502 microprocessor that was the heart of the Apple II.

Chuck Peddle, the engineer who designed the 6502, took only four months to slap together the $795 Commodore PET, which debuted at the same time as the $1,298 Apple II. Peddle admits the frivolous name was inspired by the Pet Rock craze of the era, although the acronym officially stood for Personal Electronic Transactor or Programmable Educational Terminal, depending on whom you asked.

Courtesy of Michael Swaine

Instead of buying Apple, Commodore bought MOS Technology, which designed the PET.

The boxy PET was an all-in-one computer with a built-in monochrome video display, cassette deck, and keyboard, but it was the stuff it didn't include that caused many industry insiders to deride the klugy machine as Peddle's Ego Trip. "They left out expandability, color, good memory, high-resolution graphics, a nice keyboard, the ability to use your TV ... all sorts of things," recalls Woz. Considering the relative lifespans of the PET versus the Apple II, it's doubtful Jack Tramiel could ever forget his mistake in passing up Apple.

Following Commodore's refusal to buy out Apple, Jobs eventually got the necessary funding and managerial experience from Mike Markkula. The revolutionary Apple II was introduced during the first West Coast Computer Faire in San Francisco on April 17, 1977, and took the fledgling computer industry by storm. After enjoying limited success with its Mac-like Amiga computer, a moribund Commodore announced that it was going out of business on April 29, 1994.

The first time Apple exhibited at the Consumer Electronics Show in Chicago, the small band of employees working the booth was complaining about how sore their feet were from standing all day long. Even though he spent most of his time in bare feet or sandals, Jobs wasn't complaining. He proudly shared his solution for refreshing himself: He would periodically go to the rest room, sit on top of a toilet tank, plop his feet into the toilet bowl, then flush repeatedly to create a poor man's whirlpool.

VisiCalc

HP, Atari, and Commodore aren't the only companies that failed to recognize a good thing when they saw it. Apple is guilty of passing up tremendous opportunities itself. Case in point: VisiCalc.

In January 1979, Daniel Fylstra, from Boston-based Personal Software, Inc., showed Mike Markkula and Steve Jobs a prototype of an Applesoft BASIC program called Calculedger. Written in an attic by 26-year-old Daniel Bricklin, a first-year Harvard Business School MBA student, and his MIT friend Robert Frankston, Calculedger was a cross between a calculator and a ledger sheet that solved very complex "what if" financial planning problems by establishing mathematical relationships between numbers.

Courtesy of Michael Swaine

Dan Bricklin, co-author of VisiCalc, one of the best-selling computer programs ever.

Fylstra offered to sell this revolutionary program for $1 million, but Apple turned him down. The wizards in Cupertino were not alone in failing to grasp the importance of the program. Bill Gates also declined to purchase the program because Microsoft was too busy selling BASIC directly to computer manufacturers to get involved in publishing applications, stating, "We do not talk to any end users."

By the time it was unveiled publicly at the West Coast Computer Faire in San Francisco that May, Calculedger had been renamed VisiCalc (a contraction of "visible calculator"), and the world got its first look at an electronic spreadsheet. When finally published in October 1979, VisiCalc ran on the Apple II only and helped launch that machine as the business standard because finally a computer could do something extremely useful.

VisiCalc was arguably the first "killer application." It was so compelling that people bought hardware just to run it. It went on to become one of the hottest-selling software products in the personal computer industry, selling 200,000 copies in two years.

A patent attorney advised Personal Software that programs were not eligible for patent protection, so they never got rich from inventing the spreadsheet. Today Bricklin is working on Trellix (www.trellix.com), which he describes as "a spreadsheet for words." Bob Frankston maintains a web site at frankston.ne.mediaone.net.

According to Frankston, Bricklin tested VisiCalc by analyzing the ad campaign of a then-obscure Pepsi marketing executive named John Sculley, who would become CEO of Apple in 1983.

The first version of VisiCalc wasn't much to look at, but the world had never seen anything like it.

"I saw a video tape that we weren't supposed to see. It was prepared for the Joint Chiefs of Staff. By watching the tape, we discovered that, at least as of a few years ago, every tactical nuclear weapon in Europe manned by U.S. personnel was targeted by an Apple II computer. Now, we didn't sell computers to the military; they went out and bought them at a dealer's, I guess. But it didn't make us feel good to know that our computers were being used to target nuclear weapons in Europe. The only bright side of it was that at least they weren't [Radio Shack] TRS-80s! Thank God for that."

Steve Jobs
(Playboy, *February 1985*)

Personal Software was ultimately renamed VisiCorp in recognition of its reliance on its flagship product. VisiCorp would again impress the world at the 1982 Fall COMDEX in Las Vegas, Nevada, by demonstrating VisiOn (code-named Quasar), a graphical interface for souped-up IBM PCs. Keep in mind, Apple hadn't even announced Lisa yet, so this was most people's first look at a WIMP system (windows, icons, mice, and pointers).

Unfortunately for VisiCorp, its window of opportunity had already shut when VisiOn shipped a year later. Since VisiOn couldn't run DOS applications, to make it useful you had to shell out a total of $1,765 for a package that included a spreadsheet, graphing program, word processor, and mouse. In addition to being late and overpriced, VisiOn was slow, buggy, and had onerous hardware requirements. In August 1983, Control Data bought VisiOn, which disappeared from sight thereafter. However, Lotus Development (www.lotus.com) bought the rights to VisiCalc in 1985, and the world's first spreadsheet technology continues to live on in the form of Lotus 1-2-3.

MacBASIC

Some analysts credit Microsoft's current dominance of the industry to the wisdom and ruthless business practices of its founder and chairman, William Henry Gates III. But even big bad Bill has blundered at times, perhaps never more so than when it came to the curious case of MacBASIC.

In August 1977, Apple agreed to pay $21,000 for an eight-year license to Microsoft's version of the BASIC programming language. After some fiddling by a high-schooler named Randy Wigginton (who went on to create MacWrite), Microsoft's modified code was released as Applesoft BASIC and burned into the ROMs of every Apple II. Tens of thousands of useful programs were written in BASIC for the Apple II, contributing in a large part to the computer's popularity.

Mindful of the role BASIC played in the success of the Apple II, in 1982 Steve Jobs encouraged Microsoft to develop a BASIC programming language for the Macintosh, which it agreed to do. Oddly enough, Jobs then returned to Cupertino and instructed programmer Donn Denman to begin work on Apple's own implementation called MacBASIC, which was originally scheduled to ship in the second quarter of 1984 for $99.

Having gotten wind of Jobs' plan and anxious to reap the financial rewards of being first to market, Gates rushed Microsoft BASIC to completion and released it upon the introduction of the Mac in January

Courtesy of Microsoft Corp.

In 1985, youthful Microsoft chairman Bill Gates dictated that Apple kill MacBASIC, which he would later call "one of the stupidest deals...ever."

According to *The Journey Is The Reward*, Jobs appeared at Apple's first annual Halloween party in 1977 dressed as Jesus Christ. Actually, Jobs was merely wearing a toga, as were the woman who would later give birth to his daughter, and employee Dan Kottke— both Jobs' roommates at the time. In contrast, Bill Gates attended the 1985 Microsoft Halloween/30th birthday party in a Bellevue, Washington, roller rink dressed as F. Scott Fitzgerald's wealthy character Jay Gatsby.

1984. By most accounts, Microsoft BASIC was a dog that didn't even take advantage of many of the Mac's unique features such as the powerful Toolbox routines. According to Denman, it was "a really crappy, slow implementation," so he felt confident that he had time to perfect MacBASIC, which was widely available in a beta version and receiving very favorable responses.

Gates must have realized that MacBASIC would eat his lunch in the open market, but he had an ace in the hole. When the Applesoft license came up for renewal in 1985, the Apple II line was still the company's cash cow and BASIC was absolutely crucial to the venerable Apple II. Failing to grasp the fact that he had the boys from Cupertino over a barrel and was in a position to extract damn near anything he wanted at the negotiating table, Gates simply demanded that Apple halt development of MacBASIC.

After a fair amount of huffing and puffing, Apple caved in, correctly reasoning that the Mac was designed as an information appliance for which a hobbyist programming language was hardly a necessity. So Apple got off easy by agreeing to kill MacBASIC. In exchange, it got a new lease on life for the Apple II and the company.

Microsoft BASIC never set the world on fire (in fact, it was eventually withdrawn in disgrace), but the Apple II continued to contribute significantly to Apple's bottom line for years to come. It wasn't discontinued officially until November 1993. Gates would later realize the error of his ways and refer to the whole episode as "one of the stupidest deals I have ever done."

Incidentally, Denman didn't learn he had been sold out until Arthur Luehrmann, an outside writer working on a MacBASIC tutorial book, called to tell him that the book the two were collaborating on had been canceled because MacBASIC was deep-sixed.

Broken Breakout Promises

Before co-founding Apple in April 1976, Steve Jobs was one of the first 50 employees at Atari, the legendary Silicon Valley game company founded by Nolan Kay Bushnell in 1972. Atari's Pong, a simple electronic version of ping-pong, had caught on like wildfire in arcades and homes across the country, and Bushnell was anxious to come up with a successor. He envisioned a variation on Pong called Breakout, in which the player bounced a ball off a paddle at the bottom of the screen in an attempt to smash the bricks in a wall at the top.

Bushnell turned to Jobs, a technician, to design the circuitry. Initially Jobs tried to do the work himself, but soon realized he was in way over his head and asked his friend Steve Wozniak to bail him out. "Steve wasn't capable of designing anything that complex. He came

To make ends meet in the summer of 1972, Woz, Jobs, and Jobs' girlfriend took $3-per-hour jobs at the Westgate Mall in San Jose, California, dressing up as *Alice In Wonderland* characters. Jobs and Woz alternated as the White Rabbit and the Mad Hatter.

Conceived by Bushnell, Breakout was originally designed by Wozniak and Jobs.

"He was the only person I met who knew more about electronics than me."
Steve Jobs, *explaining his initial fascination with Woz*

"Steve didn't know very much about electronics."
Steve Wozniak

to me and said Atari would like a game and described how it would work," recalls Wozniak. "There was a catch: I had to do it in four days. In retrospect, I think it was because Steve needed the money to buy into a farm up north."

Designing a complex game in such a short period of time was a challenge, so even though Wozniak was working full-time at Hewlett-Packard, he and Jobs put in four all-nighters in a row and finished a working prototype. Both came down with mononucleosis as a result, yet Woz remembers it as an incredible experience. "I was so proud of designing a product like that," recalls Wozniak. "Nolan Bushnell wanted a game with as few chips as possible. Steve said if there were less than 50 chips, we got paid $700 and split it in half. Less than 40 chips, $1,000. After four nights, it was 42 chips. I wasn't about to spend another second trying to reduce it by two more chips; I'll settle for $700."

Nolan Bushnell went on to found the Chuck E. Cheese Pizza Time Theater restaurant chain and PlayNet Technologies—a maker of pay-per-play Internet games for bars, restaurants, and hotels—which filed to liquidate itself in June 1998.

After delivering the game to Atari, Jobs put off paying Woz, explaining that there was some problem getting the money, but he finally wrote a check for $350 and immediately split for the All-One Farm in Oregon. Jobs was happy because his friend had helped him get in good with his boss. Bushnell was thrilled because Breakout was designed in record time and used so few chips. Woz was happy earning some pocket money doing what he loved best. "I would have done it for a quarter," says Wozniak.

> "Steve [Jobs] will use anybody to his own advantage. He will say one thing and anybody who heard it would think that he was saying 'Maybe yes' or 'Maybe no.' You could never tell what he was thinking."
>
> **Steve Wozniak**

It wasn't until 1984 that Woz discovered the unpleasant truth about the Breakout project and his "good friend," Steve Jobs. "I was on a plane going to a user group club in Fort Lauderdale to promote the Mac, along with some other members of the Mac team," recalls Wozniak. "Andy Hertzfeld had just read *Zap!*, a book about Atari which said that Steve Jobs designed Breakout. I explained to him that we both worked on it and got paid $700. Andy corrected me, 'No, it says here it was $5,000.' When I read in the book how Nolan Bushnell had actually paid Steve $5,000, I just cried."

Ironically, Woz's design for Breakout was so brilliant that none of the Atari engineers could figure out exactly how it worked, which made it impossible to test, so the whole thing had to be redesigned in-house before it shipped.

It wasn't the money that bothered Woz. Had Jobs asked, Wozniak would have done the project for free because he was turned on by such technological challenges. What hurt was being misled by his friend. Looking back on the incident, Wozniak realized Jobs' behavior was completely in character. "Steve had worked in surplus electronics and said if you can buy a part for 30 cents and sell it to this guy at the surplus store for $6, you don't have to tell him what you paid for it. It's worth $6 to the guy. And that was his philosophy of running a business," says Wozniak.

Breakout, The Easter Egg

The legacy of Breakout lived on at Apple. Woz was so taken with the game that he specifically designed the Apple II to accept the addition of paddles as input devices, and Apple later shipped the computer with a version of the game called Little Brickout. More recently, Breakout can be found on the Mac hiding in the form of an Easter egg. If you are running System 7.5, launch SimpleText or choose Note Pad from the Apple menu (or open any other Drag Manager-enabled word processor), type *secret about box*; select the text, then drag it to the Finder's desktop. Out pops a simple Breakout-style game with the names of the System 7.5 team appearing in the bricks. When the ball drops in a few seconds, use the mouse to move your paddle so that the ball bounces toward the bricks and destroys them. If you miss the ball, don't worry; you get as many balls as you need. When all of the bricks are gone, a new batch appears. When this simple game grows tiresome, click the mouse button to close the window.

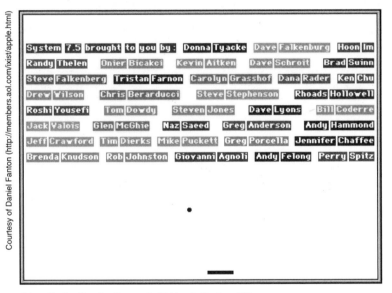

Courtesy of Daniel Fanton (http://members.aol.com/ixist/apple.html)

A functioning Breakout game is hidden in System 7.5.

The Breakout game appears only in System 7.5. If you're running System 7.5.2 or later on certain newer Macs, instead of a Breakout game, the screen is filled with a color photograph of the interior courtyard of Apple's headquarters on Infinite Loop in Cupertino. Programmer credits scroll below the scene and in the foreground is a fluttering flag bearing the image of a large green iguana and the slogan "iguana iguana powersurgius." You can control the direction that the

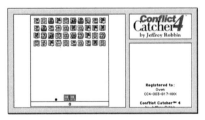

Another Breakout Easter egg can be found in Conflict Catcher 4.0 from Casady & Greene (www.casadyg.com). Open the control panel and click the version number in the lower right. In the About box that follows, type *play* to start the game. The arrow keys control the paddle movement. You get only one ball, so your reflexes better be quick. Click the mouse button to quit.

flag waves by moving the mouse. You can even snap the flag off the pole and watch it float to the ground by rapidly moving the mouse back and forth just right (it's not easy, but it can be done). Click anywhere to return things to normal.

What's the meaning of "iguana iguana powersurgius," you ask? Bill Coderre made up the fake Latin-sounding slogan as an homage to engineer Dave Evans' pet iguana, Herman, the mascot for the System 7.5.2 programming team. As for "powersurgius," System 7.5.2 was designed specifically for the PCI family of Macs, which was code-named PowerSurge.

A fluttering flag at Apple's headquarters replaced the Breakout Easter egg starting with System 7.5.2 on certain late-model Macs.

There are a few hidden options in this Easter egg. After selecting *secret about box* and while you are dragging it to the desktop, press and hold the *P* key to replace the iguana flag with one depicting the System 7.5.2 programming team or the Mac OS logo (if you are running System 7.5.3). Likewise, press and hold *Q* while dragging to see a pink flag and blank background with the message "QuickTime required for images"; this is what you would see if you accessed this Easter egg without QuickTime installed.

The Apple III Fiasco

After two years of development, the Apple III was announced on May 19, 1980, during the National Computer Conference (NCC) in Anaheim, California. With Apple's typical flair for spectacle, the company rented Disneyland for five hours the following night at a cost of $42,000 and transported an estimated 7,000 NCC attendees to the site in British double-decker buses.

Apple was proud of the Apple III because it represented many firsts for the company. Foremost, it was the company's first attempt at building a powerful business computer. It was also the company's first major departure from the tried-and-true Apple II architecture. It would prove the company's first bona fide failure. Unfortunately, instead of learning from the experience, Apple repeated many of the same mistakes with the Lisa and the Mac.

The Apple III was sold in two different configurations ranging in price from $4,340 to $7,800. At the heart of each was a Synertek 8-bit 6502A microprocessor running at 2MHz (twice the speed of the Apple II), a maximum of 128K of random access memory (RAM), built-in keyboard with numeric keypad, and one internal 143K, 5.25-inch disk drive manufactured by Shugart. In effect, the Apple III came standard with everything most people eventually added to the Apple II. If that wasn't enough, there were four internal slots that accepted Apple II peripheral cards, plus you could add additional devices via the two serial ports on the back.

Although it had an Apple II emulation mode, the Apple III worked best with software written specifically to take advantage of its proprietary Sophisticated Operating System and new features such as a built-in real-time clock and video capable of generating 24 lines of 80-column text and up to 560 by 192 pixels in the monochrome graphics mode. On paper, all the specifications were quite impressive, but implementing them proved a humbling experience for Apple.

Apple originally promised to ship the Apple III in July, but production problems plagued the product throughout the summer and into the

The Apple III was code-named Sara after chief engineer Wendell Sander's daughter.

The Apple III (shown here with a 5MB ProFile hard drive) was the firm's first failure.

"We had to put chips in to disable some Apple II features so people's heads would have the right image that Apple IIIs are for business and Apple IIs are for home and hobby."
Steve Wozniak

> "The Apple III was kind of like a baby conceived during a group orgy, and [later] everybody had this bad headache and there's this bastard child, and everyone says, 'It's not mine.'"
>
> *Apple employee #6*
> **Randy Wigginton**

> "[Jobs] could see that horizon out there, a thousand miles out. But he could never see the details of each little mile that had to be covered to get there. That was his genius and his downfall."
>
> *Apple's head of human resources*
> **Jay Elliott**

> "We had to replace fourteen thousand of them. I must say that, as far as enhancing our reputation, this operation was a success. We received thank-you letters telling us that General Motors would never have done the same."
>
> *General manager of Apple France*
> **Jean-Louis Gassée**

fall. Unlike the Apple I and II, which were essentially the work of one man, Steve Wozniak, the Apple III was designed by a committee headed by Steve Jobs, who would demand one thing one day, then the opposite the next. The shipping delays threatened to mar Apple's initial public offering in December (see "Millionaire Mania," page 37), so managers ignored the dire warnings of engineers who knew what would happen if they pushed the Apple III out the door before its time. As soon as units began trickling into distribution in late November, the worst fears of the engineers were realized.

On February 10, 1981, Apple announced that the Apple III would no longer contain the built-in clock/calendar features because National Semiconductor's clock chip didn't meet Apple's specifications. How the flaky parts got into a shipping product nobody was willing to say. Apple dropped the price of the Apple III to $4,190 and gave a $50 rebate to everybody who had purchased an Apple III up to that date.

When the first volume shipments began in March 1981, it became apparent that dropping the clock chip was just a finger in the dike. Approximately 20 percent of all Apple IIIs were dead on arrival primarily because chips fell out of loose sockets during shipping. Those that did work initially often failed after minimal use thanks to Jobs' insistence that the Apple III not have a fan (a design demand he would make again on the Mac). He reasoned that in addition to reducing radio-frequency interference emissions, the internal aluminum chassis would conduct heat and keep the delicate components cool. He was wrong.

Compounding the problem was that Jobs dictated the size and shape of the case without concern for the demands of the electrical engineers, who were then forced to cram boards into small spaces with little or no ventilation. As the computer was used, its chips got hot, expanded slightly, and slowly worked their way out of their sockets, at which point the computer simply died. Apple's solution was to recommend lifting the front of the computer six inches off the desktop, then letting it drop with the hope that the chips would reseat themselves!

The problems with loose chips were exacerbated by short cables between internal components and non-gold connectors that suffered from corrosion. To its credit, Apple didn't bury the problem; on April 15, 1981, Mike Markkula, president and CEO, admitted to *The Wall Street Journal*, "It would be dishonest for me to sit here and say it's perfect." Apple instituted a liberal repair policy, swapping brand new Apple IIIs for bad ones on the spot, no questions asked. To everyone's dismay, the replacements often failed, too.

On November 9, Apple announced a revised Apple III with a base price of $3,495. The company steadfastly claimed that the original problems were linked to shortcomings in manufacturing and quality-control procedures rather than the underlying design of the computer. Nonetheless, the new Apple III featured different sockets, updated software, memory expansion up to 256K, and an optional 5MB hard disk drive. Based upon the Seagate ST506 mechanism, the $3,495 ProFile was an important addition to the system since IBM didn't yet offer a hard drive for its PC, which had been introduced that August. Of the 7,200 original Apple IIIs that had been sold, 2,000 were replaced for free when the new version became available in mid-December.

The ProFile (code-named Pippin) cost $700 per megabyte in 1981. Compare that to hard drives selling for less than 8¢ per megabyte in 1998!

Even after the Apple III had been revised, sales remained disappointing. Analysts estimate that Apple sold 3,000 to 3,500 units a month, just one-tenth the sales rate of the venerable Apple II. According to InfoCorp, a Santa Clara research firm, the Apple III had an installed base of only 75,000 units by December 1983, compared to 1.3 million Apple IIs. Potential buyers had been turned off by the bad publicity as well as by a lack of useful software that took advantage of the Apple III's unique Sophisticated Operating System. Industry experts openly referred to the operating system by its distress-signal initials, SOS, although Apple preferred the phonetic nickname "applesauce."

In a last-ditch effort to revive the product, Apple replaced the Apple III with the $2,995 Apple III Plus in December 1983. In addition to a lower price, the new model came standard with 256K of RAM, a built-in clock that actually worked, a new logic board, SOS version 1.3, improved peripheral ports with standard DB-25 connectors, and a modified slot housing for easier card installation. It was a classic case of too little, too late.

> "It just wasn't a good enough machine and it had so many flaws from the start that when we reintroduced it we should have called it the Apple IV."
>
> ***Steve Wozniak***

Although the Apple III Plus had helped boost the installed base to an estimated 120,000 units, Apple abruptly dropped the line on April 24, 1984. "While the Apple III is an excellent business computer," wrote David Fradin, Apple III business unit manager, in a memo to his staff, "it is a generally accepted view by Apple's product managers that Apple can best serve the future needs of our business customers by expanding the Apple II and Apple 32 [Lisa and Mac] product families, and by concentrating future development, marketing and sales efforts on these products. Therefore, we have decided that no further product development efforts shall be initiated and undertaken for the Apple III product line, effective immediately." After losing over $60 million on the Apple III product line, Apple quietly removed it from the product list in September 1985.

"The Apple III is designed to have a 10-year lifespan."
Apple CEO **Mike Markkula**
(The Wall Street Journal,
April 15, 1981)

"Apple is firmly and totally committed to supporting the Apple III and is maintaining and increasing our commitment to the Apple III as a major product for the next five to seven years."
Mike Markkula
(Computer Systems News,
November 16/23, 1981)

"The Apple III will be a serious contender in the business computer marketplace for a long time to come."
Apple III manager **David Fradin**
(The Peninsula Times Tribune,
November 21, 1983)

"No further product development efforts shall be initiated and undertaken for the Apple III product line, effective immediately."
David Fradin
(*internal memo, April 24, 1984*)

Apple III Timeline

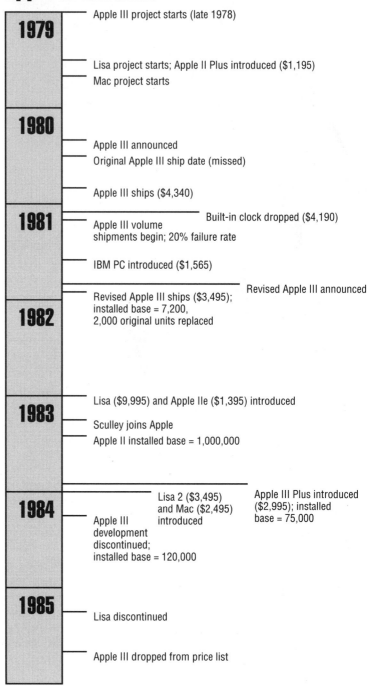

1979 — Apple III project starts (late 1978)
Lisa project starts; Apple II Plus introduced ($1,195)
Mac project starts

1980 — Apple III announced
Original Apple III ship date (missed)
Apple III ships ($4,340)

1981 — Apple III volume shipments begin; 20% failure rate — Built-in clock dropped ($4,190)
IBM PC introduced ($1,565)
Revised Apple III ships ($3,495); installed base = 7,200, 2,000 original units replaced — Revised Apple III announced

1982

1983 — Lisa ($9,995) and Apple IIe ($1,395) introduced
Sculley joins Apple
Apple II installed base = 1,000,000

1984 — Lisa 2 ($3,495) and Mac ($2,495) introduced — Apple III Plus introduced ($2,995); installed base = 75,000
Apple III development discontinued; installed base = 120,000

1985 — Lisa discontinued
Apple III dropped from price list

Code Names Uncovered

Apple's research and development facilities, located on Infinite Loop in Cupertino, are some of the most secure buildings on the Apple campus. Confidential papers are discarded into locked wastebaskets lest they fall into the hands of Dumpster-diving competitors or reporters; guards are posted at all entrances; and employees must pass their electronic identification badges in front of wall plates that verify access privileges and monitor personnel movement. Apple has come a long way from the days when Jobs and Woz eagerly showed off what they were doing in the Los Altos garage, but it hasn't gotten paranoid. Like most high-tech companies, Apple is simply trying to maintain the security of the many new proprietary technologies and products it is constantly designing.

An essential part of security is the use of code names. Before Apple publicly announces a product by its official name, that product is internally referred to by a code name. Usually lead engineers or managers get to name their own projects whatever they want, but a few recurring trends are evident. Early in its incarnation, Apple favored female names for projects. More often than not, the projects were named after the children, girlfriends, or wives of the team members (for example, the Lisa was named after Jobs' oldest daughter). Jef Raskin rebelled against the sexist notion of female code names and looked instead to apple varieties as the inspiration for his Macintosh project, purposely misspelling McIntosh. For a while, the names of different types of apples (Pippin, Jonathan) were often whispered in the R&D labs. Having exhausted the various types of apples, project managers now tend to choose whimsical code names that either reflect pop culture or contain awful puns. Perusing the list of code names is like walking down memory lane, checking out the fads and trends that swept through Apple cubicles and lab benches over the years.

Apple takes the code-naming business seriously, often assigning the same project different code names, one to be used internally, and another for external use. Also, a single project may have separate code names associated with hardware, software, documentation, industrial design, and marketing. Furthermore, outsiders—such as developers and the press—may be told about the same project, but each will be told a different code name. Just to keep everybody guessing, Apple sometimes changes code names in the middle of a project, or reuses old code names for new projects. Not only does all this create confusion in Apple watchers, it also serves as an audit trail to trace leaks to their sources.

This list isn't perfect, so if you're an Apple employee or devout Mac fan and you spot a code-name error or omission, please bring it to my attention at OWL@Bigfoot.com for correction in a subsequent printing of this book.

Despite Apple's best efforts to keep this sort of thing from becoming public, I've compiled an extensive list of code names that have escaped from Cupertino and other Mac-related firms over the years. In some cases, I've even been able to uncover why a particular code name was chosen.

Apple II

Apple II High Speed SCSI Card: Cocoon

Apple IIc: Annie, Bert, Chels, Elf, E.T., Jason, Lollie, Moby, Pippin, Sherry, Teddy (short for Testing Every Day), IIb (for book-sized), IIp (for portable), VLC (Very Low Cost), Yoda, Zelda

Apple IIc Plus: Adam Ant (because the team was adamant about keeping the project alive), Pizza (because of its pizza-box shape), Propeller (because a team member had a propeller beanie in his office), Raisin (after the testers won second place for their California Raisins costumes at a Halloween party)

Apple IIe: Diana, LCA (Low Cost Apple), Super II

Apple IIGS: Cortland, Phoenix (the project was revived after being canceled), Rambo (the design team had to fight for approval), Gumby (from an Apple Halloween parade impersonation)

Apple IIGS Video Overlay Card: Gumby, Pokey

Before becoming Federal Reserve Board chairman, Alan Greenspan gushed about the merits of using an Apple IIc to achieve financial success in an early Apple ad.

Courtesy of Motorola

Motorola's speedy PowerPC 604e CPU was code-named Mach 5 and Sirocco.

CPUs

PowerPC 603e Upgrade Card for PowerBook 500 series: Malcolm
PowerPC 603/603e, 603et, 603ev: Stretch, Goldeneye, Valiant
PowerPC 604/604e, 604er, 604ev: Sirocco, Mach 5, Helm Wind
PowerPC 620: Trident
PowerPC 630: Boxer, Dino
PowerPC 750: Arthur, G3, Typhoon

Drives

Apple 871: Twiggy
Apple Hard Disk 400SC: A Ts'ah (Japanese for eagle), Eagle
Apple PC Drive Card: Emerald City
Apple PowerCD: Tulip
AppleCD 600: Hollywood
AppleCD 800: Stingray
CD Setup: Monarch
Drive Setup: Dragonfly

The PowerCD drive, one of Apple's first attempts at a consumer electronics product, was code-named Tulip.

Input Devices

ADB Mouse II: Topolino (Italy's equivalent to Mickey Mouse)
Adjustable Keyboard: Norsi
Extended Keyboard: Dörfer (Ed Colby's nickname), Saratoga (it's
    so large it's named after an aircraft carrier; prototypes were
    adorned with small model aircraft)
Extended Keyboard II: Gatsby, Nimitz (another aircraft carrier)
OneScanner: Half-Dome, Ping-Pong
OneScanner for Windows: WinDome
OneScanner 600/27: Rio
OneScanner 1200/30: New Orleans
QuickTake 100: Venus
Standard Keyboard: Eastwood
Standard Keyboard II: Elmer

The ergonomic Adjustable Keyboard was code-named Norsi.

Centris

Centris 610: Econoline, QFC (quick, fast, cheap), WLCD
Centris 650 all-metal case: Lego
Centris 650: Wombat 25
Centris 660AV: Tempest

Classic Macs

Mac 512K: Fat Mac (four times the memory of the original Mac)
Mac Classic: XO
Mac Classic II: Apollo (a class of sailboat), Montana
Mac Color Classic: Slice
Mac Plus: Mr. T (perhaps of *The A Team*, but Apple's former chief
    scientist Larry Tesler shares this nickname), Turbo Mac
Mac SE: Aladdin, Chablis, Freeport, Mac plus or minus, Maui,
    Plus Plus
Mac SE/30: Double Stuffed (4MB version), Fafnir, Green Jade, Oreo
    (basic unit), Roadrunner, Single Stuffed (2MB version)

Like a lot of models developed around the same time, the Mac Classic II's code name (Apollo) indicated a class of sailboat.

Mac II Series

Mac II: Becks (the engineers' favorite beer), Cabernet, Ikki (Japanese for bottoms up), Little Big Mac, Milwaukee (engineer Mike Dhuey's hometown), Paris (homage to Jean-Louis Gassée), Reno (in honor of the expansion slots), Uzi

Mac II 32-bit ROMs: Squeaky (as in "squeaky clean," since earlier "dirty" ROMs didn't properly use all 32 bits)

Mac IIci: Aurora II, Cobra II, Pacific, Stingray

Mac IIci Cache Card: American Express, Optima (both are "cash cards," get it?)

Mac IIcx: Atlantic, Aurora, Avanti, Cobra

Mac IIfx: Blackbird, F-16, F-19, Four Square, Stealth, IIxi, Weed-Whacker, Zone 5 (military term for pushing an aircraft to its design limits)

Mac IIsi: Erickson (a class of sailboat), Oceanic, Raffica, Raffika, Ray Ban (as in "the future's so bright, you gotta wear shades" … It shipped to developers with a pair of sunglasses), Spin

Mac IIvi: Brazil 16

Mac IIvx: Brazil 32c

Mac IIvx Sony floppy drive without auto-insert: Wolfpack

Mac IIx: Spock, Stratos

Mac LC Series

Mac LC: Elsie (as in the Borden cow … try pronouncing the letters *L* and *C*), Pinball (low-slung case design looks like a pinball machine to some), Prism

Mac LC Apple IIe card: Double Exposure

Mac LC II: Foster Farms

Mac LC III: Vail, Elsie III

Mac LC 475: Primus

Mac LC 520: Hook 25

Mac LC 550: Hook 33

Mac LC 575: Optimus

Mac LC 630: Show & Tell (for its multimedia capabilities)

Oddball Macs

iMac Revision A: C1, Columbus, Elroy

iMac Revision C (five different colors): C1.5

Mac TV: Peter Pan, LD50 (in the medical world, LD50 is the abbreviation for Lethal Dose 50 percent, the dosage that kills half of those who take it)

Macintosh Coprocessor Platform: Roman, Zorro

Twentieth Anniversary Mac: Pomona, Smoke & Mirrors, Spartacus

In keeping with the agricultural theme begun with the Mac LC's code name of Elsie, the Mac LC II was known as Foster Farms.

Performas

Performa 200: Lady Kenmore

Performa 400: Lady Kenmore, Vail

Performa 460, 466, and 467: Route 66

Performa 475 and 476: Aladdin, Primus

Performa 550: Hook 33

Performa 600: Brazil 32, IIvm (consumer testing showed that users thought the suffix was an abbreviation for "virtual memory," so the model became the Performa 600)

Performa 630: Show, Show & Tell

Performa 5200: Bongo, Rebound, Transformer, Trailblazer

Performa 6400: Hacksaw, Instatower

Performa 6400 logicboard design: Alchemy

Performa 6400 logicboard design, enhanced: Gazelle

Power Macs

Power Mac project: Cognac (in honor of a RISC pioneer with a surname identical to the after-dinner liqueur)

Power Mac AV Card: Planaria

Power Mac 5200: Bongo, Rebound, Transformer

Power Mac 5400: Excalibur

Power Mac 5400 logic-board design: Alchemy

Power Mac 5400/120: Chimera

Power Mac 6100/60: PDM (Piltdown Man)

Power Mac 6100 intelligent connector: HPV (high-power video)

Power Mac 6300: Crusader

Power Mac 7000 series: Outrigger (when opened, the chassis swings outside the enclosure)

Power Mac 7100/66: BHA, Carl Sagan, LAW

Power Mac 7200/90: Catalyst

Power Mac 7500/100: TNT (The New Tesseract, tesseract being the code name of a project developed in parallel with the 601 Power Macs only to be discontinued in late 1994)

Power Mac 8100/80: Cold Fusion

Power Mac 8100/110: Flagship

Power Mac 8500/120: Nitro

Power Mac 8600 and 9600 tower case: K2

Power Mac 8600 and 9600 with PowerPC 604e: Kansas

Power Mac 9500/120: Tsunami (for its amazing power)

Power Mac 9500/150: Autobahn

Power Mac G3 series: Gossamer (motherboard), Outrigger (case)

Power Mac Upgrade Card: STP (an automobile fuel additive)

Power Mac Upgrade enabler: Rocinante (Don Quixote's horse)

Power Macs with PCI bus and 603 and 604 CPUs: PowerSurge

The curvaceous Performa 6400 was code-named Instatower.

The code name for the Power Macintosh 7100/66 started as Carl Sagan, then was changed to BHA (Butt-Head Astronomer), and ended up as LAW (Lawyers Are Wimps). For the complete story, see "Trademark Tiffs," page 207.

Apple's 68040-based PowerBook 540 project was code-named Blackbird, after the high-flying SR-71 reconnaissance plane because both feature dark colors, curves, and speed. However, it was known informally inside Apple as the Spruce Goose because some people felt that introducing a 7-pound laptop in 1994 was as ill-fated an idea as Howard Hughes' huge aircraft, which flew only once. On a related note, the Blackbird's innovative new Trackpad was code-named Midas, after the Phrygian king who turned whatever he touched into gold.

The PowerBook Duo had a host of code names, but was commonly called BOB W because Apple felt that a dockable portable computer offered the Best Of Both Worlds.

PowerBooks

Mac Portable: Esprit, Guinness, Laguna, Malibu, Riviera

Mac Portable (with backlit display): Aruba, Love Shack, Mulligan

PowerBook 100 series hard drives from Conner Peripherals: Elwood (40MB), Jake (20MB)

PowerBook 100 series internal modems: O'Shanter & Bess

PowerBook 100: Asahi, Classic, Derringer (a sailboat), Rosebud

PowerBook 140: Leary, Replacements, Tim LC (a class of sailboat), Tim Lite

PowerBook 145: Colt 45

PowerBook 145B: Pikes Peak

PowerBook 150: JeDI (Just Did It)

PowerBook 160: Brooks

PowerBook 165: Dart LC

PowerBook 165c: Monet

PowerBook 170: Road Warrior, Tim (a class of sailboat)

PowerBook 180: Converse, Dartanian

PowerBook 180c: Hokusai (after the Japanese woodblock carver)

PowerBook 190: Omega

PowerBook 520 and 520c: Blackbird LC (low cost)

PowerBook 540: Blackbird, Spruce Goose, SR-71

PowerBook 540c: Blackbird LC (low cost)

PowerBook 1400: Epic

PowerBook 2400c: Comet, Nautilus, Mighty Cat (souped up configuration), Minihooper

PowerBook 3400c: Hooper

PowerBook 3400c PCI bus technology: PowerStar

PowerBook 5300 series: Anvil, M2 (the model of a mountain bike from Specialized Bicycles)

PowerBook Duo 210 and Duo 230: BOB W ("Best Of Both Worlds," because it's a portable computer that's also a desktop machine when inserted into its dock), Cinnamon, Companion, DB-Lite (the lightweight machine was named one night over a few brewskies in a club called Das Boot)

PowerBook Duo 250: Ansel

PowerBook Duo 270c: Escher

PowerBook Duo 280 and Duo 280c: Yeager

PowerBook Duo 2300: AJ

PowerBook Duo Dock II: Atlantis

PowerBook Duo Floppy Adapter: Blackwatch

PowerBook Duo MiniDock: Spaniard

PowerBook G3: Kanga, PowerBook 3500

PowerBook G3 (second release): WallStreet, PDQ

PowerBook Trackpad: Midas (after the king with the golden touch)

Quadras

Quadra 605: Aladdin, ELB (extremely low budget), Primus

Quadra 610: Speedbump 610 (when the Centris 610 was renamed the Quadra 610, its speed was increased from 20 to 25MHz)

Quadra 610 DOS PDS card: Houdini, Royal Scam

Quadra 630: Crusader, Show Biz, Show & Tell (for its multimedia capabilities)

Quadra 630 removable motherboard: Tell

Quadra 650: Speedbump 650 (when the Centris 650 was renamed the Quadra 650, its speed was increased from 25 to 33MHz)

Quadra 660AV: Tempest

Quadra 700: Evo 200, Shadow (shadow of Quadra 900), Spike (a class of sailboat, and "Gonna spike NeXT"), IIce

Quadra 800: Fridge, Wombat 33

Quadra 840AV: Cyclone, Quadra 1000

Quadra 840AV floppy disk controller chip set from NEC: New Age

Quadra 900: Darwin, Eclipse (a class of sailboat, and "Going to eclipse NeXT"), Premise 500, IIex

Quadra 950: Amazon, Zydeco

Seated next to a two-page monitor, it's easy to understand why the squat Quadra 800 mini-tower was code-named Fridge.

Servers

Network Server 500: Shiner LE

Network Server 700: Shiner HE

Workgroup Server 60 and 80: Blugu

Workgroup Server 95 A/UX: Barracuda

Workgroup Server 95 AppleShare: Fugu

Workgroup Server 95 project: Menagine

Workgroup Server 95: Chinook

Workgroup Server 6150/60, 8150/80, and 9150/80: Starbucks

Workgroup Server 7250/120 and 8550/132: Summit

Miscellaneous

1MB Apple Inline Cache: Sam-I-Am

AISS: Making Waves

Apple MPEG Card: Cannes (after the French film festival)

AppleDesign Powered Speakers: Badger

AppleDesign Powered Speakers II: Baby Badger

PC Compatibility Card (586): Gaucho

PC Compatibility Card (Pentium): Grand Illusion

Designed for low-cost multimedia, the second iteration of the AppleDesign Powered Speakers was known as Baby Badger.

The Macintosh 16-inch Color Display was code-named Goldfish.

Killer Rabbits on the Rampage

AppleShare 3.0 was code-named Killer Rabbit, after the blood-sucking character in the movie *Monty Python and the Holy Grail*. Although it was renamed before release, vestiges of its former incarnation can be found in the shipping version. If you have ever activated File Sharing under System 7, look inside the File Sharing folder in the Preferences folder in the System folder. Normally, the Mac writes an invisible PDS (Parallel Data Structure) file to each volume that is mounted while File Sharing is on. However, in the cases of write-protected or read-only volumes (such as CD-ROMs), the Mac writes visible PDS files to the startup disk. These files are used to help manage File Sharing and they have an icon of a Killer Rabbit.

Incidentally, the Killer Rabbit is stored as ICN# resource 20002 in the File Sharing extension (this file's creator code is hhgg, which some say stands for Douglas Adams' book *The Hitchhiker's Guide to the Galaxy*, but more likely refers to the Holy Hand Grenade, which killed the Killer Rabbit).

Monitors

Apple AudioVision 14 Display: Telecaster
Apple Color Plus 14-Inch Display: Dragon
Apple High-Res. Monochrome Monitor Video Card: Bob the Card
AppleColor High-Resolution RGB Monitor Video Card: Toby
AppleVision 1710 Display: Hammerhead
AppleVision 1710AV Display: Sousa
Macintosh 12-inch RGB Display: Mai Tai
Macintosh 16-inch Color Display: Goldfish
Macintosh 21-inch Color Display: Vesuvio
Two-Page Monochrome Display: Fred, Kong (its colossal size is reminiscent of the great ape)
Two-Page Monochrome Video Card: Barney

Networking

Apple Freedom Network: Frogger
Apple Token Ring: Frodo (from J.R.R. Tolkien's *Lord Of The Rings*)
AppleShare 1.0: 007
AppleShare 3.0: Killer Rabbit
AppleTalk Internet Router (1989): North (after Lieutenant Colonel Oliver North, who routed Iranian arms sale proceeds to the Nicaraguan Contras)
AppleTalk Internet Router (1992 update): Betelgeuse (the star Alpha Orionis)
AppleTalk Network Card for Apple II: Bullwinkle (companion to Rocky, the canceled Apple II-based server using a 5MB ProFile)
AppleTalk Remote Access: 976 (a prefix for many phone-sex hotlines)
LocalTalk: AppleBus, AppleTalk
LocalTalk serial card: Livonia
Network Software Installer 1.0: Lumahai
Network Software Installer 2.0: Balihai
Network Software Installer 3.0: Why-o-wai
PowerTalk APIs: Ventoux (a French resort known for bicycle races)
SNA•ps 5250: B52

Newton

eMate 300: Project K, Schoolbook, Shay
Newton Keyboard: Bazooka
Newton MessagePad 100: Junior, Wedge
Newton MessagePad 110: Lindy (the brand name of a pen)
Newton MessagePad 110 Charging Station: Crib
Newton MessagePad 120: Gelato (came in two flavors, 1 or 2 MB)
Newton MessagePad 2000: Q
Newton OS 2.0: Dante
Newton OS 2.0 print-only handwriting recognizer: Rosetta (after
    the stone that helped decipher hieroglyphics)

Printers

Color LaserWriter 12/600 PS: Cobra
Color StyleWriter 2200: Calamari
Color StyleWriter 2400: Aurora
Color StyleWriter Pro: Fantasia, Logo
ImageWriter II: Express
LaserWriter: LightWriter
LaserWriter 12/640 PS: Mongoose
LaserWriter IIf: Kirin Dry (a Japanese beer)
LaserWriter IIg: Kirin (a Japanese beer)
LaserWriter IINT: Leia
LaserWriter IINTX: Darth Vader
LaserWriter IISC: Solo
LaserWriter Pro 600: Tollhouse
LaserWriter Select 300: Ninja
LaserWriter Select 360: Viper
Personal LaserWriter: Capriccio
Personal LaserWriter 300: Comet
Personal LaserWriter 320: Photon
Personal LaserWriter LS: Nike
Personal LaserWriter NT: Twist
Personal LaserWriter SC: Shout
StyleWriter: Franklin, Mighty Mouse, Salsa, Tabasco
StyleWriter II: Speedracer
StyleWriter 4100: Cabo
StyleWriter 4500: Baja

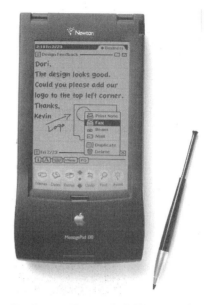

The Newton MessagePad 130 was code-named Dante, after the author of *Inferno*, because creating it was a project from hell.

The code name for the StyleWriter II, Speedracer, was a reference to its improved print performance.

Software

32-bit QuickDraw: Jackson Pollock (after the colorful painter)
A/UX 1.0: Pigs in Space
A/UX 1.1.1: Circle K
A/UX 2.0: Perestroika, Space Cadet
A/UX 3.0: Hulk Hogan
Apple File Exchange: Renault
Apple Font Pack: Big Sur
Apple Guide: Reno
AppleScript 1.0: Cheeze Whiz, Gustav (engineer Donn Denman's
    rottweiler, the team mascot), Toy Surprise
AppleScript 1.1: Guava Surprise, Pure Guava
AppleSearch: Bogart
At Ease: Tiny Toon
Cocoa: Kidsim
Cyberdog search engine/info-access tool kit: V-Twin
Data Access Manager: SnarfMan
Dylan: Denali, Ralph
Edition Manager: Diet Coke
Graphing Calculator: NuCalc
HyperCard: WildCard (hence the creator code WILD)
HyperCard 2.0: Hot Water, Snow
HyperCard IIGS: Bulfinch (after author Thomas Bulfinch), Iduna
Layer Manager: Glass Plus
MacDraw: Mackelangelo
MacDraw Pro 1.0: Chameleon, Maui
Macintosh Application Environment (MAE): Cat-in-the-Hat
MacsBug: Motorola Advanced Computer Systems debugger
MacWrite: Macauthor
MacWrite Pro 1.0: Old Pro
MacWrite Pro 1.5: Cue Ball
MacWrite Pro 1.5v3: Shakespeare
MacX: DeXter (saxophonist "Long Tail Dexter" Gordon), Malcom
MultiFinder: Juggler, Oggler, Twitcher
OpenDoc: Amber, Exemplar, Jedi ("Jed and I," referring to Jed
    Harris and Kurt Piersol, original OpenDoc architects)
PlainTalk SR (speech recognition): Casper
QuickTime: Warhol (an early beta had a Campbell's soup can icon)
QuickTime for Windows: Ethel
QuickTime 1.5: Dali
QuickDraw 3D: Escher
QuickDraw 3D Accelerator Card: White Magic
QuickDraw GX: El Kabong, Serrano, Skia
QuickTime Conferencing: Alexander, MovieTalk
Sound Manager: DJ, Party Line

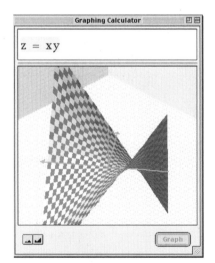

Graphing Calculator was developed under the code name NuCalc.

The original 1987 document describing the Mac's Sound Manager was titled "Software Architecture for a Device-Independent Sound Manager," which can be abbreviated SADISM.

System Software

System 6.0.4: Antares

System 6.0.5: Big Deal

System 6.0.6: SixPack (never released outside of Apple)

System 6.0.8: Terminator (the last version of System 6 ever released)

System 7: Big Bang, Blue, M80 (a powerful firecracker), Pleiades

System 7 Finder: Furnishings 2000 (a defunct furniture store in the San Francisco Bay Area)

System 7 Tune-Up: 7-Up

System 7.0.1: Beta Cheese, Regatta (this release ran on Macs with nautical code names), Road Warrior

System 7.1: Cube-E, I Tripoli (both because the project was to conform to IEEE standards)

System 7.1 Pro: Jirocho

System 7.5: Capone (like the gangster, it was to strike fear in the heart of Chicago, the code name for Windows 95), Mozart

System 7.5 Update 1.0: Danook (from Gary Larson's *Far Side*)

System 7.5 Update 2.0: Thag (from Gary Larson's *Far Side*), Zhag (a corruption of Thag and Zeus)

System 7.5 Version 7.5.3: Unity

System 7.5.2: Marconi (named after Guglielmo Marconi, 19th-century Italian engineer and inventor)

System 7.5.3 Revision 2: Buster

System 7.5.5: Son of Buster (engineers liked the SOB abbreviation)

System 7.6: Harmony

System 7.6.1: Ides of Buster

Mac OS 8.0: Copland, Maxwell, Tempo

Mac OS 8.1: Bride of Buster

Mac OS 8.5: Allegro

Mac OS 8.6: Veronica (after aunt of Brian Bechtel, technical lead)

Mac OS Extended Format (HFS+): Sequoia (after the giant tree)

Taligent OS: Defiant, Pink

Telecommuications

Apple Internet Connection Kit: Cyberpup (stripped-down Cyberdog)

Data Modem 2400: Funnelweb (a poisonous Australian spider)

eWorld 1.0: Aladdin

eWorld 1.1: Golden Gate

ISDN NuBus card: CarCraft

MacTCP: Verduras (Spanish for vegetables)

MacTerminal 2.0: SuperPrawn

MacTerminal II: Killer Bees

PPP 1.0: Paris

System 7 was code-named Blue because that was the color of the index cards used to hold its feature set wish list during a March 1987 brainstorming session. That same meeting also gave rise to Pink, the object-oriented operating system that would form the basis for the Taligent venture with IBM.

Introducing Mac OS 8

What eventually shipped as Mac OS 8 was code-named Tempo, but the ill-fated Copland was expected to use that number until the project was canceled.

Third-Party Products

Adobe Acrobat: Houdini
Adobe Illustrator 7.0: Simba
Avid Cinema: San Francisco
Bandai Power Player: Pippin
Borland dBASE IV 2.0: X-15
Claris CAD: Blackjack
Claris FileMaker Pro: Banza, Ninja, Samurai
Claris MacProject: Road Runner
Claris OfficeMail: RotoRouter
ClarisDraw: Expressway
ClarisImpact: Wall Street (due to its appeal to business users)
ClarisWorks: Terminator (designed to terminate Microsoft Works)
Dantz DiskFit Direct: Paris
Dantz Retrospect 2.0: Warpaint
Dantz Retrospect 3.0: Peary (after the explorer)
dBase Mac: Dottie
Full Impact: Glass
FullWrite: Ozone
IBM PC: Acorn, Chess
IBM PC AT: Bigtop, Salmon
Iomega Jaz: Viper
Lotus MarketPlace: Surfer
Macromind MacroModel: Gummo (Silicon Graphics version),
    Harpo (PC version), Zeppo (Mac version)
Microsoft Excel: Odyssey
Microsoft Mail 4.0: Capone
Microsoft Windows 95: Cairo, Chicago
Microsoft Windows 95 Net Update: Nashville
Microsoft Windows 98: Memphis
Netscape Navigator 4.0: Galileo
Newer Technology SpellTools: Octopod
NeXT Computer: Big Mac, 3M
Power Computing PowerWave 604 series: TidalWave
Power Computing PPCP system: Project Grail
Quattro Pro 1.0: Buddha (it would assume the Lotus position)
Quattro Pro 2.0: Splash
Radius flat-panel pivoting color LCD: Ptolemy
RasterOps ColorBoard264: Cheapskate
SuperMac 8•24 PDQ: Snap
SuperMac Thunder/8: Crackle
SuperMac Thunder/24: Pop (the Rice Krispies series; "Milk" never
    saw the light of day)
SyQuest EZ135: RoadRunner

Microsoft Excel was developed under the code name Odyssey (no relation to John Sculley's book, I'm sure), and when it came time to sell the spreadsheet, Microsoft considered calling it Number Buddy, Mr. Spreadsheet, Sigma, and Plansheet, but ultimately it was a district manager who suggested Excel. Immediately upon Excel's release, Microsoft was sued by Manufacturers Hanover Trust because it owned the rights to the Excel name for its computerized banking service. The two firms eventually settled out of court, with Manufacturers Hanover Trust allowing the use of the word Excel as long as it is always preceded by the name Microsoft.

Millionaire Mania

Getting a company off the ground always requires sacrifices, and in that regard Apple was no different than any other. To scrape together the cost of producing the original Apple I printed circuit board in May 1976, Steve Jobs parted with his red and white Volkswagen bus for $1,500 and Steve Wozniak sold his beloved Hewlett-Packard 65 programmable calculator for $250. The company was hobbling along at the beginning of 1977, when retired businessman Mike Markkula poured $92,000 into Apple's coffers and secured a $250,000 line of credit at Bank of America.

Courtesy of Volkswagen of America and Hewlett-Packard

Jobs and Woz sold a VW bus and HP calculator, respectively, to finance the Apple I.

The time and money each of the three sacrificed to make Apple a success were amply rewarded on December 12, 1980, when underwriters Morgan Stanley and Hambrecht & Quist took the company public. Originally filed to sell at $14 a share, the stock opened at $22 and all 4.6 million shares sold out in minutes. The stock rose almost 32 percent that day to close at $29, giving the company a market valuation of $1.778 billion. Jobs, the single largest stockholder with 7.5 million shares, suddenly had a net worth exceeding $217 million. Not too shabby for a college dropout. Woz's 4 million shares were worth a respectable $116 million. Pretty good for a wire-head who never wanted to build a company. Even Markkula couldn't complain. His 7 million shares were valued at $203 million, for an unbelievable 55,943 percent annualized return on his original 1977 stake!

The three founders of Apple Computer Inc. weren't the only ones who did well that fateful day in December. Of Apple's 1,000

Apple's initial public offering was the largest IPO since the Ford Motor Company went public in 1956. Nonetheless, it sold out in minutes. Unfortunately, not everyone was allowed to get in on the ground floor. For fiscal year 1980, Apple showed a profit of $11.7 million, or 24 cents a share, on revenue of $118 million. That priced the IPO at 92 times earnings. Since Massachusetts' securities law didn't allow offerings with prices of more than 20 times earnings, the state banned individual residents from participating in the IPO, deeming it "too risky." After the IPO, the state determined that residents had been made aware of the risks and decided to allow trading. On May 27, 1981, a second offering of 2.6 million shares of stock was completed.

"When I was 23, I had a net worth of over a million dollars. At 24 it was over $10 million, and at 25 it was over $100 million."

Steve Jobs

Jobs first appeared on the *Forbes* Four Hundred list of richest Americans in 1982. After he sold NeXT to Apple and took Pixar public, *Forbes* estimated his net worth at $710 million in 1997. In the fall of 1998, the 43-year-old Jobs was worth $1 billion, according to *Forbes*.

Apple Computer stock trades in the over the counter (OTC) market and is listed on NASDAQ under the symbol AAPL, on the Tokyo Stock Exchange under the symbol APPLE, and on the Frankfurt Stock Exchange under the symbol APCD.

employees, more than 40 became instant millionaires thanks to their stock options. (An option is a form of compensation that grants an employee the right to purchase stock at a specified exercise price.) Stock options are a way of life in Silicon Valley, and in the late 1970s Apple routinely enticed candidates for employment with options on a few thousand shares of stock with exercise prices of roughly $4.

Courtesy of Michael Jamison

By 1982, certificates featuring the Apple II (inset) had replaced ornate pre-IPO shares.

Each share of stock issued prior to April 1979 was known as a "founder's share." Thanks to the five stock splits prior to the initial public offering (IPO), each founder's share multiplied into 32 shares. So anyone who owned a little over 1,000 founder's shares went to bed a millionaire on December 12, 1980.

But not everyone who helped build Apple was richly rewarded. Stock options were reserved for salaried employees such as engineers, not hourly employees such as technicians. Many of Apple's earliest employees were either too inexperienced or too naive to demand stock options. Let's face it, many of them were just teenagers and college kids. A telling example is Daniel G. Kottke, who had been Jobs' best friend at Reed College and who traveled to India with him in 1974 seeking spiritual enlightenment.

Originally called in to help stuff Apple I circuit boards in 1976, Kottke became employee #12 in June 1977 and was paid minimum wage to assemble and test Apple II motherboards. By 1980, Kottke was doing

"I'm the only person I know that's lost a quarter of a billion dollars in one year. … it's very character building."

Steve Jobs, *discussing what it's like having so much of your net worth tied to a volatile stock such as Apple*

much more demanding work, building and troubleshooting the Apple III prototype, but he remained an hourly technician. "I kept my head down and was working in the lab," recalls Kottke. "I was very naive. I just thought I would do good work and eventually get rewarded. What an idiot."

Courtesy of Dan Kottke

Dan Kottke (left) displaying the Apple I with Steve Jobs at the PC-76 show in Atlantic City.

Kottke wanted the title of engineer more than the options that went with the position, but he wasn't a complete idiot. "I wanted to invest in the company. I had been working there since it started and I wasn't intending to leave. I deserved to invest," believed Kottke, who at the time was sharing a house in Cupertino with Jobs and Jobs' former girlfriend (who would later bear Jobs' child, Lisa Nicole).

Rod Holt, engineering VP, was so uncomfortable with the inequity of the situation that he personally approached Jobs and suggested they both give Kottke some stock by matching each other's contribution. Jobs reportedly exclaimed, "Great! I'll give him zero."

Even though his "best friend" was unwilling to grant him any options, Kottke eventually managed to get some shares. Holt unilaterally gave Kottke 100 shares out of his own pocket, and just before Apple went public, Kottke went to chairman Markkula and president Mike Scott and told them how unhappy he was because he hadn't gotten any shares. "I told them that I was going to leave the company," recalls Kottke. "They gave me options on 1,000 shares at around $8, but it was too late" for the splits that made others fabulously wealthy.

Kottke's allotment was augmented through the generosity of Wozniak, who felt that it was unfair that many of the earliest Apple employees—including Chris Espinosa (employee #8) and Bill Fernandez (employee #4)—failed to get stock options.

Prior to the IPO in 1980, Woz wanted to sell $2 million worth of stock to buy a house and get a car. He had an outside buyer lined up to buy the stock and the two had agreed upon what they considered to be a

> "I kept asking Steve about stock options and he would always put me off, saying that I had to talk to my supervisors. I found out a couple of years later that Jobs was the head of the Compensation Committee in charge of distributing options."
>
> *Apple employee #12* ***Dan Kottke***

> "People think I'm an asshole, don't they?"
>
> ***Steve Jobs***

fair price, even though it was pretty obvious that the stock was going to be worth a lot more when Apple went public. "I had an offer from a qualified buyer, so I just thought I'd sell it at that price to Apple employees," says Woz. So he set up a program called the WozPlan that allowed certain employees to buy up to 2,000 shares each.

Initially Apple's lawyers had a problem with Woz selling to "unqualified buyers," because they didn't want to upset the Securities and Exchange Commission, but when the details were made clear, chief counsel Albert A. Eisenstat gave the OK. In the end, about 80 people participated in the WozPlan, with some buying shares at a very advantageous price, and a select few receiving outright gifts.

"I had much more money than I could ever dream of, and I felt that everyone who had participated in engineering and marketing should be part owners of the company," recalls Woz. "A few of us were going to be making a huge amount of money, yet the others weren't really valued. Mike Markkula's opinion was that these people weren't worthy and weren't entitled to stock. Only the managers with the right college backgrounds who were hired above them got the stock options and were going to make a lot of money. I just wanted to help the others because they were important, too."

Even though Jobs remarked that "Woz ended up giving stock to all the wrong people," Wozniak takes great pleasure from his good deed. "Over the years, a lot of people have called to thank me for making it possible for them to do things—buy houses, send kids to college, etc.— that they otherwise would never have been able to afford. That makes it all worthwhile."

> ## "A person like him shouldn't have that much money."
> **Jerry Wozniak**, *after finding $250,000 worth of uncashed checks strewn about his son's Porsche, which bore the license plate "APPLE II"*

Taking Stock of Apple

Detailed financial information about Apple Computer is available on the Internet from all of the standard stock and personal finance sites, and Apple maintains its own site at www.apple.com/investor. Furthermore, you can request printed copies of Apple's annual reports, SEC filings, and quarterly financial results by contacting

Apple Investor Relations
1 Infinite Loop MS 75-7IR
Cupertino, CA 95014
(408) 974-3123

If you have lost or misplaced an Apple stock certificate, contact First National Bank of Boston, care of Boston EquiServe at (800) 733-5001.

Monthly Closing Price of Apple Computer Common Stock (split-adjusted)

On July 8, 1982, Apple's stock traded at an all-time low of $5.50. It reached an all-time high of $73.25 on April 12, 1991.

On March 18, 1992, the Federal Reserve Board added Apple stock to its list of securities that can be bought on margin (credit).

On December 15, 1992, Apple's stock closed higher than IBM's stock for the first time. Apple closed at $56.875 versus $56.125 for IBM.

Apple's first formal business plan, drawn up by Mike Markkula in November 1976, set a goal for sales to grow from virtually nothing to $500 million in ten years. As it turns out, the company passed that mark in half the time between fiscal 1981 and 1982.

"It was almost like a World War I plane going at Mach 2."
*Employee #68 **Trip Hawkins**, on Apple's early sales growth*

On June 14, 1982, Apple Computer was included in the *"Fortune* Double 500" for the first time at number 598. In May 1983, Apple entered the *Fortune* 500 in under five years at number 411, the fastest ascent in business history.

In December 1982, Apple became the first personal computer company to reach $1 billion annual sales rate. To celebrate, it threw a "Billion Dollar Party" for employees.

"It takes a long time to kill a $11-billion-a-year company. Apple's already down to around $8 billion a year. I give it another three years, until the millennium, to fall the rest of the way to the ground."
*Venture capitalist **Stewart Alsop***

Net Sales (in millions of dollars)

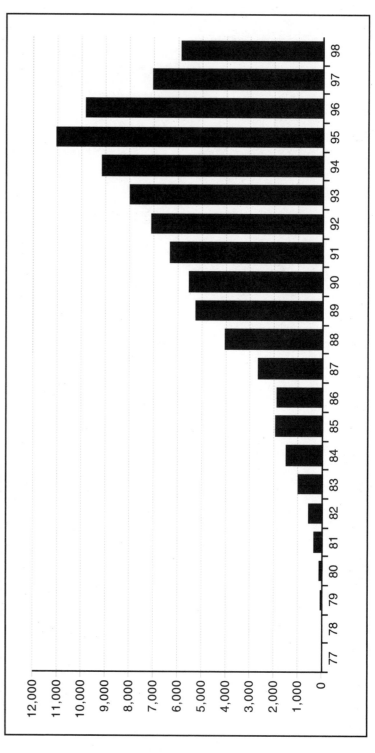

Net Income (in millions of dollars)

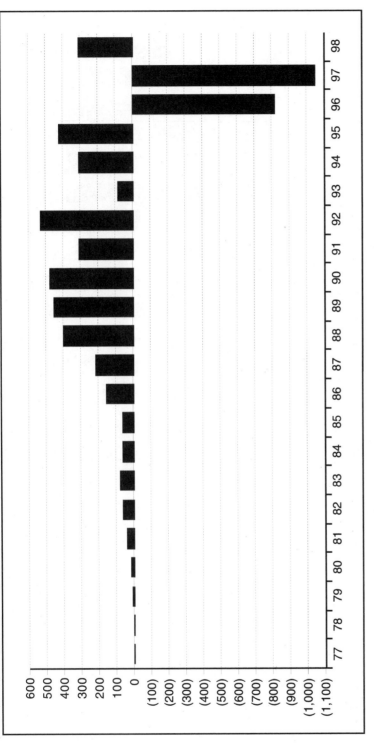

In April 1987, Apple announced its first (and so far, only) stock split. Shares split two-for-one effective May 15, 1987. At the time, Apple declared its first quarterly cash dividend of $0.06 per share (post-split).

Apple continued paying dividends until the second quarter of 1996, at which time it suspended paying dividends on its common stock in an effort to conserve cash. Apple anticipates that, for the foreseeable future, it will retain any earnings for use in the operation of its business.

CEO
05/77	Mike Scott
03/81	Mike Markkula
04/83	John Sculley
06/93	Michael Spindler
02/96	Gil Amelio
07/97	Steve Jobs (interim)

President
05/77	Mike Scott
03/81	Mike Markkula
04/83	John Sculley
06/93	Michael Spindler
02/96	vacant

Chairman
01/77	Mike Markkula
03/81	Steve Jobs
09/85	vacant
01/86	John Sculley
10/93	Mike Markkula
02/96	Gil Amelio
07/97	vacant

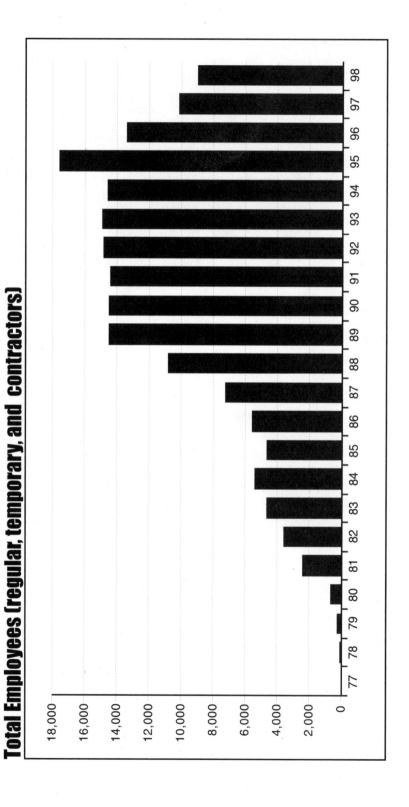

Total Employees (regular, temporary, and contractors)

The Strangest Bedfellow of All

In the late 1970s, Apple was the standout in the crowded personal computer field. The Apple II sold briskly into the home and education markets and had even made headway into business offices, thanks to the popularity of VisiCalc. The entire personal computer industry was enjoying phenomenal growth, and Apple was leading the pack. But Apple knew it was only a matter of time before it faced the most formidable competitor of all, International Business Machines (www.ibm.com) of Armonk, New York. The day of reckoning arrived on August 12, 1981, when IBM introduced its $1,565 personal computer with a single 5.25-inch floppy disk drive and 16K of memory.

Courtesy of IBM Corp.

The boxy IBM Personal Computer didn't break any new technological barriers, but the mere fact that it came from the world's largest computing firm validated the microcomputer market that Apple had dominated so far.

At first Apple was confident it could hold its own against IBM. "We're going to out-market IBM," said chairman Steve Jobs. "We've got our shit together." President Mike Markkula was equally upbeat, stating,

"It's curious to me that the largest computer company in the world [IBM] couldn't even match the Apple II, which was designed in a garage six years ago."
Steve Jobs

"I was at Apple the day IBM announced [its PC]. They didn't seem to care. It took them a year to realize what had happened."
Microsoft CEO **Bill Gates**

"The IBM PC is beneath comment. It's been known for 12 years how to do a good-looking display and IBM didn't put one on its machine. You can't have any favorable comment beyond that. That is the ultimate in know-nothingness."
Apple Fellow **Alan Kay**

"We've been planning and waiting for IBM to get into the marketplace for four years. We're the guys in the driver's seat. We're the guys with one-third of a million installed base. We're the guys with a software library. We're the guys with distribution. It's IBM who is reacting and responding to Apple. They'll have to do a lot more reacting and responding. IBM hasn't the foggiest notion of how to sell to individuals. It took us four years to learn about it. They must learn about distribution structure and independent dealers. You cannot reduce time by throwing money at it. Short of World War III nothing is going to knock us out of the box."

"As it turned out, the original welcome was like Little Red Ridinghood's welcoming the wolf into her grandmother's home. There is a very fine line between being self-confident and getting cocky about it."

John Sculley

Welcome, IBM. Seriously.

Welcome to the most exciting and important marketplace since the computer revolution began 35 years ago.

And congratulations on your first personal computer.

Putting real computer power in the hands of the individual is already improving the way people work, think, learn, communicate, and spend their leisure hours.

Computer literacy is fast becoming as fundamental a skill as reading or writing.

When we invented the first personal computer system, we estimated that over 140,000,000 people worldwide could justify the purchase of one, if only they understood its benefits.

Next year alone, we project that well over 1,000,000 will come to that understanding. Over the next decade, the growth of the personal computer will continue in logarithmic leaps.

We look forward to responsible competition in the massive effort to distribute this American technology to the world.

And we appreciate the magnitutde of your commitment.

Because what we are doing is increasing social capital by enhancing individual productivity.

Welcome to the task. apple

Apple actually welcomed IBM into the PC market, but urged "responsible competition."

On August 24, Apple responded to IBM's PC introduction in an amazing display of bravado by placing a now-famous, full-page advertisement in *The Wall Street Journal* welcoming the pin-striped corporate behemoth into the market that Apple practically saw as its birthright.

While Apple clearly viewed the IBM PC as second-rate technology, the buying public didn't look much farther than those magic initials, which represented stability, service, and reliability. To them, it didn't much matter what was inside the box, the IBM PC was a serious business machine from a serious company, and it didn't take long for Apple to realize it was in serious trouble. By the end of the year, IBM had sold 50,000 computers, and after two years passed Apple in dollar sales of the machines. In 1983, Apple's market share of personal computers edged up from 20 to 21 percent, while IBM's rose dramatically from 18 to 26 percent, according to Future Computing, a Texas-based consulting firm.

Apple tried to stem the tide with the January 1983 introduction of the Lisa. By all accounts, the Lisa was a revolutionary computer, but as far as the business community was concerned, it had two major flaws. First, its $9,995 price tag was too expensive. Second, and perhaps most importantly, it wasn't compatible with anything else on the market. The IBM PC and Microsoft's MS-DOS had established a standard to

which clone manufacturers flocked, but Apple resisted the temptation to go with the flow. Right or wrong, Apple has always felt that its technology was better, if not the best, and if it just waited long enough, the world would recognize this fact and be willing to pay a premium to buy a computer from Cupertino.

By 1984, it was clear that the Lisa was a sales disappointment, and industry pundits were decrying the Apple II as dated technology destined to die any day now (a flawed assessment "experts" would repeat many times over the decade; the Apple II remained on the price list until November 15, 1993). Apple desperately needed a hit to combat IBM, and Jobs had made up his mind to bet everything on the Macintosh. Part of his strategy was to get the public thinking of Apple versus IBM in terms of a two-horse race like Coke and Pepsi, Avis and Hertz, *Newsweek* and *Time.* Never was this strategy executed as effectively as in the landmark *1984* commercial, which heralded the introduction of the Macintosh on January 24, 1984. As Jobs put it in a 1985 *Playboy* interview, "It really is coming down to just Apple and IBM. If, for some reason, we make some giant mistake and IBM wins, my personal feeling is that we are going to enter sort of a computer Dark Ages for about 20 years."

Throughout the 1980s, Apple tenaciously fought to maintain its modest market share against encroachment from IBM and the many clone makers, but after enjoying years of gross margins as high as 53 percent, price wars late in the decade began slashing margins to the bone. Still, Apple steadfastly resisted calls for it to license the Mac or go head-to-head against IBM with its own PC clones. While mulling over Apple's predicament, John Sculley had an epiphany when he finally came to accept what many people had been saying all along: Apple's real strength isn't hardware, it's software—specifically, the Mac's easy-to-use operating system. Therefore, Apple's real enemy isn't IBM, but Microsoft. In an about-face that shocked the industry, Apple decided to join forces with its old adversary in Armonk to take on its new nemesis to the north.

On April 12, 1991, Sculley gave a secret demo to a group of IBM's top engineers. They saw Apple's secret object-oriented operating system (code-named Pink, after the color of the index cards on which the feature set was written during a March 1987 brainstorming session) running on an IBM PS/2 Model 70, making it look and feel a lot like a Mac running System 7, Apple's latest OS that was to be released the following month. Impressed, IBM signed a letter of intent with Apple on July 3, pledging to help finish Pink and give Apple a license to its RISC (reduced instruction set computing) processor, the PowerPC.

> **"IBM wants to wipe us off the face of the earth."**
> *Steve Jobs*

> **"It would be easy for us to come out with an IBM look-alike product, and put the Apple logo on it, and sell a lot of Apples. Our earnings per share would go up and our stockholders would be happy, but we think that would be the wrong thing to do."**
> *John Sculley*

> **"We're not going to sell five million [Macs] a year by being IBM-compatible. We're going to do it by making a second industry standard."**
> *Steve Jobs*

The most Macs Apple ever sold in a single year was 4.5 million in 1995.

Q. What do you get when you cross
   Apple and IBM?
A. IBM.

> "[PowerPC supporters] are smoking dope. There's no way it's going to work."
> *Compaq VP of corporate development*
> **Robert W. Stearns**

IBM's Jack Kuehler (left) and Apple's John Sculley proudly presenting their "marriage certificate," which laid out plans to cooperate on PowerPC, Taligent, and Kaleida.

On October 2, the historic alliance became official when Apple and IBM signed the papers during a press conference at the Fairmont Hotel in San Francisco. "We want to be a major player in the computer industry, not a niche player," explained Sculley. "The only way to do that is to work with another major player." The two former enemies agreed to work on computers based upon the PowerPC chip manufactured by Motorola and established two spin-off companies called Taligent and Kaleida. Taligent would complete Pink while Kaleida worked on ScriptX, a brand-new multimedia engine.

Some speculated that IBM was simply hedging its bets against the possibility of Apple winning its 1988 "look and feel" lawsuit against Microsoft and then coming after IBM for Presentation Manager, which was similar to Windows. As it happened, Apple's suit started heading south at just about the same time the company got into bed with IBM and was eventually dismissed in 1993 (see "Windows: What Went Wrong," page 133).

> "Putting Presentation Manager on an IBM [computer] is like putting Bernaise on a hot dog."
> *Apple Fellow* **Alan Kay**, *speaking to attendees at the Boston Macworld Expo on August 6, 1988*

For all the great expectations, only one item of substance came out of the famous Apple-IBM pact of 1991. Apple's Power Macs, based upon the first-generation PowerPC 601 from Motorola, were introduced as scheduled on March 14, 1994, and garnered favorable reviews for their speed and excellent compatibility with existing Mac software and hardware. The Mac faithful snapped them up in record numbers, but

Apple failed to capitalize on its newfound price / performance lead to expand its market share. While the PowerPC chips have continued to this day to outpace offerings from rival Intel, they haven't become an industry standard, even after Apple, IBM, and Motorola increased their level of cooperation by developing the PowerPC Reference Platform (see "The Clone Quandary," page 193). In June 1998, IBM's Microelectronics Division ended its participation in the PowerPC alliance. Motorola's RISC Microprocessor Division took sole ownership of the Somerset Design Center in Austin, Texas, where the companies developed the PowerPC.

If the PowerPC was a disappointment, Kaleida and Taligent were disasters. Both fell behind schedule almost immediately because of squabbling between Apple and IBM camps over conflicting ideas about what should go into the software products they were developing. A series of cost-cutting moves at Apple forced Kaleida Labs to lay off 20 percent of its employees on May 9, 1994. Seeking to lessen its financial obligations to Taligent, Apple brought in Hewlett-Packard as an investor in 1994.

Both of the joint ventures eventually managed to ship products. On December 19, 1994, Kaleida Labs released its Media Player and ScriptX language, both of which were considered technologically sound, but rival firm Macromedia (www.macromedia.com) had beaten them to market with Shockwave for Director and built up a commanding lead. Taligent's first product, CommonPoint for AIX, shipped in July 1995. CommonPoint comprised more than 100 object-oriented frameworks, providing developers with a powerful platform-independent model that supported interactive collaboration. IBM also released CommonPoint for OS/2, and Apple planned to deliver it for the Mac, but never did.

By late 1995, Kaleida Labs had consumed $150 to $200 million in funding from Apple and IBM. Taligent had burned through an additional $400 million. Apple was in turmoil and couldn't afford to continue playing the role of sugar daddy. On November 17, the plug was pulled on Kaleida Labs, with Apple picking up its technologies and key employees. The other shoe fell on December 19, with Taligent becoming a wholly owned subsidiary of IBM. Each partner retained a license to the technologies held by the other, and each pledged to continue development of what they picked up in the restructurings.

Some of the ideas formulated at Kaleida Labs were used as the basis for Apple's QuickTime classes for Java. Apple also managed to salvage Taligent's Unicode text classes for use in Mac OS 8's Text Encoding Convertor as well as in Java. Other than these small contributions to the advancement of the Mac computing experience, little more was ever heard from either group once they were brought inside the firms that had spawned them with such hope just four years before.

From Xerox,
With Love

Putting the Mac into proper historical perspective is impossible without considering its forerunner, Apple's ill-fated Lisa computer. The Lisa began life in the fall of 1978 when Steve Jobs and William "Trip" Hawkins III, manager of marketing planning, began brainstorming about a next-generation project that would break from the Apple II mold. But it wasn't until July 30, 1979, that the Lisa project really got under way when Ken Rothmuller was hired as project manager. As conceived, the Lisa was nothing like the Mac. For that matter, Lisa, the project, bore little resemblance to Lisa, the product.

In 1979, Lisa existed only as a set of specifications calling for a $2,000 business computer to ship in March 1981 with a built-in green phosphor display, keyboard, and rather traditional user interface. The basic idea of designing the computer around a bit-slice microprocessor was discarded when it became apparent that it would be far too expensive. As it turned out, hardly anything from the original plan made it into the shipping product besides the name. What caused Apple to radically change the Lisa? In a word: Xerox.

Courtesy of Xerox Corp. and Brian Tramontana of Xerox PARC

The Xerox Palo Alto Research Center is the birthplace of many computing firsts.

In 1970, anxious to be on the cutting edge of information technology, the Xerox Corporation (www.xerox.com) gathered many of the best minds in the computer industry and ensconced them in the Palo Alto Research Center (PARC) at 3333 Coyote Hill Road in Palo Alto, California. Their mission was to create the future without worrying about the practicality of actually marketing their creations as commercial products.

By 1973, they had succeeded in giving birth to the Xerox Alto, the embodiment of many computing firsts. It was the first personal computer in the sense that it was designed to be used by a single person. Rather than putting fully formed characters on screen one at a time, the Alto created both text and graphics out of individually controlled pixels using a process called bit mapping. Using Ethernet, another PARC creation, the Alto could network with other Alto computers and laser printers, yet another PARC invention. It had an object-oriented programming language—Smalltalk—with reusable, self-contained modules of code. It also featured a funny pointing device, a three-button mouse, invented in the 1960s by Doug Engelbert, a researcher at the Stanford Research Institute think tank.

The Alto was a revolutionary creation, but it wasn't a product. If it had been sold commercially with the industry's customary gross margins, it might have cost as much as $40,000.

> "It doesn't matter how great the computer is if nobody buys it. Xerox proved that."
>
> *Mac documentation leader*
> **Chris Espinosa**

Courtesy of Xerox Corp. and Brian Tramontana of Xerox PARC

Many Lisa features were borrowed from the groundbreaking Xerox Alto.

Even though the Alto was never sold to the public, it was well known in Silicon Valley. The PARC researchers were proud of their creations and willingly showed them off to many curious visitors who dropped by the campus during the early years. One person in particular who had been impressed with their work was Jef Raskin, an Apple employee who was heading up a small, obscure research project code-named Macintosh. As a visiting scholar at the Stanford Artificial Intelligence Laboratory in the early 1970s, Raskin spent a lot of time at PARC and thought what the researchers and engineers were doing there was wonderful.

Raskin says he tried convincing Jobs to go see the wonderful stuff at Xerox PARC, but in his binary way of viewing the world at the time, Jobs considered Raskin a "shithead who could do no good," so he ignored Raskin's recommendation. However, Raskin had an ally in software engineer Bill Atkinson, who had been his student at the University of California at San Diego and now worked on LisaGraf primitives, the basic graphics routines of the Lisa (ultimately these would be named QuickDraw, a term Raskin coined in his 1967 Penn State thesis). In Jobs' eyes, Atkinson was a hero who could do no wrong, so when Atkinson pushed Jobs to visit Xerox PARC, Jobs readily agreed. By then the Smalltalk group had tired of holding open houses, and Xerox had tightened security at the facility. Fortunately, Jobs had just what it took to open the doors.

Jobs approached the Xerox Development Corporation, the venture capital branch of the copier giant, and boldly told them, "I will let you invest a million dollars in Apple if you will sort of open the kimono at Xerox PARC."

At the time, Apple was enjoying meteoric growth and was in the midst of its second private investment placement. Xerox was anxious to get a piece of the action and was more than willing to allow an Apple contingent to take a peek at PARC. After all, an investment in Apple was likely to turn a handsome profit when the company eventually went public, whereas the stuff in the PARC labs was an intangible asset that would probably never make it to market—it had already languished for six years. Xerox signed an agreement never to purchase more than 5 percent of Apple's shares and invested $1 million by buying 100,000 shares at $10 each (within a year these split into 800,000 shares worth $17.6 million when Apple went public).

In return, Apple was allowed two visits to the PARC labs. When Jobs first visited (with Atkinson) in November 1979, he saw with his own eyes what all the fuss was about. He was so excited that he returned in December with Hawkins, Rothmuller, Richard Page (hardware engineer), John Dennis Couch (VP of software), Michael M. Scott (president), Dr. Thomas M. Whitney (executive VP of engineering), and Bruce Daniels (software engineer). Xerox researchers Adele Goldberg, Diana Merry, and Lawrence Tesler planned to give the same dog-and-pony Smalltalk show (running on a Dorado, a very fast "big brother" of the Alto) that Xerox had put on many times before, but it didn't take long to realize that the guys from Apple were different.

They "got it" immediately, in large part because they had been extensively briefed by Raskin. They understood the importance of what they were shown, recognizing the subtle details that made it better than everything else. They asked all the right questions. Jobs began jumping around, shouting, "Why aren't you doing anything

"The original Lisa was a character-generator machine. I spent days with the Lisa team trying to explain that it could be done all in graphics, like the Alto. In that regard, I had a very strong influence on the Lisa; I was trying to make it more like the Mac. I thought they were headed in the wrong direction."
Father of the Mac project **Jef Raskin**

"You could argue about the number of years it would take, you could argue about who the winners and losers in terms of companies in the industry might be, but I don't think rational people could argue that every computer wouldn't work this way someday."
Steve Jobs, *on the graphical user interface he saw at Xerox*

"We had very few visitors who were multiple-hundred-dollar millionaires, in their twenties, and heads of companies, so most of the people who visited were not able to simply go back and, by fiat, say this is what we want."

*Xerox researcher **Alan Kay**, explaining why Jobs' PARC visits were different from the many others*

After a stint as chief scientist at Atari Computer, Alan Kay became an Apple Fellow on May 1, 1984. Twelve years later, Kay left for Walt Disney Imagineering of Burbank, California, to become a Disney Fellow and VP of R&D.

Alan Kay was one of many PARC researchers who would eventually join Apple.

"Apple is an Ellis Island company. Apple is built on refugees from other companies. These are the extremely bright individual contributors who were troublemakers at other companies."

Steve Jobs

with this? This is the greatest thing! This is revolutionary!" If Xerox didn't recognize the value of its own employees' work, Jobs certainly did. When he saw Smalltalk running with its movable overlapping windows and pop-up menus, he knew that's what he wanted and he instructed the Lisa crew to begin working in that direction.

It's often been reported that Apple stole the Alto from Xerox and marketed it as the Lisa, but that shortchanges the brilliance and hard work of the Lisa team. Apple didn't get blueprints from Xerox, but rather inspiration. "Just like the Russians and the A-bomb," observed PARC's director, George Pake, "they developed it very quickly once they knew it was doable."

Actually, development of the Lisa didn't go so quickly or smoothly, even after the PARC visit. Jobs was trying to distance himself from the Apple III, which he had helped botch, so he began meddling with the Lisa project, arguing over almost every design decision. Nonetheless, by March 1980, Hawkins had completed a marketing-requirements document that specified a graphical user interface, a mouse, a local area network, file servers, and innovative software applications. After complaining that there was no way they could incorporate all these features and stick to the original schedule and $2,000 target, Rothmuller was fired for being uncooperative (of course, he would be proven correct in due time). In July, Tesler left Xerox and joined Apple to work with Atkinson on defining the ground rules of the Lisa's user interface. Eventually more than 15 Xerox employees would defect to Apple, including Bob Belleville, Steve Capps, Owen Densmore, Bruce Horn, Alan Kay, Barbara Koalkin, and Tom Malloy.

Just as the Lisa project was coming into focus, Scott reorganized Apple along product lines in the fall of 1980. Jobs desperately wanted control of the high-visibility Lisa project, which was now part of the Personal Office Systems (POS) division, but Scott was no fool. He knew first-hand that Jobs was an extremely combative manager who lacked technical expertise, a fact that was becoming painfully apparent as the Apple III floundered because of some of Jobs' design mandates. There was no way Scott was going to put Jobs in charge of a project as vitally important as Lisa. Instead, Scott named John Couch VP and general manager of POS and tried to soften the blow to Jobs by asking him to act as the corporate spokesman as Apple prepared for its initial public offering, which would take place that December. Jobs, the media darling and

Courtesy of The 3DO Company

Trip Hawkins modified the Lisa's marketing requirements to match Jobs' vision.

consummate showman, was born for the role, but he would never forgive Scott for denying him the opportunity to bring Lisa to market.

Even with Jobs out of the way, the Lisa was slow to market because the Lisa team refused to simply churn out an Apple-ized Alto. Sure, it borrowed pop-up menus, overlapping windows, and scroll bars from Smalltalk, but it improved them and also invented the concepts of the menu bar, pull-down menus, the one-button mouse, cutting and pasting with the Clipboard, and the Trash can.

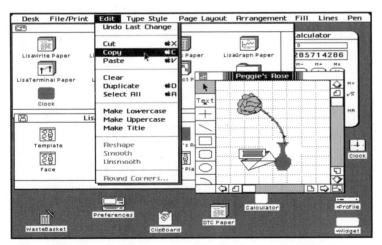

Lisa clearly owes much to the work done at Xerox, but it introduced its fair share of new user interface concepts, including pull-down menus.

> "Steve had an incredible ability to rally people towards some common cause by painting an incredibly glorious cosmic objective. One of his favorite statements about the Lisa was, 'Let's make a dent in the universe. We'll make it so important that it will make a dent in the universe.'"
>
> *Manager of marketing planning for Lisa*
> **Trip Hawkins**

After leaving Apple, Hawkins went on to found the entertainment software publisher Electronic Arts (www.ea.com) and, later, video game manufacturer The 3DO Company (www.3do.com).

On December 14, 1989, almost seven years after the Lisa's introduction, Xerox filed a suit in U.S. District Court for Northern California challenging the validity of Apple's copyrights covering the Lisa and Mac graphical user interfaces. On March 23, 1990, the court dismissed all but one of Xerox's counts.

> "Xerox is incapable of turning a vision into a product. Xerox can't even sue you on time."
>
> *Apple Evangelist* **Guy Kawasaki**,
> *speaking at the Demo '92 trade show*

After seeing the $16,595 Xerox Star (a variation on the Alto) at the June 1981 National Computer Conference in Houston, as well as the work Bruce Horn was doing on the Mac's Finder, a small band of Lisa software engineers led by Atkinson felt confident they were on the right track with some fundamental changes they had made to the operating system's user interface, resulting in icons that you could drag and double-click to open. Everything fell into place nicely after that. On July 30, 1982, the Lisa team managed to get its entire collection of applications to function together for the first time. By September 1, the Lisa was officially declared ready for market, so the following months were devoted to squashing the long list of known bugs.

> "We're going to blow IBM away. There's nothing they can do when this computer comes out. This is so revolutionary, it's incredible."
>
> **Steve Jobs**, *describing the Lisa to John Sculley*

The Lisa made its sales force debut on October 10, 1982, at Apple's annual sales meeting, held that year in Acapulco. According to long-time Apple employee Chris Espinosa, "The story is that ... there was instability in the Mexican government at that time. We had a plan that if a coup occurred and martial law was imposed, we would rent a boat and take all the pre-production Lisas out into the ocean and dump them, so they wouldn't be seized by the military. Come to think of it, that wouldn't have been a bad thing to do anyway."

After more than 200 person-years of hard work (compared to only 2 person-years for the Apple II) and $50 million in development costs, the Lisa was formally introduced on January 19, 1983, during Apple's annual shareholder meeting at De Anza College's Flint Center in Cupertino (the $1,395 Apple IIe was introduced simultaneously under the theme "Evolution and Revolution").

> "We want to drive this industry. We could have introduced Lisa a year ago, but we wanted to make it perfect. We're prepared to live with Lisa for the next ten years."
>
> **Steve Jobs**
> (Time, *January 31, 1983*)

As it turned out, the Lisa's lifespan would be less than two years.

While innovative, the Lisa (with dual Twiggy drives) was expensive and sold poorly.

The Lisa weighed 48 pounds and featured a Motorola 68000 microprocessor running at 5MHz, 1MB of RAM, two 5.25-inch 860K floppy disk drives, a 5MB hard disk (the same ProFile originally designed for the Apple III), a detachable keyboard, a one-button mouse, and a built-in 12-inch, 720-by-364 pixel, bitmapped monochrome display.

Since it was incompatible with everything else on the market, the Lisa was bundled with seven applications: a spreadsheet, drawing program, graphing program, file manager, project manager, terminal emulator, and word processor. The Lisa came with everything and a a list price to match: $9,995. As Rothmuller had warned three years earlier, feature creep boosted the price of the computer to the point where only well-heeled businesses could afford it. Instead of its traditional personal computer competitors Atari, Commodore, and Radio Shack (Tandy), Apple found itself going up against the big guns of Digital Equipment Corp. (DEC), IBM, Wang, and Xerox.

Formidable competition wasn't the only factor inhibiting Lisa's market acceptance. In large measure, Apple contributed to its own undoing. First there was that list price just shy of $10,000. Apple simply had no experience selling computers at such a high price point, so it had to build an elitist, 100-person sales staff from the ground up. Then there was all that bundled software. Giving the customer everything they could possibly need must have seemed like a good idea at the time, but it stifled third-party development efforts. Also, the Lisa was so slow that it inspired a popular "knock knock" joke wherein the response to "Who's there?" was a fifteen-second pause followed by the word "Lisa."

If all that wasn't bad enough, Apple was also bedeviled by the Lisa's floppy disk drives, which Jobs had stubbornly insisted on developing in-house, despite the fact that nobody at Apple had any experience designing a drive from scratch. The Apple 871 disk drive—code-named Twiggy after the 1960s "mod" British fashion model because both were thin—provided an impressive 860K of storage, but was notoriously unreliable. Richard Jordan, an engineer who worked on the project, unsuccessfully begged Jobs to "take out your .45 and shoot the friggin' horse in the head," but Jobs resisted the pleas to license a drive from an outside source.

Finally, and perhaps most damaging, even before the Lisa began shipping in June, the press was full of intentionally leaked rumors about a fall release of a "baby Lisa" that would work in much the same way, only faster and cheaper. Its name: Macintosh.

> **"We're really banking everything on Lisa's technology. If Lisa fails, we'll be just another half-billion or billion-dollar computer company."**
> **Steve Jobs**, *carefully specifying Lisa technology, not the Lisa itself*

Despite Lisa's failure, Apple's sales peaked at $11 billion in fiscal 1995.

The 1983 Lisa television commercial entitled *Breakfast* starred a then-unknown actor named Kevin Costner.

> **"The Lisa failed because it was very under-powered, and so while it did beautiful things, it did them very slowly."**
> **Alan Kay**

> **"Lisa is going to be incredibly great. It will sell twelve thousand units in the first six months and fifty thousand in the first year."**
> **Steve Jobs**

According to a confidential internal document, Apple planned to sell at least 10,000 units in the first half of fiscal year 1983 and 42,000 units in fiscal 1984. InfoCorp estimates the Lisa sold only 60,000 units over its two-year lifespan.

"Whatever Apple's plans are, we think it extremely unlikely that it would introduce a similar product that would undercut their Lisa system so soon after its costly development and introduction. Indeed, we cannot see the benefit that would be gained by such action. So, whatever MacIntosh [sic] may turn out to be and whenever it finally appears, we think it is more likely that it will be clearly differentiated from the Lisa offering."

*Journalist **Joseph L. Ehardt**,*
who would soon eat his words

The revamped Lisa 2 (with 400K Sony drive) was introduced along with the Mac.

Apple recognized some of its mistakes, and on September 12, 1983, it unbundled the suite of software and began selling the Lisa hardware at the reduced price of $6,995. Then on January 24, 1984, when Apple introduced the Macintosh, it also announced the revamped Lisa 2 series. The base model now cost $3,495, had half the memory of the original and twice the speed. The high-end model, the Lisa 2/10, had more memory and a 10MB hard disk drive. Instead of the troublesome Twiggy, both used a new robust 3.5-inch 400K Sony disk drive borrowed from the Mac.

Lisa sales began picking up as the Mac pulled people into dealer showrooms and many realized they needed more power than the Mac offered. Still, Apple shipped three times as many Macs in its first 100 days than Lisas in its first year. In an attempt to consolidate the product line in January 1985, Apple changed the name of the Lisa 2/10 to Macintosh XL, dropped the other Lisa models, and introduced MacWorks, an emulation program that could run Mac software. The renamed Lisa began holding its own, but ironically it would soon be killed by the very man who had brought it to life: Steve Jobs.

A lot had happened since Mike Scott denied Jobs the chance to head the Lisa project in 1980. In March 1981, Markkula took over the presidency from Scott, and Jobs succeeded Markkula as chairman. In April 1983, Jobs convinced John Sculley to leave Pepsi-Cola to become president and CEO of Apple. Impressed by his young suitor, Sculley gave Jobs free rein over the Mac division, and in November, the Lisa and Mac divisions were combined into the Apple 32 SuperMicro division with Jobs at the helm. His power thus consolidated, Jobs decided to put the newly renamed Lisa out of its misery.

By Sculley's own account, "Steve and several members of the Macintosh team believed the original design of the Lisa wasn't good enough and that it never would have the quality of a Macintosh. They felt it wasn't a priority product and wanted it phased out. We obviously couldn't phase a product out that had just been introduced. So someone in the Macintosh division simply neglected, perhaps deliberately, to order parts and components to allow us to continue the manufacture of the Macintosh XL."

Apple officially discontinued the Macintosh XL, née Lisa, on April 29, 1985, and the last Lisa rolled off the assembly line at the Carrollton, Texas, factory on May 15. Sun Remarketing of Logan, Utah, purchased the 5,000 unsold Lisas in inventory and took several thousand more used and broken units on consignment.

Courtesy of Kevin Rice

Sun Remarketing was doing pretty well selling the leftover Lisas after upgrading them with the latest Mac technology, but in mid-September 1989, Apple decided to literally bury the Lisa once and for all. Under the watchful eyes of armed security guards, 2,700 Lisas that Sun had on consignment were interred at the landfill in Logan, Utah (requiring 880 cubic yards at $1.95 a yard), so Apple could receive a tax write-off that year.

The last of the Lisas were buried unceremoniously in a landfill in Logan, Utah.

> "You guys really fucked up. I'm going to have to lay a lot of you off."
>
> ***Steve Jobs***, *to the Lisa troops, after consolidating the Lisa and Mac divisions*

> "We had to abandon [the Lisa] without honor or glory since we failed to raise sales to an adequate profit margin at a time when market growth was slowing down. All of which proves that it is difficult to revive a product that has made a poor start."
>
> *President of Apple Products*
> ***Jean-Louis Gassée***

Sun Remarketing sells and services Apple equipment and still fulfills special orders for Lisas: P.O. Box 4059, Logan, UT 84323-4059. (800) 821-3221 or (801) 755-3360, www.sunrem.com.

> "[The Lisa] was a great machine. We just couldn't sell any."
>
> *Apple human interface guru*
> ***Bruce Tognazzini***

Code Name Confusion

Like the Macintosh, the ill-fated Lisa made it to market with its code name intact. There are many conflicting rumors about the origin of the name. The most widely circulated story is that the Lisa was named after Steve Jobs' first daughter, who was born out of wedlock. This much is fact: On June 17, 1978, in Oregon, Jobs' high-school sweetheart and former live-in girlfriend gave birth to a girl, whom the 23-year-old Jobs helped name Lisa Nicole. In 1979, Lisa's mother filed a paternity suit against Jobs. Even after a blood test performed by the University of California concluded that the probability of Jobs being Lisa's father was 94.4 percent, Jobs dismissed the results. Nonetheless, he didn't want the suit dragging on—Apple would soon go public, making him exceedingly rich—so he agreed to pay child support of $385 a month, provide health insurance for Lisa, and reimburse public assistance for the baby in the amount of $5,856. Though they got off to a rough start, Jobs eventually came to accept Lisa as his daughter. In recent years the two have often been spotted together in Palo Alto, where Jobs lives on Waverly Street with his wife and other kids.

Still, the question remains, was the Lisa named for Jobs' daughter? The project began several months after the birth of Lisa Nicole, so the timing is right. Also, during this period at Apple, it was customary to name projects after daughters of project leaders. While many therefore believe that the Lisa must have been named after Jobs' daughter, Steve Wozniak disagrees. "I know for a fact that Lisa was not named for Steve Jobs' illegitimate daughter," insists Woz. "It's not the truth. John Couch headed the Lisa program, and he told me it was named after Ken Rothmuller's daughter, another key person behind the Lisa." Sadly for this interpretation of events, Rothmuller's only daughter is named Cheryl, and as he put it, "Jobs is such an egomaniac, do you really think he would have allowed such an important project to be named after anybody but his own child?"

No matter who the computer was named after, Apple figured it needed a more professional-sounding name to appeal to the business market, so it hired an outside consulting firm to recommend a new name. Among others, they suggested Applause, Apple IV, Apple 400, The Coach, Esprit, Teacher, and The World. Quite an effort went into thinking up a different name, but the forthcoming computer had already received so much press coverage under its code name that Apple reverse-engineered the explanation that Lisa stood for "Local Integrated Software Architecture." This was so obviously contrived that industry wags suggested a more accurate explanation was that Lisa stood for "Let's Invent Some Acronym."

Jobs, 36, married Laurene Powell, 27, a Stanford University MBA student, at the Ahwahnee Hotel in Yosemite National Park on March 18, 1991. Their first child, Reed Paul (named after the Oregon college that Jobs dropped out of), was born that September. Their second child, a girl, was born in August 1995.

Lisa Timeline

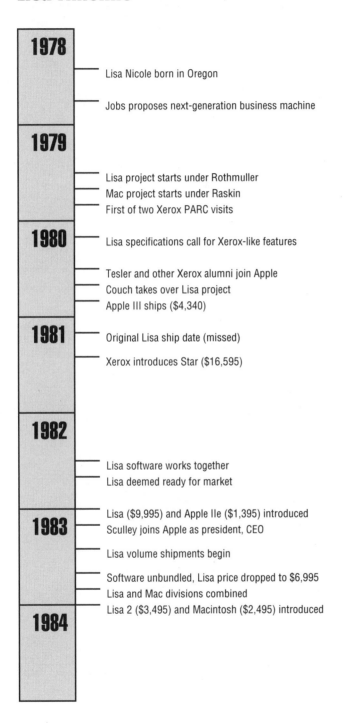

1978
— Lisa Nicole born in Oregon

— Jobs proposes next-generation business machine

1979

— Lisa project starts under Rothmuller
— Mac project starts under Raskin
— First of two Xerox PARC visits

1980
— Lisa specifications call for Xerox-like features

— Tesler and other Xerox alumni join Apple
— Couch takes over Lisa project
— Apple III ships ($4,340)

1981
— Original Lisa ship date (missed)

— Xerox introduces Star ($16,595)

1982

— Lisa software works together
— Lisa deemed ready for market

— Lisa ($9,995) and Apple IIe ($1,395) introduced
1983
— Sculley joins Apple as president, CEO

— Lisa volume shipments begin

— Software unbundled, Lisa price dropped to $6,995
— Lisa and Mac divisions combined
— Lisa 2 ($3,495) and Macintosh ($2,495) introduced
1984

On September 23, 1981, an employee task force issued a memo codifying the company's culture in a list of Apple Values that were defined as "the qualities, customs, standards, and principles that the company as a whole regards as desirable. They are the basis for what we do and how we do it. Taken together, they identify Apple as a unique company. [We] recognize that these values are goals. We don't always live up to them … Identifying our values is important, but fostering them in practice is even more important." As you examine the following Apple Values written in the early 1980s, take a moment to consider if they're still evident in the Apple of today:

- One person, one computer.
- We are going for it and we will set aggressive goals.
- We are all on the adventure together.
- We build products we believe in.
- We are here to make a positive difference in society, as well as make a profit.
- Each person is important; each has the opportunity and the obligation to make a difference.
- We are all in it together, win or lose.
- We are enthusiastic!
- We are creative; we set the pace.
- We want everyone to enjoy the adventure we are on together
- We care about what we do.
- We want to create an environment in which Apple values flourish.

Lisa Timeline (continued)

In honor of John Sculley's previous employer, the Lisa 2 was code-named Pepsi before being renamed the Macintosh XL. While XL was supposed to convey the impression of an extra-large Macintosh, insiders joked that it really stood for "eX-Lisa" or "eXtra Lisas" in inventory.

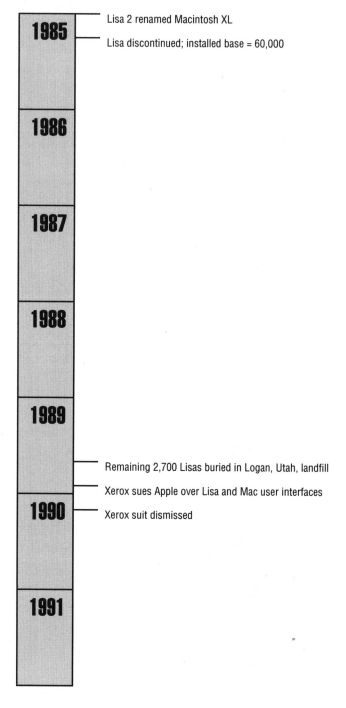

1985 — Lisa 2 renamed Macintosh XL

Lisa discontinued; installed base = 60,000

1986

1987

1988

1989

Remaining 2,700 Lisas buried in Logan, Utah, landfill

Xerox sues Apple over Lisa and Mac user interfaces

1990 — Xerox suit dismissed

1991

The Making of Macintosh

Steve Jobs and the Macintosh are inextricably linked in the minds of most people. So it may come somewhat as a surprise to learn that the Mac wasn't his idea at all. In fact, he actually wanted to kill the project in its infancy. Lucky for Apple and millions of dedicated Mac users everywhere, he wasn't successful. The story of how the Mac came to be is a fascinating tale of one man's inspiration, another man's ego, and the dedication of a small band of "pirates" that forever changed the way the world computes.

In 1994, while Apple and all the major Macintosh publications were celebrating the Mac's 10th anniversary, one man was quietly celebrating its 15th. That man is Jef Raskin, the true father of the Macintosh.

Courtesy of Michael Swaine

Early Apple employees (from left to right) Michael Scott, Steve Jobs, Jef Raskin, Chris Espinosa, and Steve Wozniak, shown here in a hotel room in 1977.

Raskin, a professor turned computer consultant, wrote the Integer BASIC manual for the Apple II in 1976. When he joined Apple on January 3, 1978 (exactly one year after its incorporation), as employee #31, the 34-year-old Raskin was manager of the publications department. Over time he started a new product review division and an application software division.

In the spring of 1979, chairman Mike Markkula asked Raskin if he would work on a project code-named Annie, the goal of which was to produce a $500 game machine (shades of the ill-fated Bandai Pippin). At the time, Jobs and cohorts were working on the business-oriented Lisa, and the company felt it needed a lower-cost product than the Apple II, which was selling for well over $1,000 in a basic configuration without a disk drive or monitor.

"I told him it was a fine project, but I wasn't terribly interested in a game machine," remembers Raskin. "However, there was this thing that I'd been dreaming of for some time which I called Macintosh. The biggest thing about it was that it would be designed from a human factors perspective, which at that time was totally incomprehensible." Markkula was intrigued and asked Raskin to elaborate on his ideas and investigate the feasibility of putting them into practice.

By late May, Raskin had sketched out the basic ideas behind a computer for the "Person in the Street," known as the PITS, for short. Raskin had grown increasingly frustrated at the complexity of the Apple II. Its open architecture was good in the sense that you could fill its slots with anything you wanted, but that flexibility forced the user to be a pseudo-technician and made it extremely difficult for developers to create products that worked with all configurations.

"Considerations such as these led me to conceive the basic architecture and guiding principles of the Macintosh project," explains Raskin. "There were to be no peripheral slots so that customers never had to see the inside of the machine (although external ports would be provided); there was a fixed memory size so that all applications would run on all Macintoshes; the screen, keyboard, and mass storage device (and, we hoped, a printer) were to be built in so that the customer got a truly complete system, and so that we could control the appearance of characters and graphics."

Physically, the computer would be contained in an all-in-one case without cables. Raskin expected people to grow so attached to their Macs that they would never want to leave home without them, so portability was a key concern. He envisioned a weight just under 20

"Adam Osborne is always dumping on Apple. He was going on and on about Lisa and when we would ship Lisa and then he started joking about Mac. I was trying to keep my cool and be polite but he kept asking, 'What's this Mac we're hearing about? Is it real?' He started getting under my collar so much that I told him, 'Adam, it's so good that even after it puts your company out of business, you'll still want to go out and buy it for your kids.'"

Steve Jobs

Osborne Computer Corp. was founded in 1980 and made a name for itself with a portable computer the size of a sewing machine. The company went bankrupt in 1983 when sales dried up after founder Adam Osborne pre-announced an improved model that everyone waited for instead of buying the current one.

Cold Cash for a Code Name

In naming his Macintosh project, Raskin bucked the trend of using female code names. He thought the practice was sexist, and it was. The Annie project, for which Markkula originally tried to recruit Raskin, was a thinly veiled reference to Little Annie Fanny, the well-endowed cartoon character (created by Harvey Kurtzman and Willy Elder) that regularly appeared in *Playboy* back then.

It's often reported that Raskin misspelled the name of his favorite variety of apples, but that's unlikely given that he was manager of publications. "I intentionally changed the spelling," insists Raskin. "I'm a pretty good speller. Writing is one of the things I do well. The name of the apple is McIntosh. I thought that would lead us to a conflict with McIntosh Laboratory, the hi-fi manufacturer. So I used the spelling Macintosh, figuring that if it conflicted with the overcoat, who cares?" Unfortunately, the slight spelling change wasn't enough to keep Apple in the clear.

When Apple attempted to trademark the name Macintosh in 1982, the request was denied because it phonetically infringed on the trademark already owned by an American manufacturer of audio equipment. McIntosh Laboratory (www.mcintoshlabs.com) of Binghamton, New York, operates at the very high end of the high-fidelity food chain, selling CD players for $2,000 and speakers that go from $1,600 to $25,000 a pair. On November 16, 1982, Steve Jobs wrote a letter to the president of McIntosh Labs, Gordon Gow, requesting a worldwide release for the name Macintosh for use in the computer industry. "We have become very attached to the name Macintosh. Much like one's own child, our product has developed a very definite personality," wrote Jobs.

Gow visited Cupertino shortly thereafter to take a look at what Apple was developing, but on the advice of his legal counsel, he rejected Jobs' request. Apple considered shortening Macintosh to MAC, which would stand for "Mouse-Activated Computer" outside the company, and "Meaningless Acronym Computer" internally. However, in late March 1983, Apple managed to license the rights to the name and in 1986 purchased the trademark outright.

Although the terms of these agreements remain confidential to this day, it has been reported that Apple paid $100,000 in cash for the Macintosh name. According to McIntosh's legal counsel, that's "substantially off the mark" and the real pay-off was "significantly higher."

"Throw thirty million dollars of advertising at it and it will sound great."
Venture capitalist **Ben Rosen**, when Jobs asked his opinion of the name Macintosh

pounds and an internal battery providing up to two hours of operation. His wish list also included an 8-bit microprocessor with 64K of RAM, one serial port, modem, real-time clock, printer, 4- or 5-inch diagonal screen with bitmapped graphics, and a 200K, 5.25-inch floppy disk drive all built in.

BASIC and FORTH programming languages were to be contained in read only memory (ROM), as were "self-instructional" programs that were so easy to use, manuals would be unnecessary. Raskin described a user interface in which everything—writing, calculating, drafting, painting, etc.—was accomplished in a graphical word processor-type environment with a few consistent and easily learned concepts. "For example, the calculator abilities will apply to numbers that are entered the same way any text is entered. The traditional concept of an operating system is replaced by an extension of the idea of an on-line editor." While that may not sound much like the Mac as we know it today, his reasoning was that there should be no modes or levels, a concept that has endured.

> "The standard way [Jobs] operated was picking your brain. He would immediately poo-poo the idea, then a week later, he'd come back and say, 'Hey, I've got a great idea!' The idea that he gave back to you was your own. We called him the Reality Distortion Field."
>
> **Jef Raskin**

> "With Steve [Jobs] you never know exactly where an idea comes from."
>
> **Steve Wozniak**

Raskin even proposed an official name for his Macintosh computer: the Apple V. He figured that it could go into production by September 1981, for sale that Christmas with an initial end-user price of $500. As volume increased, he expected the price to drop to $300 after 18 months. "Jobs hated the idea," Raskin recalls. "He ran around saying 'No! No! It'll never work.' He was one of the Macintosh's hardest critics and he was always putting it down at board meetings. When he became convinced that it would work, and that it would be an exciting new product, he started to take over … He was dead set against the Macintosh for the first two years. He said it was the dumbest thing on earth and that it would never sell. When he decided to take it over, he told everybody that he had invented it." Although Jobs strongly opposed the Macintosh when it was first proposed, Raskin nonetheless won the board's approval to begin a formal research project in September 1979.

As he brainstormed, Raskin kept coming up with more wonderful things to add to his computer. It didn't take him long to realize that he couldn't include everything he wanted and still produce a computer with a $500 price tag, so he settled on a new goal of $1,000. "There is no doubt that we want more—more mass storage, a built-in printer, color graphics—but we feel that low price and portability are the most important attributes, and we have kept strenuously to these goals," Raskin wrote in one of his memos.

Careful What You Ask For

By September 27, 1979, a preliminary cost investigation revealed that with Apple's customary 400% cost of goods mark-up, there was no way Raskin's proposed Macintosh could sell for the initial target price of $500, even without a disk drive and printer. A more realistic figure was $1,500 for a fully loaded Mac. On October 2, Jobs told Raskin, "Don't worry about price, just specify the computer's abilities."

Raskin replied with a sarcastic memo specifying:

A small, lightweight computer with an excellent, typewriter style keyboard. It is accompanied by a 96 character by 66 line display that has almost no depth, and a letter-quality printer that also doesn't weigh much, and takes ordinary paper and produces text at one page per second (not so fast so that you can't catch them as they come out). The printer can also produce any graphics the screen can show (with at least 1000 by 1200 points of resolution). In color.

The printer should weigh only a fraction of a pound, and never need a ribbon or mechanical adjustment. It should print in any font. There is about 200K bytes of main storage besides screen memory and a miniature, pocketable, storage element that holds a megabyte and costs $.50, in unit quantity.

When you buy the computer, you get a free unlimited access to the ARPAnet, the various timesharing services, and other informational, computer accessible data bases. Besides an unexcelled collection of application programs, the software includes BASIC, Pascal, LISP, FORTRAN, APL, PL\1, COBOL, and an emulator for every processor since the IBM 650.

Let's include speech synthesis and recognition, with a vocabulary of 34,000 words. It can also synthesize music, even simulate Caruso singing with the Mormon Tabernacle Choir, with variable reverberation.

Conclusion: starting with the abilities is nonsense. We must start both with a price goal, and a set of abilities, and keep an eye on today's and the immediate future's technology. These factors must be all juggled simultaneously.

It's easy to see why Raskin's defiant manner rankled Jobs, but he unwittingly described many of the technologies that the Mac would eventually come to include.

Steve Jobs took singer Joan Baez to the Macintosh Christmas party held at the St. Francis Hotel in San Francisco in February 1983.

"I was in an executive staff meeting with all the officers in the company, and Steve turns to me and says, 'Can I talk to you for a minute?' So we go sit in his office. At the time, I was going out with a woman six years older than me who had children. Steve started to ask me all these questions about what it's like. And then he starts telling me he's going out with a woman who's older and has some kids. We talk about it for 45 minutes. It was a delightful conversation; it wasn't until about four months later that I figured out he was talking about Joan Baez."

Apple manager of marketing planning
Trip Hawkins

The Evolution of the Macintosh

Here are the Mac's specifications at various times during its development, based upon official Apple documents.

DATE	5/29/79	9/27/79	9/28/79	10/12/79
Price	$500	$1,500	$500	$500
INTERNAL				
Processor	8-bit CPU	6809E	6809E	6809E
Memory	64K	64K	64K	64K
ROM	na	32K	32K	32K
Mass storage	200K 5.25" floppy	200K 5.25" floppy	optional	optional
Battery	2 hours	2 hours	2 hours	optional
Serial port	one	one	one	one
Modem	built-in	built-in	built-in	built-in
Real-time clock	built-in	built-in	built-in	built-in
VIDEO				
Display	built-in	built-in	use TV	use TV
Diagonal	4" or 5"	4" or 5"	4" or 5"	4" or 5"
Characters	na	na	64 per line	64 per line
Pixels	na	na	na	na
INPUT				
Keyboard	built-in	built-in	built-in	built-in
Input device	na	na	na	na
Speech recognition	na	na	na	optional
Microphone	na	na	na	na
OUTPUT				
Printer	built-in	built-in	optional	optional
Speaker	na	na	na	built-in
Speech synthesis	na	na	na	optional
PHYSICAL				
Weight	20 pounds	na	10 pounds	na
H x W x D	na	na	13" x 13" x 5"	na
SOFTWARE				
BASIC	built-in	built-in	built-in	na
Calculator	na	na	na	built-in
Communications	na	na	na	na
FORTH	built-in	na	na	na
Word processor	na	na	na	built-in

	1/12/80	7/1/80	2/16/81	1/24/84
DATE				
Price	$1,000	$1,300	$1,500	$2,495
INTERNAL				
Processor	6809E	6809E	68000	68000
Memory	64K	64K	64K	128K
ROM	32K	32K	32K	64K
Mass storage	200K 5.25" floppy	200K cassette	200K 5.25" floppy	400K 3.5" floppy
Battery	optional	optional	na	na
Serial port	one	one	one	two
Modem	built-in	built-in	built-in	na
Real-time clock	built-in	built-in	built-in	built-in
VIDEO				
Display	built-in	built-in	built-in	built-in
Diagonal	7"	7"	9"	9"
Characters	70 chars x 25 lines	70 chars x 25 lines	96 chars x 25 lines	na
Pixels	256 x 256	256 x 256	384 x 256	512 x 342
INPUT				
Keyboard	built-in	built-in	built-in	detached
Input device	lightpen	joystick	joystick	mouse
Speech recognition	optional	optional	optional	na
Microphone	built-in	built-in	na	na
OUTPUT				
Printer	optional	optional	optional	optional
Speaker	built-in	built-in	built-in	built-in
Speech synthesis	optional	optional	optional	limited
PHYSICAL				
Weight	22 pounds	na	na	16.7 pounds
H x W x D	na	na	na	13.5" x 9.7" x 10.9"
SOFTWARE				
BASIC	disk resident	na	na	third-party
Calculator	built-in	built-in	built-in	desk accessory
Communications	na	built-in	built-in	na
FORTH	na	na	na	na
Word processor	built-in	built-in	built-in	MacWrite

The first graphical image ever displayed on Burrell Smith's Mac prototype was a picture of Scrooge McDuck playing the fiddle while sitting on some money bags.

Raskin needed someone to turn his ideas into prototypes. His former UCSD student, Bill Atkinson, was a respected member of the Lisa team, and Atkinson was impressed with the outstanding work Burrell Carver Smith was doing as a repairman in the Apple II maintenance department. Atkinson introduced Smith to Raskin as "the man who's going to design your Macintosh," to which Raskin replied, "We'll see about that." Smith whipped together a makeshift prototype using a Motorola 6809E microprocessor, a television monitor, and the guts of an Apple II. Duly impressed, Raskin made him the second member of the Mac team.

In time, Raskin took on an assistant, and Steve Wozniak began part-time work on the Mac, but Smith continued doing most of the detailed electronic design and breadboarding. This skeleton crew toiled in what had been Apple's first office and the birthplace of the Apple II and Lisa: Suite B3 at 20833 Stevens Creek Boulevard, near the Good Earth restaurant in Cupertino. The Macintosh remained a research project and was not destined to become an actual product anytime soon. Still, Raskin remained obsessed with designing a computer that could be sold at a low price and manufactured in large quantities. Raskin did everything he could to "keep the project from burgeoning into a huge, expensive, and time-consuming effort."

Every feature required a trade-off between price and performance. They wanted a color monitor, but monochrome would have to do. The Lisa's 68000 microprocessor was desired, but the 6809E was much cheaper. A floppy disk drive would be great, but a digital cassette drive kept the cost down. More memory would nice, but 64K was considered adequate.

While Raskin's small team was quietly toiling in the Mac "skunkworks," turmoil was brewing elsewhere at Apple. Following the fateful visits to Xerox PARC, Jobs was making waves and enemies as he steered the Lisa project away from its original mandate as a $2,000 business computer into a much more expensive downsized Xerox Alto. In September 1980, the board of directors wanted to cancel the Macintosh project to concentrate on getting the jinxed Apple III out the door and getting the Lisa project under control, but Raskin pleaded for and won a three-month reprieve. During this time, president Mike Scott restructured the company and removed Jobs from the Lisa project. Jobs was furious, and to cool his heels Scott sent him out on the road to represent Apple prior to its initial public offering of stock on December 12, 1980.

When the IPO was over, "Jobs was at loose ends because finally [the board] realized that he was totally incompetent as a manager," recalls Raskin. Jobs set his sights on the Macintosh project. As software wizard Andy Hertzfeld remembers it, "The Lisa team in general told Steve to fuck off. Steve said, 'I'll get this team that'll make a cheap computer and that will blow them off the face of the earth.' Then Steve saw that Raskin had critical mass: He had a hardware engineer and a software engineer. Since Steve was a bigger kid than Raskin, he said, 'I like that toy!' and took it." One of Jobs' first moves was an attempt to rename the computer "Bicycle," but nobody followed his lead, so he quietly dropped the idea.

> "[Jobs] would try to push himself into everything. No matter what you were doing, he had to have something to do with it. Nobody at Apple wanted him involved with their projects. I had started the Macintosh team and we didn't want him either."
>
> **Jef Raskin**

Although Jobs' attempt to rename the Mac "Bicycle" failed, the concept survived as the logo for the Apple University Consortium's "Wheels for the Mind" promotion.

The board was only too happy to let Jobs go off and spin his wheels on the Mac, which they viewed as a relatively unimportant research project. The board may have seen it that way, but Jobs viewed it as his opportunity to prove his worth as a technological innovator. At first, Jobs was content to manage only the hardware side of the project, leaving Raskin in charge of software and documentation. "I was more interested in the interface than the chips inside," says Raskin, so the move didn't trouble him too much. Besides, with Jobs on board, perhaps the project would get the funding and support needed to actually create a product. Would it ever!

Raskin's Secret Memo
Steve Jobs began rubbing Jef Raskin the wrong way not long after muscling his way into the Mac project in January 1981. On February 19, 1981, a year before he resigned from Apple, Raskin sent a confidential, four-page memo to president Mike Scott detailing the specific problems he had working with Jobs:

1. Jobs regularly misses appointments.
2. He acts without thinking and with bad judgement.
3. He does not give credit where due.
4. Jobs often reacts ad hominem.
5. He makes absurd and wasteful decisions by trying to be paternal.
6. He interrupts and doesn't listen.
7. He does not keep promises or meet commitments.
8. He makes decisions ex cathedra.
9. Optimistic estimates.
10. Jobs is often irresponsible and inconsiderate.
11. He is a bad manager of software projects.

"The most important thing Steve [Jobs] did was erect a giant shit-deflecting umbrella that protected the project from the evil suits across the street."

Mac software wizard **Andy Hertzfeld**

"Other than having a pirate flag fluttering over it, the Mac headquarters was an ordinary one-story, boring Silicon Valley office building that affected a quasi-Spanish style. We could tell that Steve [Jobs] was in, because his blue Mercedes was parked in the handicap zone in front. As I was to learn, Steve always parked there. He parked there because when he parked to the side, or to the back of the building, disgruntled Apple employees from the Lisa or Apple II division would come by and scratch his Mercedes with their keys."

Macworld publisher **David Bunnell**

"It's better to be a pirate than to join the Navy."

Steve Jobs, explaining the appeal of being part of the original Mac team

Soon after Jobs got involved, the Mac team took over the second floor in a small two-story building known as Texaco Towers due to its proximity to a gas station on the corner of De Anza and Stevens Creek Boulevards. (The gas station is vacant now, Texaco Towers is occupied by a different company, and Apple's former City Center office complex across the street dominates the intersection.) There was no sign on 20431 Stevens Creek Boulevard, and the office wasn't even listed in the company's telephone directory. They were out in the boonies, which was perfect for the maverick project Jobs had in mind.

The Mac quickly went from being a research project to a full-blown product development effort with several dozen employees. Jobs seriously underestimated the amount of work yet to be done and the time it would take. He figured his team would ship the Macintosh in early 1982, just a year away. So confident was he in this prediction that he bet Lisa project manager John Couch $5,000 that the Mac would beat Lisa to market, even though the Lisa had been under serious development for more than two years and the Mac project was just starting in earnest.

When the Mac missed the 1982 ship date, chairman Markkula presented Jobs with a woman's black slip and told him to make sure the garment was "the Mac's last slip." The Lisa appeared on January 19, 1983, more than a year before the Mac, and Steve Jobs made good on his $5,000 bet with John Couch.

One of the most significant advances in the Macintosh project had come when Smith figured out an ingenious way to replace the 6809E microprocessor with the more powerful 68000 used by the Lisa. Although Raskin resisted at first because it would drive up the cost of the computer, Jobs was all for the change. With Mac and Lisa sharing the same microprocessor, it was easier for the Mac team to use some of the Lisa technologies and software, including Atkinson's amazing QuickDraw routines. However, Jobs steadfastly refused to make the Mac compatible with the Lisa or vice versa.

Symbolizing Jobs' defiant attitude and Apple's internecine rivalry was the Jolly Roger that flew over the Mac team's newest building, Bandley III (10460 Bandley Drive). Jobs referred to his group as pirates, and in keeping with that spirit, he began systematically raiding the Lisa project for key technologies and people (such as Atkinson and Steve Capps) without regard for the overall well-being of Apple. As Hertzfeld explained, "We looked for any place where we could beg, borrow, or steal code."

Needless to say, the Mac began looking a lot like a little Lisa. QuickDraw and other Lisa routines increased the size of the Mac's ROM. It soon became apparent that the Mac would share so much of the Lisa's interface that a mouse was a necessity, much to Raskin's dismay; he was leaning toward a lightpen or joystick as a graphic input device. "I couldn't stand the mouse," says Raskin. "Jobs gets 100 percent credit for insisting that a mouse be on the Mac." However, Raskin did prevail in convincing the team not to use a three-button mouse like the Alto, but rather a one-button version that would be much easier for novices.

Working with industrial designer Jerrold C. Manock, Jobs also pushed for the Mac's distinctive Cuisinart-inspired upright case, and that necessitated a detached keyboard. With a rough idea of what the computer would look like physically, the design of the Mac's completely automated factory in Fremont, California, got under way in the fall of 1981, even though Smith was still furiously working on yet another Mac prototype and many of the technical details had yet to be finalized. By February 1982, the case design was fixed and the signatures of the team members were collected and transferred to the mold for the inside of the case (see "Macintosh Insiders," page 81).

Things were really picking up steam that February when Jobs approached Raskin and cavalierly announced, "Well, I'm going to take over software and you can run documentation." That was more than Raskin could bear, and he replied, "No, you can have documentation too, I resign." The showdown was inevitable, according to Dan Kottke, one of the Mac engineers. "Jef Raskin and Steve Jobs both have large egos. Jef could have stayed on if he hadn't gone against Steve. But he feels very strongly about certain things and won't shut up."

Jobs and Markkula asked Raskin to reconsider, so he took a one-month leave of absence. Upon his return, Raskin was offered the leadership of a new research division. "Been there, done that," was the essence of his reply, so on March 1, 1982, he officially tendered his resignation.

Jobs was hell-bent on proving that he could produce a better computer than the Lisa, but it was becoming painfully apparent that the real competition was not with the Lisa division, but rather with International Business Machines. IBM had introduced its Personal Computer on August 12, 1981, and the market had responded favorably, to say the least. Much to its dismay, Apple began losing market share (sliding from 29 to 24 percent in 1982) to what it considered a clearly inferior product.

> ## "A lot of people think we ripped off Xerox. But really, we ripped off Lisa."
> *Finder co-author* **Steve Capps**

Jobs wanted to avoid licensing copyrighted typefaces—such as Times, Century, Helvetica, and Gothic—for the Mac, so he instructed artist Susan Kare (www.kare.com) to design knockoffs. Kare, who had grown up in the suburbs of Philadelphia, wanted to name her fonts after the railroad stations of the Paoli Local train: Ardmore, Merion, Rosemont, etc. Jobs liked the idea of using city names, but insisted on world-class cities that corresponded to the original typefaces: New York (Times), Geneva (Helvetica), London (Old English), etc. The frivolous font known as San Francisco was originally named Ransom, because documents created with it looked like kidnappers' notes. By the way, Kare designed all the original Mac fonts except Venice, which was the creation of Bill Atkinson.

> ## "When we started this project, IBM didn't have a machine. But we looked very carefully at their PC when they released it. At first it was embarrassing how bad their machine was. Then we were horrified [at its success]. We hope the Macintosh will show people what the IBM PC was—a half-assed, hackneyed attempt at the old technology."
> *Mac documentation leader* **Chris Espinosa**

Although the Mac team derided the IBM PC in public, privately they realized Big Blue was a formidable competitor and that they had better get their own product out the door. The window of opportunity was slowly closing, and if Apple didn't finish the Mac soon, it might lose out altogether. "We had been saying, 'We're going to finish in six months' for two years," recalls Hertzfeld, but Jobs laid down the law and pushed to ship Macintosh on May 16, 1983, at the National Computer Conference in Anaheim, California.

Facing a hard deadline forced the team to make several major decisions which resulted in a sort of domino effect. High-resolution graphics had always been a primary goal for the Mac, but even as late as 1982 the 9-inch diagonal monitor could display only 384 by 256 pixels. That was certainly acceptable for graphics, but not exactly at the leading edge of technology. George Crow, analog manager, increased the resolution to the final dimensions of 512 by 342 pixels, allowing the Mac to display 80 columns of fixed-pitch (monospaced) text.

With the increased resolution of the bitmapped display, more memory was needed. Like Raskin before him, Jobs thought that 64K of memory was acceptable, but the team convinced him that 128K was needed (actually, they wanted more, so they secretly designed a way to easily increase memory by swapping chips).

More memory meant larger programs, and the 200K, 5.25-inch floppy disk drive no longer seemed like an adequate mass-storage device. Unbeknownst to Jobs, his engineers had anticipated this problem and were already working on a solution based upon a new 400K, 3.5-inch drive from Sony.

The May 1983 ship date came and went, and still the Mac wasn't complete. Each of the hardware changes took longer than expected, but nothing took as much time as completing the software. Even though Jobs had assembled many of Apple's brightest minds in the Mac division, doing the impossible takes time, especially when you have a perfectionist like Jobs as a boss. "Tact is a word you don't use to describe him," says Espinosa. "Steve will just walk up to your desk, look at what you're doing and say, 'That's shit.'"

Despite the unbelievable pressure they were under, Mac team members were spotted around the Apple campus wearing T-shirts that read "90 HRS/WK AND LOVING IT." This dedicated band of pirates had bought into Jobs' dream of changing the world, and they worked themselves to exhaustion to make the Macintosh the best damn computer they could.

Finally, after spending $78 million in development costs, Apple introduced the Macintosh to wildly cheering crowds at the annual shareholder meeting on January 24, 1984 (ironically, the stock closed down 1.625 at $27.25). The Macintosh was considerably smaller, faster, and cheaper than the ground-breaking Lisa introduced the previous year. It had a 68000 microprocessor running at 7.83MHz, 128K of RAM, one 400K, 3.5-inch floppy disk drive, and a 9-inch monochrome display. The Mac came bundled with MacPaint (written by Bill Atkinson), MacWrite (written by Randy Wigginton), and the Finder (written by Bruce Horn and Steve Capps).

Instead of letting the Mac team members wallow in obscurity, Apple broke with industry tradition and heavily promoted them as avant-garde artists. Shown here are (left to right) Bill Atkinson, Andy Hertzfeld, Chris Espinosa, George Crow, Joanna Hoffman, Burrell Smith, and Jerry Manock.

Until the last moment before introduction, Apple executives argued over the Mac's price. Jobs had hoped that the Mac could sell for $1,495. As it turned out, the Mac cost $500 to build (83 percent materials, 16 percent overhead, 1 percent labor), and with Apple's standard mark-up, the price should have been $1,995. But president John Sculley had ordered an aggressive $15-million, 100-day advertising blitz, which kicked off with the *1984* commercial during Super Bowl XVIII. To pay for this campaign, Sculley tacked on a hefty premium, and the list price for the original Mac was set at $2,495. So much for Raskin's $500 computer that would appeal to the person in the street. The Macintosh was now "The Computer for the Rest of Us," defined as those with several grand burning holes in their pockets.

"The Mac is meant to supplant the PC on the desks of corporate America, just as the PC supplanted our own Apples over the last 18 months."

John Sculley
(Forbes, *February 13, 1984*)

Q. How many Macintosh Division employees do you need to change a lightbulb?
A. One. He holds the bulb up and lets the universe revolve around him.

The Great Mac Giveaway
In an effort to curry favor with celebrities and generate some favorable press upon the introduction of the Macintosh, Apple gave 50 machines to a select group of luminaries and key decision-makers. Among them:

Bob Ciano, *Life* magazine art director
Dianne Feinstein, San Francisco mayor
Milton Glaser, designer
Jim Henson, Muppet creator
Lee Iacocca, Chrysler chairman
Sean Lennon, son of late Beatle
Maya Lin, Vietnam Vet Mem. designer
Peter Martins, ballet master
David Rockefeller, really rich guy
Stephen Sondheim, composer/lyricist
Ted Turner, entrepreneur
Kurt Vonnegut, novelist
Andy Warhol, pop artist

For a complete, up-to-date list of celebrities that are known Mac users, visit The Celebrity Macintosh Page: www.owt.com/users/sdechter/celeb.html

Software Seed List

Apple was astute enough to realize that in breaking with the IBM-DOS standard, the Mac must have a wide variety of third-party products available as soon after introduction as possible. Evangelists (yup, that's what it said on their business cards) Mike Boich and Guy Kawasaki approached a wide variety of software publishers and hardware manufacturers and begged, bribed, and berated them until they promised to create products for the Mac, even though that entailed the purchase of a Lisa as a development system.

By the time the Macintosh Product Introduction Plan was codified on October 7, 1983, the following developers had been selected "according to their marketing ability, technical expertise, end-user support capabilities, and desirability of application." Just for kicks, tally up the number of early Mac developers that are still around today.

Aardvark
Accountant's Microsystem
Addison-Wesley
Applied Software Technology
Ashton-Tate
Ask Micro
BBN Communications Corp.
Bill Duvall
Brøderbund
BPI
Brady Company
Business Solutions
CBS
Chang Labs
Compu-Law
CompuServe
Continental Software
Cygnet Technologies
Data Resources
Datasoft
Davong Systems Inc.
DB Master Associates
Debbie Wilrett
Desktop Computer Software
Digital Marketing
Digital Research
Dilithium Software
Dow Jones
Execuware

(continued on next page)

Even at its artificially inflated price, Jobs predicted Apple would sell 50,000 Macs in the 100 days following introduction and half a million units by the end of 1984; Sculley's figure was a more realistic quarter million units. Although they were both way off base with their annual forecasts, Apple reached the 100-day goal on Day 73 (April 6), and on Day 100 (May 3), after having sold 72,000 Macs, product marketing manager Barbara Koalkin boasted to *USA Today,* "We could have sold 200,000 Macintoshes if we could have built them."

Confident that sales would pick up during the Christmas months, Apple began building inventory at a rate of 110,000 units a month. Unfortunately, after the initial burst of sales to early adopters (plus computer dealers, developers, and college students who paid far less than list price thanks to special promotions), Mac sales tapered off dramatically to roughly 20,000 Macs a month. In fact, it took until September 1985 to sell 500,000 Macs, and Apple didn't reach the one million mark until March 1987.

On March 17, 1987, Apple Computer pulled six Mac Plus computers off the assembly line and designated each the one millionth Mac. In recognition of his being the true father of the Macintosh, Jef Raskin was presented with one of these Macs. Ironically, this Mac Plus was the first Macintosh Raskin ever owned. It's still in use today at his home in Pacifica, California, along with several PowerBooks and an IBM ThinkPad.

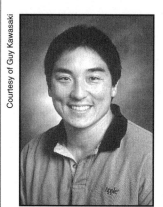

Courtesy of Guy Kawasaki

"Good software is like pornography: very difficult to describe but you know it when you see it. Good software is art: you can see the 'soul' of a programmer or programmers. Good software is fun: it should bring a smile to your face when you use it. Good software causes an erection in the mind of a software evangelist."

Mac evangelist **Guy Kawasaki**

Macintosh Timeline

1979
- Raskin proposes Mac project
- Lisa project starts under Rothmuller
- Mac project starts under Raskin

1980
- Board grants three-month reprieve to Mac project
- Apple initial public offering

1981
- Jobs muscles into Mac project
- IBM PC introduced
- Fremont factory gets under way
- Raskin's original Mac ship date (missed)

1982
- Case design finalized
- Raskin resigns; Jobs' original Mac ship date (missed)

1983
- Lisa ($9,995) and Apple IIe ($1,395) introduced
- Jobs' revised Mac ship date (missed)
- Lisa and Mac divisions combined

1984
- Lisa 2 ($3,495) and Macintosh ($2,495) introduced
- Mac installed base = 72,000
- Mac installed base = 300,000

1985
- Mac installed base = 500,000

This lovable little Mac logo wasn't what Jobs originally wanted.

For more information on Jean-Michel Folon, visit the Folon's Friends Club at www.europictures.com/folon.

Beginning with System 7.5.1, the "Welcome to Macintosh" startup message changed to "Welcome to Mac OS," and it featured a new Mac icon with two smiling faces.

Folon's Forgotten Logo

When you turn on any of the early Mac models, the first thing you see (unless you have a customized StartupScreen in your System Folder) is the familiar and reassuring "Welcome to Macintosh" greeting beside a Picasso-inspired line drawing of the original Mac. That little drawing is so universally known as the artistic representation of the soul of the Macintosh, that it's difficult to imagine any other image evoking the same response. Therefore it may surprise you to learn that it was not what Apple had originally planned.

Long before the Mac was complete, Steve Jobs had become quite taken with the work of Belgian-born poster artist Jean-Michel Folon and paid him an advance of $30,000 to design a logo to represent the new computer. Folon came up with a character he called Mac Man and depicted him in a color pastel drawing called "The Macintosh Spirit."

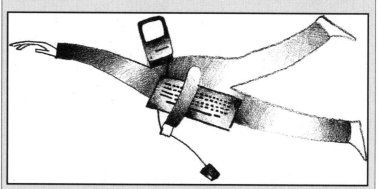

Jobs passed on Folon's "The Macintosh Spirit" depicted here.

Courtesy of Donn Denman and Dan Kottke

In addition to his hefty advance, Folon was to be paid an unprecedented royalty of $1 for every Mac sold. With almost 30 million Macs sold as of 1998, the Macintosh commission would have easily been Folon's most lucrative undertaking. But after Folon submitted "The Macintosh Spirit," the mercurial Jobs changed his mind. In June 1983, he turned instead to the Mac art director, Tom Hughes, asking him to come up with something a little more practical. Working with John Casado, Hughes created the colorful, simple drawing of the Mac that we've come to know and love.

Canon Cat

In 1987, Jef Raskin finally got his chance to more fully realize the embodiment of his original Macintosh design goals with a "work processor" called the Canon Cat, which had word processor, spreadsheet, and telecommunications features built in. Most people have never heard of the Cat, and with good reason. After only six months on the market, Canon abruptly dropped the Cat without explanation. It's not as if the Canon Cat was a dog, if you'll forgive the pun. The $1,495 Cat was well received by the public, selling a respectable 20,000 units and winning many design awards. Why, then, did Canon put the Cat to sleep?

The Canon Cat looks suspiciously like Raskin's early Mac prototypes.

Over the years, Raskin received two anonymous telephone calls from people claiming to be Canon employees. They offered conflicting motives for Canon's actions. One explained that the electronic typewriter division and the computer division were fighting for control of the Cat. The new president of Canon USA wanted to exert his power and told the two divisions to settle the matter quickly or he would do it for them. They continued to fight over the Cat, so he killed the project outright to teach them a lesson.

The second caller painted a more sinister scenario involving Raskin's old nemesis, Steve Jobs. Shortly after the Cat was introduced, Canon was exploring the possibility of investing in Jobs' new venture, NeXT (see "Jobs After Apple: To NeXT and Beyond," page 167). Unwilling to share the corporate attention of Canon with Raskin, Jobs allegedly told Canon that unless they dropped the Cat, he wouldn't allow them to invest in NeXT. Although Raskin has never been able to verify either story, Canon did pay $100 million for a 16.67 percent share of NeXT in June 1989. Kinda makes you wonder …

Macintosh Insiders

If you've ever cracked open the case of an early Macintosh, you may have noticed a bunch of signatures in raised plastic on the inside back panel. Steve Jobs felt that the Macintosh was a piece of art, and since real artists sign their masterpieces, he and the other employees of the Macintosh division in 1982 affixed their signatures to a large sheet of paper. When everyone had signed, a film negative was made from the paper, and the signatures were chemically etched into the core of the tooling for the inside of the original Macintosh.

Since not everyone has access to an early Mac, the following pages reproduce the internal signatures as they appear on the original master. Mac fanatics will no doubt notice the absence of some prestigious members of the Mac division, such as programmer Steve Capps and graphic designer Susan Kare. They weren't left out on purpose. It's just that they weren't on the team when the signatures were collected in early 1982, a time when Steve Jobs felt that shipping was imminent. Of course, it was almost two years too soon, further proof that almost everything about the Mac was ahead of its time. Please note that some signatures were added (such as Steve Balog) over time and others were dropped (ostensibly to accommodate changes in the case design for the Mac SE).

It's been said that in addition to popularizing the graphical user interface, Apple Computer's greatest contribution to the industry has been as a training ground for high-technology employees who have carried Apple's idealism to other firms. Here's a brief look at the people who created the Mac and an update on what they are doing today, more than sixteen years later. Silicon Valley is infamous for its "burn and turn" approach to human resources, so don't be surprised if people are no longer at the companies listed.

Special thanks to Guy Kawasaki for the initial research upon which this chapter is based.

Apple continued using case molds with signatures until sometime during the production of the Mac SE, at which time signature-free molds were substituted for the classic-style, all-in-one Mac. However, the practice was revised with the Mac IIci and IIcx, both of which contain signatures of the Product Design Team inscribed along the left side of the case, below the motherboard: Gavin Ivester, Pat Jackson, Jimmy Melton, Grant Ross, Terry Smith, Tom Toedtman, Lada Zajicek, and Laszlo Zsidek.

"Going out of the eighties, you know there won't be a Mac group. Burrell [Smith] will be off in Oregon playing his guitar. Andy [Hertzfeld] will be writing the next great American novel. Who knows what. But we'll be scattered all over the globe doing other amazing stuff."

Steve Jobs, *prior to the Mac's intro*

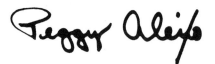

Peggy Alexio

Then: Area associate
Now: Left Apple; whereabouts unknown

Collette Askeland

Then: Designed the printed circuit board for the main logic board
Now: Left Apple in 1998; most recently dir. of engineering services

Bill Atkinson

Then: Wrote QuickDraw and MacPaint
Now: Left Apple in 1990; photographer (www.natureimages.com)

Robert L. Belleville

Then: Engineering manager
Now: Left Apple in 1986; retired, building electronic pendulum clocks

Mike Boich

Then: Software evangelist
Now: Left Apple in 1985; founded Radius, now between engagements

Bill Bull

Then: Worked on "no-fan solution," plus cables, keyboard, and mouse
Now: Manager of product design for Input Device Group

Matt Carter

Then: Mac manufacturing manager
Now: Left Apple in 1983; starting a new company

Berry Cash

Then: Marketing and sales consultant
Now: Left Apple; venture capitalist in Texas

Debi Coleman

Then: Controller of the Macintosh division
Now: Left Apple in 1992; CEO of Merix (www.merix.com)

George Crow

Then: Designed the analog board, video, and power supply
Now: Left Apple in 1985; returned in 1998 as dir. prod. engineering

Donn Denman

Then: Wrote Alarm Clock, NotePad desk accessory, and MacBASIC
Now: Left Apple in 1994; senior software engineer at PowerTV
(www.powertv.com)

Christopher Espinosa

Then: Supervised the manuals and technical documentation
Now: Head of Apple's Components & Scripting Group

Bill Fernandez

Then: Engineering jack-of-all-trades
Now: Left Apple in 1993; freelance user interface architect in
Albuquerque, New Mexico

Martin P. Haeberli

Then: Worked on Memory Manager and co-authored MacTerminal
Now: Left Apple in 1996; CEO of startup called Oversea Systems,
managing shipping containers

Andy Hertzfeld

Then: Software wizard; wrote most of the Macintosh Toolbox
Now: Left Apple in 1984; VP and programmer at General Magic until
1997, now an Internet hobbyist and open source enthusiast

Joanna K. Hoffman

Then: Wrote the first marketing plan for the division
Now: Left Apple in 1985; retired and raising her two boys

Rod Holt

Then: Worked on the power supply
Now: Left Apple in 1987; retired and sailing boats

Bruce Horn

Then: Designed the Finder and completed it with Steve Capps
Now: Left Apple in 1982; writing Finder companion, Context, for
Ingenuity Software (www.ingenuitysoftware.com)

Harrison S. Horn

Then: Linear circuit designer
Now: Left Apple in 1983; retired, living in Los Altos, California

Brian R. Howard

Then: Ensured digital designs would work and be manufacturable
Now: Distinguished engineer, scientist, technologist working on hardware architecture of chip sets

Steven Jobs

Then: General manager of the division
Now: Left Apple in 1985; CEO of Pixar, interim CEO of Apple

Larry Kenyon

Then: Worked on the file system, drivers, and boot code
Now: Left Apple in 1997; WebTV senior manager of system software

Patti King

Then: Managed the engineering department's software library
Now: Left Apple in 1985; full-time mom, married to Larry Kenyon

Daniel Kottke

Then: Built prototypes and troubleshot board-level problems
Now: Left Apple in 1985; Firmware engineer at Vertical Networks

Angeline Lo

Then: Programmer
Now: Left Apple in 1982; whereabouts unknown

Ivan Mach

Then: Optimized main logic and power sweep boards for factory automation
Now: Left Apple in 1982; director of manufacturing technology at Tessera working on micro ball grid array package

Jerrold C. Manock

Then: Managed the industrial design engineers
Now: Left Apple in 1985; president of MCD, Inc., a product design engineering consulting firm in Burlington, Vermont

Mary Ellen McCammon

Then: Area associate for the marketing group
Now: Left Apple in 1986; completed a master's degree in psychology, active arts community volunteer in San Jose, California

Vicki Milledge

Then: Human resources liason

Now: Left Apple 1988; professor of organizational behavior at University of Massachusetts, Boston

Michael R. Murray

Then: Director of marketing

Now: Left Apple in 1985; VP of human resources and administration at Microsoft

Ronald H. Nicholson Jr.

Then: Digital hardware engineer

Now: Left Apple in 1983; engineer at Silicon Graphics (www.sgi)

Terry A. Oyama

Then: Worked on the product design of housing

Now: Left Apple in 1985; whereabouts unknown

Benjamin Pang

Then: Worked on the industrial design of Macintosh

Now: Left Apple in 1998; whereabouts unknown

Jef Raskin

Then: Father of the original Macintosh project in 1979

Now: Left Apple in 1982; human interface design consultant and technology writer

Ed Riddle

Then: Worked on the design of the keyboard

Now: Left Apple in 1981; writer in the areas of technical, marketing, and spiritual issues

Brian Robertson

Then: Managed purchasing and supplier sourcing

Now: Left Apple in 1997; whereabouts unknown

David H. Roots

Then: Worked on the product design of keyboard, external disk drive

Now: Left Apple in 1989; whereabouts unknown

Patricia Sharp

Then: Steve Jobs' administrative assistant
Now: Left Apple in 1997; whereabouts unknown

Burrell Carver Smith

Then: Hardware wizard; designed the digital board
Now: Left Apple in 1985; doing research in Palo Alto, California

Bryan Stearns

Then: Worked on the user interface for MacBASIC
Now: Left Apple in 1995; senior engineer at Excite (www.excite.com)

Lynn Takahashi

Then: Steve Jobs' area associate
Now: Left Apple in 1985; whereabouts unknown

Guy L. Tribble III

Then: Manager of software engineering
Now: Left Apple in 1985; VP of Architecture and Technology at Sun

Randy Wigginton

Then: Wrote MacWrite on contract
Now: Left Apple in 1981; partner at consulting firm MediaLane

Linda Wilkin

Then: Managed engineering documentation
Now: Left Apple in 1986; studying Exercise Physiology at Ohio State

Steve Wozniak

Then: Had to quit team after crashing his plane
Now: Teaching fifth graders to use computers at UNUSON

Pamela G. Wyman

Then: User manual designer/production editor
Now: Left Apple in 1985; whereabouts unknown

Laszlo Zsidek

Then: Tooling and manufacturing engineer
Now: Works in the portable computing division of Apple

The Greatest Commercial That Almost Never Aired

Every true Macintosh fanatic has seen, or at least heard about, the famous *1984* television commercial that heralded the introduction of the Macintosh. The spot, with its distinctive Orwellian vision, is indelibly imprinted in the minds of Mac users the world over. What you don't know about the commercial will surprise you; what you think you know is probably wrong.

First of all, the commercial was not inspired by the Macintosh. In late 1982, Apple's advertising agency, Chiat/Day (www.chiatday.com), had devised a corporate print campaign featuring the Apple II for *The Wall Street Journal* that was designed to play off George Orwell's totalitarian vision of the future.

"Six months before we knew about Mac, we had this new ad that read, 'Why 1984 won't be like *1984*,'" reveals Lee Clow, creative director at Chiat/Day. "It explained Apple's philosophy and purpose—that people, not just government and big corporations, should run technology. If computers aren't to take over our lives, they have to be accessible."

The ad never ran and was filed away, only to be dusted off in the spring of 1983 by Steve Hayden, the agency's copywriter, and Brent Thomas, the art director, who were looking for some hook to make a bold statement about the incredible new Macintosh. With considerable reworking, the Chiat/Day team put together a storyboard of the *1984* commercial they proposed to shoot.

The mini-movie would show an athletic young woman, chased by helmeted storm troopers, bursting into a dank auditorium in which rows upon rows of slack-jawed, drone-like workers watched an image of Big Brother spouting an ideological diatribe on a huge screen. The heroine, wearing bright red jogging shorts and a white Mac T-shirt, would smash the screen with a baseball bat (later changed to a

> "Am I getting anything I should give a shit about?"
> **Steve Jobs**, *upon first meeting Lee Clow, creative director for Chiat/Day*

On January 24th, Apple Computer will introduce Macintosh. And you'll see why 1984 won't be like "1984."

This famous tag line was originally intended for the Apple II, not the Macintosh.

sledgehammer for dramatic effect) and a refreshing burst of fresh air would pass over the masses as they literally "saw the light."

In the closing shot, a solemn voice would intone "On January 24th, Apple Computer will introduce Macintosh. And you'll see why 1984 won't be like *1984.*" The computer itself would never be shown.

After Chiat/Day presented the storyboard to Apple, John Sculley was apprehensive, but Steve Jobs insisted that the Mac deserved such a radical spot. They gave the authorization to shoot the commercial and purchase time to air it during the upcoming Super Bowl.

> "We wanted people to say, 'What the hell is this product?' The idea was to use the commercial as a tease, not a product introduction; to make sure the world knew a new product was here and that it was a significant event."
>
> *Chiat/Day director of planning*
> **Mary Terese Rainey**

On the strength of his successful science-fiction films *Alien* and *Blade Runner*, Chiat/Day gave Ridley Scott a budget of $900,000 to direct the *1984* spot as well as a Lisa commercial called *Alone Again*, in which, believe it or not, Apple actually emphasized the fact that the Lisa was incompatible with all established standards.

In September, Scott assembled a cast of 200 for a week of filming at London's Shepperton Studios. To play the part of the despondent, bald-headed workers, Scott recruited authentic British skinheads and paid amateurs $125 a day to shave off their hair. Casting the heroine proved trickier. Many of the professional fashion models and actresses had difficulty spinning in place and then accurately throwing the sledgehammer as called for in the script. In fact, one errant sledgehammer toss almost killed an old lady walking down a path in

The beautiful, athletic heroine was the embodiment of Apple's youthful self-image.

Hyde Park, where the casting call was being held. As luck would have it, one model, Anya Major, was also an experienced discus thrower. She was hired to play the female lead because she looked the part and didn't get dizzy when spinning around preparing to hurl the hammer.

When the rough cut was assembled, Chiat/Day proudly presented it to Jobs and Sculley. Jobs loved the commercial, and Sculley thought it was crazy enough that it just might work. On October 23, the commercial was aired publicly for the first time at Apple's annual sales conference in Honolulu's civic auditorium. The 750 sales reps went wild when they saw the piece.

Jobs and Sculley clearly thought they had a winner on their hands, so in late December, they asked marketing manager Mike Murray to screen the commercial for the other members of Apple's board of directors: Mike Markkula (Apple founder), Dr. Henry E. Singleton (Teledyne founder), Arthur Rock (venture capitalist), Peter O. Crisp (managing partner in Rockefeller's Venrock Associates), and Philip S. Schlein (CEO of Macy's California).

When the lights came back up after the spot played, the room on De Anza Boulevard was silent. Schlein was sitting with his head on the table. Markkula stared in amazement. Murray thought Markkula was overcome by the wonderful commercial until he broke the silence to ask, "Who wants to move to find a new agency?" In his memoirs, Sculley recalled, "The others just looked at each other, dazed expressions on their faces ... Most of them felt it was the worst commercial they had ever seen. Not a single outside board member liked it."

> ## "Some of them liked it, some of them didn't."
>
> *Spin doctor **Steve Jobs**, describing the board's reaction to* 1984

The board didn't demand the commercial be killed, nonetheless Sculley asked Chiat/Day to sell back the one and one half minutes of Super Bowl television time that they had purchased. The original plan was to play the full-length, 60-second *1984* spot to catch everyone's attention, then hammer home the message during a subsequent commercial break with an additional airing of an edited 30-second version.

Defying Sculley's request, Jay Chiat told his media director, Camille Johnson, "Just sell off the 30." Johnson laughed, thinking it would be impossible to sell any of the time at so late a date, but miraculously, she managed to find a buyer for the 30-second slot. That still left Apple with a 60-second slot for which it had paid $800,000.

Campbell went on to head Claris, GO, and Intuit. He was named to the Apple board in 1997. Kvamme eventually made partner at the venture capital firm Kleiner, Perkins, Caufield & Byers (www.kpcb.com).

Still pushing for *1984*, Jobs sought the support of Steve Wozniak, who normally didn't like to get involved in such political issues. Recalls Wozniak, "One evening I was over at the Macintosh group, which I was about to join, and Steve grabbed me and said 'Hey, come over here and look at this.' He pulled up a 3/4-inch VCR and played the ad. I was astounded. I thought it was the most incredible thing. Then he told me that the board decided not to show it. He didn't say why. I was so shocked. Steve said we were going to run it during the Super Bowl. I asked how much it was going to cost, and he told me $800,000. I said, 'Well, I'll pay half of it if you will.' I figured it was a problem with the company justifying the expenditure. I thought an ad that was so great a piece of science fiction should have its chance to be seen." Fortunately for Wozniak, Jobs didn't take him up on his offer to pony up half the cost.

"It broke all the rules; and the reaction has been, in a word, unprecedented."
*Chiat/Day copywriter **Steve Hayden***

Perhaps seeking to cover himself in the event the commercial flopped, Sculley left the decision of whether to run *1984* up to William V. Campbell (VP of marketing) and E. Floyd Kvamme (executive VP of marketing and sales). If they couldn't sell the remaining Super Bowl minute and decided against airing *1984*, the backup plan was to run *Manuals*, a rather straightforward product-benefit spot that challenged viewers to decide which was the more sophisticated computer: the IBM PC, with its huge pile of documentation that came crashing down beside the computer, or the Macintosh, with its light-as-a-feather user's guide floating to rest next to the mouse.

Campbell and Kvamme threw caution to the wind and decided to run the *1984* commercial after all, kicking off a $15-million, 100-day advertising blitz for the Mac. On January 22, 1984, the controversial commercial aired to an audience of 96 million early in the third quarter of Super Bowl XVIII, in which the Los Angeles Raiders defeated the Washington Redskins 38 to 9 in Tampa Stadium.

Any apprehension Apple may have harbored regarding *1984* disappeared seconds after the spot ran. Switchboards immediately lit up at CBS, Chiat/Day, and Apple with calls demanding to know, "What was that?!" Love it or hate it, the commercial demanded attention and sparked widespread controversy. It would ultimately garner an estimated $5 million in free publicity; all three television networks and nearly 50 local stations aired news stories about the spot, most replaying it in its entirety, and hundreds of newspapers and magazines wrote about the phenomenon.

A.C. Nielsen estimated the commercial reached 46.4 percent of the households in America, a full 50 percent of the nation's men, and 36 percent of the women. The commercial garnered astronomical recall scores and went on to win the Grand Prize of Cannes as well as over 30 other advertising industry awards.

The *1984* commercial was the first example of what Sculley called "event marketing," the goal of which is to create a promotion so ground-breaking that it deserves as much coverage as the product itself. Apple fed the media frenzy surrounding *1984* by announcing that the commercial would never be aired again.

To this day, if you ask most Apple employees about the commercial, they will claim that the only time Apple ever paid to run the commercial was during the Super Bowl. It's been repeated convincingly so many times by so many sincere people that it's now accepted as gospel. The only problem is it isn't true.

In keeping with industry tradition, Chiat/Day paid $10 to run *1984* in the 1:00 AM sign-off slot on December 15, 1983, at a small television station (KMVT, Channel 11) in Twin Falls, Idaho, thereby ensuring that the commercial would qualify for that year's advertising awards. Then beginning on January 17, the 30-second version of the commercial aired for weeks in ScreenVision, an advertising medium played in movie theaters before previews and feature presentations (some theater owners loved the commercial so much that they continued running it for months without pay).

At the same time, a five-day teaser campaign began running a full schedule during prime time in America's ten largest television markets (encompassing 30 percent of the nation's viewers), plus the relatively unimportant television market of West Palm Beach, Florida, right next door to IBM's PC headquarters. "I would love to know what they're saying in Boca Raton," Jobs smugly mused the Monday after the Super Bowl.

Ironically, it was during the same game that IBM launched the ad campaign for its ill-fated, low-cost PCjr computer, which had just begun shipping to dealers. The light-hearted commercial depicted Charlie Chaplin wheeling the PCjr into a room in a baby carriage as the announcer introduced "the bright little addition to the family." Jobs would later remark, "I expected the computer to wet all over the television set." Reflecting on IBM's use of Charlie Chaplin's *Modern Times* character, Jean-Louis Gassée found it "surprising that the Little Tramp, symbolizing the worst aspects of the assembly line, was chosen to advertise a company that is a humanistic one in every other way."

Drones were played by British skinheads and amateurs paid $125 a day to shave off their hair.

You can download the famous *1984* commercial as a QuickTime movie from the following sites, but beware, it's a multi-megabyte file:
http://www2.apple.com/whymac/ads.html
http://www.chiatday.com/product/historical_work/tv/1984/1984.html

> "We were so convinced we had a major product statement that we weren't worried about the product living up to the commercial."
> *Apple executive VP of marketing and sales **E. Floyd Kvamme***

> "It was all this horseshit from people who didn't have the balls to produce something like *1984*."
> *Chiat/Day creative director **Lee Clow**, dismissing his competitors' negative reactions to the commercial*

> "Luck is a force of nature. Everything seemed to conspire to make *1984* a hit: the timing, the product, the industry. Using the *1984* theme was such an obvious idea that I was worried someone else would beat us to it, but nobody did."
> ***Steve Hayden**, explaining the commercial's success*

An Apple II was used to generate the spurious data that appeared superimposed over Big Brother's face.

In a superb bit of irony, ten years after working on the *1984* commercial, Steve Hayden went to work for Ogilvy & Mather (www.ogilvy.com) as overseer of the entire worldwide IBM account.

Big Brother Speaks

As *1984* was originally conceived, Big Brother did not have a speaking role, but director Ridley Scott wanted to give him some lines. Copywriter Steve Hayden objected at first, but agreed to put something together when Scott threatened to write the lines himself. Apple vehemently denied that the propaganda-spouting Big Brother character in the *1984* commercial represented its $40-billion competitor, IBM. Decide for yourself as you read Big Brother's harangue from the full-length, 60-second commercial:

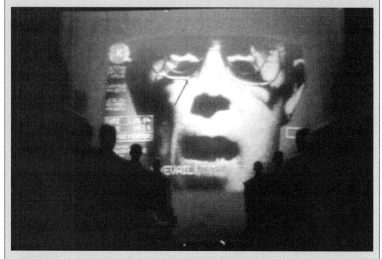

Is Big Brother really Big Blue? Apple insisted not, but the words speak volumes.

"My friends, each of you is a single cell in the great body of the State. And today, that great body has purged itself of parasites. We have triumphed over the unprincipled dissemination of facts. The thugs and wreckers have been cast out. And the poisonous weeds of disinformation have been consigned to the dustbin of history. Let each and every cell rejoice! For today we celebrate the first, glorious anniversary of the Information Purification Directive! We have created, for the first time in all history, a garden of pure ideology, where each worker may bloom secure from the pests of contradictory and confusing truths. Our Unification of Thought is a more powerful weapon than any fleet or army on Earth! We are one people. With one will. One resolve. One cause. Our enemies shall talk themselves to death. And we will bury them with their own confusion!"

The Mac
Meets the Press

When the Macintosh was introduced in 1984, Apple's public relations and marketing departments performed miracles, securing more coverage for its newborn than for any other computer in history. Looking back with the aid of 20/20 hindsight, read the following excerpts from several of the major computer publications of the time and decide for yourself which journalists were on the mark when it came to assessing the original Macintosh.

Byte

"The Lisa computer was important because it was the first commercial product to use the mouse-window-desktop environment. The Macintosh is equally important because it makes that same environment very affordable.

"The Macintosh will have three important effects. First, like the Lisa, it will be imitated but not copied ... Those companies that try to imitate the Mac on other machines will have trouble matching its price/performance combination.

"Second, the Macintosh will secure the place of the Sony 3.5-inch disk as the magnetic medium of choice for the next generation of personal computers.

"Third, the Macintosh will increase Apple's reputation in the market ... Many business users will stay with the 'safer' IBM PC. However, people new to computing and those who are maverick enough to see the value and promise of the Mac will favor it. The Mac will delay IBM's domination of the personal computer market.

"Overall, the Macintosh is a very important machine that, in my opinion, replaces the Lisa as the most important development in

> "The Mac is the first computer good enough to be criticized."
> *Apple Fellow **Alan Kay***
> (InfoWorld, *June 11, 1984*)

"Macintosh is going to be Apple's next milestone product in the industry—the Apple II being the first one in 1977, the IBM Personal Computer being the second industry milestone in 1981, and Macintosh being the third industry milestone in 1984."

Steve Jobs
(Personal Computing, *April 1984*)

computers in the last five years. The Macintosh brings us one step closer to the ideal of computer as appliance. We're not there yet—at least, not until the next set of improvements (which, in this industry, we may see fairly soon). Who knows who the next innovator will be?"

Gregg Williams
(Byte, *February 1984*)

Computer & Electronics

"Despite [the omissions of color and a parallel port], Macintosh is an impressive product and worthy of taking the 'less-traveled' road. Apparently, much of Apple's future depends on Macintosh, so its success or failure will truly make 'all the difference.'"

Vanessa Schnatmeier
(Computer & Electronics, *March 1984*)

Creative Computing

"In its current form, the Macintosh is the distilled embodiment of a promise: that software can be intuitively easy to use, while remaining just as powerful as anything else around … It should be obvious to you now that the Mac does represent a significant breakthrough, both in hardware and in software. It should also be clear that the true concern is whether the machine will live up to its undeniable promise. Fine. It is now time to lay out the 'bads.'

- The Macintosh does not have enough RAM.
- Single microfloppy storage is slow and inadequate.
- There are no internal expansion slots or external expansion busses.
- MacWrite has some severe limitations.
- The system is monochrome only.
- MS-DOS compatibility is ruled out.
- The Macintosh will not multitask.
- You can't use a Mac away from a desk.
- MacPaint has an easel size limitation.
- Forget about external video.
- Macintosh software development is an involved process.

"I simply wonder if this standard can be upheld. The thought first occurred to me as I played around with Microsoft BASIC. A BASIC program running on the Mac looks very much like a BASIC program running on any other machine, except for its windows. Without the icon/window/menu shells, the Mac is reduced to a rather average machine.

"It is up to talented programmers to make the most of Macintosh ROM in every program they develop. With it they can meet the ambitious promise that is the Apple Macintosh. Otherwise the Mac may never develop the staying power it needs.

"We are still quite some distance from the ideal machine Alan Kay envisioned back in 1971 and christened the 'Dynabook.' This is a computer the size of a [Tandy] Model 100 with the power of a hundred Macs. In a recent interview, he rather cynically predicted that it would be the Japanese who would make the Dynabook a reality. He told Allen Muro of *St. Mac* magazine that the Macintosh was in point of fact 'no big deal.'"

"That's the problem with people who are vastly ahead of their time. The times never seem to catch up. The Mac clocks in at 8 MHz, but Kay is already imagining what he could do with 12 MHz. In my last vestiges of prideful nationalism, I only hope it is Apple, not NEC, that introduces a 1000K 12 MHz machine two years from now. Perhaps I will write about it using a truly professional word processor running on a 512K hard disk Macintosh. Of course Kay will still be cranky with it, even when it does happen. If only he had 20 MHz and 5000K in a case the size of a box of Milk Duds. Then he could really make things happen. Well if anybody can pull off that kind of miracle, it is probably Apple. Those folks show a lot of promise."

John J. Anderson
(Creative Computing, *July 1984*)

inCider

"The Macintosh is the best hardware value in the history (short though it may be) of the personal computer industry. It is a machine which will appeal to the masses of people who have neither the time nor the inclination to embark upon the long learning process required to master the intricacies of the present generation of personal computers. Barring unforeseen technical glitches and assuming that a reasonable software library is in place by the end of the year, the Macintosh should establish itself as the next standard in personal computers."

Bob Ryan
(inCider, *March 1984*)

"The next generation of interesting software will be done on Macintosh, not the IBM PC."
Microsoft chairman **Bill Gates**
(BusinessWeek, *November 26, 1984*)

"Anybody who could write a good application on the 128K Mac deserves a medal."
Bill Gates

Two years later, the 1MB Mac Plus was introduced, but it would take until March 1987 to break the 8MHz barrier with the 16MHz Mac II.

On October 17, 1989, John Anderson and another *MacUser* editor, Derek Van Alstyne, died in the San Francisco earthquake. They are sorely missed.

"Borland founder Philippe Kahn was half right in January 1985, when he called the early Macintosh 'a piece of shit.' It was underpowered, had very little software, no hard drive, no compelling application like desktop publishing, and it was marketed by a company that seemed to be near death. I can't help but be amused by all the pumped-up bravado I hear and read about the people who created the Macintosh. To hold up the Macintosh experience as an example of how to create a great product, launch an industry, or spark a revolution, is a cruel joke. Anyone who models their business startup on the Macintosh startup is doomed to failure. Miracles, like the Macintosh, can only happen once."

Macworld *publisher* **David Bunnell**

InfoWorld

"Considering all of the hoopla that has preceded the Mac's introduction, we are still greatly impressed with Apple's new product. The Macintosh is a well-designed personal computer that, dollar for dollar, represents the most advanced personal computer to date. The MC68000 processor, the 3.5-inch variable-speed disk drive, the high-resolution display, the advanced operating system and user interface as well as the rich use of graphics make this machine superior to the rest of the pack. In our opinion, the success of the Macintosh will be determined by Apple's ability to provide or to encourage others to supply hardware expansions and exciting and usable software. We think Apple has at least one thing right—the Macintosh is the one machine with the potential to challenge IBM's hold on the market."

Thomas Neudecker
(InfoWorld, *March 26, 1984*)

Microcomputing

"Macintosh is a machine that is fun. As an Apple II owner, I felt uncomfortable and even suspicious about a computer that is so easy to operate. Missing was the familiar Applesoft prompt—a PR#6 before reading a disk. What I found was a machine that was so easy to operate that my eight-year-old would constantly pester me to use the Macintosh while I was writing this review. Within an hour she was well-versed in the terminology and in how to use the machine. This type of ease of use may create some resentment in the hacker in you—the machine consciously places distance between you and the operating system. In the Macintosh case, the term user transparent would be more accurate [than] user friendly. Macintosh represents state-of-the-art windowing technology at a price you might pay for just window software for the IBM PC. Its speed and sophistication place it above any window products I've seen for the PC. Its size [makes] it a welcome appliance on a desk. Plans for integrating Macintosh into a networked office system containing a Lisa at its heart and Macintoshes on most desks will appeal to almost anyone who, in Apple terminology, is a 'knowledge worker.' Whether or not you're in the market for a computer, experience a Macintosh. I bet that you will want one."

Keith Thompson
(Microcomputing, *March 1984*)

San Francisco Examiner

"A lot of ink has been spilled over the new Apple Computer—the Macintosh. The machine is praised and acclaimed by the press.

"While I personally like this new computer, I don't see it as a general hit. I hope I'm wrong. Normally, I don't like to pontificate about these things, but there are some good reasons that the computer may not become the raving success hoped for by Apple:

1. The trend toward color
2. The trend toward two disk drives
3. The trend toward IBM PC compatibility
4. The machine's main memory is limited to 128,000 characters
5. The Macintosh has no slots for expansion and is therefore restricted in versatility
6. There is no bundled software except for a word processor and a program that allows the user to 'paint'
7. The machine uses an experimental pointing device called a 'mouse'
8. The smallish keyboard has no cursor arrows and no numeric keypad
9. Who out there in the general marketplace even knows what a 'font' is?
10. What businessman knows about point size or typefaces or the value of variable point size?
11. The computer only drives a dot-matrix printer
12. The high-speed serial port is too slow for a hard disk
13. Apple's inability to sell anything but the Apple II
14. It's too expensive for a single board computer with one disk drive and a mouse.
15. The Macintosh uses icons to represent functions as though there was some intuitive knowledge on the part of the user as to what these icons mean.

"The nature of the personal computer revolution is simply not fully understood by companies like Apple (or anyone else, for that matter). Apple makes the arrogant assumption of thinking that it knows what you want and need. It, unfortunately, leaves the 'why' out of the equation—as in 'why would I want this?'"

John C. Dvorak
(San Francisco Examiner, *February 19, 1984*)

"Remember, Lisa was the first time. I guess I encourage the Mac group to understand they're the best in the world, so they tend to criticize other things, as I do, too, and that's okay. But it's also good to understand that most people [in the Mac team] have been able to stand on the Lisa people's shoulders, maybe avoid some mistakes. The Lisa people wanted to do something great. And the Mac people want to do something insanely great. The difference shows."

Steve Jobs

The Seybold Report on Professional Computing

"It's entirely reasonable to expect Mac itself to grow over time. The first logical step would be to give Mac an external Winchester [hard disk drive] like that used on Lisa … Other future steps will almost certainly include higher-capacity drives … We would certainly expect that Apple will eventually be able to offer 800K double-sided drives. Along with progress in disks, we can expect progress in computer memories … Replacing the current 64K memory chips with the new 256K chips expected onto the market this year could increase the RAM memory from 128K to 512K without requiring a larger circuit board. The machine we would dearly love to have when it becomes available would be a Macintosh with 512K of RAM, an external Winchester disk, and an 800K internal disk.

"On the positive side, everyone in our organization who has used the Mac, and every family member we have pressed into service to help us with this evaluation, has been enthusiastic about the design of the machine and the user interface. The longer you use it, the more you realize how good it is … Apple got a lot of things right with Macintosh. In many ways Mac represents the direction that desktop computers are (or at least should be) going:

- The computer as an appliance. No electronic skills required.
- A system which is truly easy to use. It is a pleasure for everyone from the computerphobe to the computer-jock.
- A compact, transportable package.
- A beautiful screen display and very quick graphics.
- An inexpensive communications bus for use as a work-area network and as a means of tying additional peripherals to the machine.
- Attractive pricing.
- A great deal of personality and user appeal.

"Apple also got some important things wrong. Our biggest worry is that Mac may be under-configured … But the dumbest thing Apple did with the whole development effort was to allow two different operating environments for Mac and Lisa."

Jonathan and Andrew M. Seybold
(The Seybold Report on Professional Computing,
Vol. 2, No. 6, PC-25 through PC-27)

Mac Models Timeline

In the infancy of the Mac market, consumers, competitors, and commentators waited eagerly for each new product announcement from Apple. The waits often seemed insufferably long. Creating the original 128K Mac was such an ordeal that after it shipped in January 1984, it was hard to keep the engineers focused on designing upgrades. They weren't resting on their laurels, they were simply exhausted.

The 512K Mac didn't ship until eight months after the original introduction, and the Mac Plus wouldn't make it to market until 1986. Power users desiring an "open" model had to wait until 1987 for the Mac II to break out of the "classic" Mac mold. Apple was giving birth to new members of the Macintosh family so slowly that it was easy to become intimately familiar with each one.

All that changed in 1992 with the introduction of the incomprehensibly numbered Performa line. In an attempt to gain market share, Apple decided to attack every market niche with its own Mac model. As you can see on the following pages, which show every Macintosh model ever made (more than 250 at last count), the result of Apple's accelerated introduction schedule is a product line that proliferated into a bewildering assortment of minutely differentiated models.

> "We were too tired, too arrogant, too stupid, I don't know what."
>
> **Guy Kawasaki**, explaining why Apple took so long to fix some of the early Mac's speed and memory problems

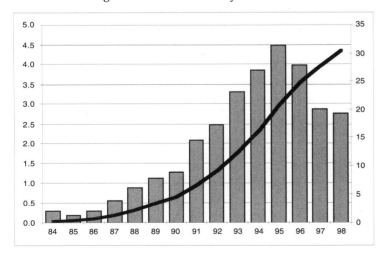

Mac unit sales (bars, left axis, in millions) increased every year from 1985 to 1995. Despite a decline in unit sales, the Macintosh installed base (line, right axis) broke 30 million during fiscal year 1998.

"I think we'll break the cumulative two million total in 1985. Sure."

Steve Jobs, *predicting Mac sales prior to its introduction*

Apple sold only 500,000 Macs by the end of 1985 and didn't break the two million mark until 1988.

The Mac Plus enjoyed the longest lifespan of any model: 1719 days.

The Mac II was the first Macintosh designed to be easily opened and expanded by end users.

If Apple had followed the naming convention established when the Mac IIx replaced the Mac II, the Mac SE/30 would have been called the Mac SEx.

"We don't want to castrate our computers to make them inexpensive. We make Hondas, we don't make Yugos."

President of Apple Products **Jean-Louis Gassée**, *defending the Mac SE/30's $4,369 price tag*

At $9,870, the Mac IIfx was the most expensive Mac ever sold.

Mac Models Timeline

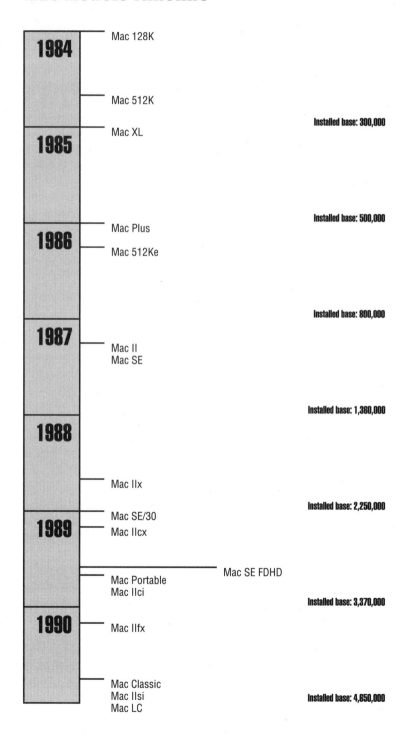

1984
Mac 128K
Mac 512K
Mac XL

1985
Installed base: 300,000

Installed base: 500,000

1986
Mac Plus
Mac 512Ke

Installed base: 800,000

1987
Mac II
Mac SE

Installed base: 1,360,000

1988
Mac IIx

Installed base: 2,250,000

1989
Mac SE/30
Mac IIcx

Mac SE FDHD

Mac Portable
Mac IIci

Installed base: 3,370,000

1990
Mac IIfx

Mac Classic
Mac IIsi
Mac LC

Installed base: 4,650,000

Mac Models Timeline (continued)

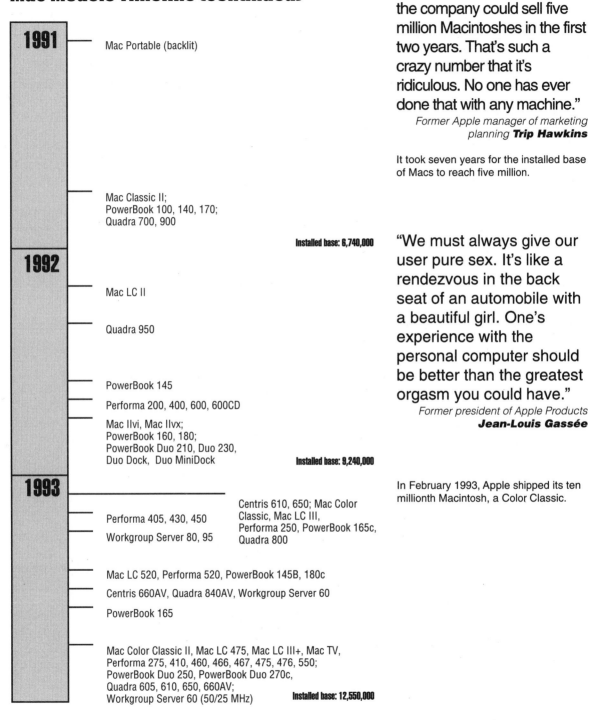

1991

Mac Portable (backlit)

Mac Classic II;
PowerBook 100, 140, 170;
Quadra 700, 900

Installed base: 6,740,000

1992

Mac LC II

Quadra 950

PowerBook 145

Performa 200, 400, 600, 600CD

Mac IIvi, Mac IIvx;
PowerBook 160, 180;
PowerBook Duo 210, Duo 230,
Duo Dock, Duo MiniDock

Installed base: 9,240,000

1993

Performa 405, 430, 450

Workgroup Server 80, 95

Centris 610, 650; Mac Color
Classic, Mac LC III,
Performa 250, PowerBook 165c,
Quadra 800

Mac LC 520, Performa 520, PowerBook 145B, 180c

Centris 660AV, Quadra 840AV, Workgroup Server 60

PowerBook 165

Mac Color Classic II, Mac LC 475, Mac LC III+, Mac TV,
Performa 275, 410, 460, 466, 467, 475, 476, 550;
PowerBook Duo 250, PowerBook Duo 270c,
Quadra 605, 610, 650, 660AV;
Workgroup Server 60 (50/25 MHz)

Installed base: 12,550,000

"[Jobs] originally believed that the company could sell five million Macintoshes in the first two years. That's such a crazy number that it's ridiculous. No one has ever done that with any machine."

Former Apple manager of marketing planning **Trip Hawkins**

It took seven years for the installed base of Macs to reach five million.

"We must always give our user pure sex. It's like a rendezvous in the back seat of an automobile with a beautiful girl. One's experience with the personal computer should be better than the greatest orgasm you could have."

Former president of Apple Products **Jean-Louis Gassée**

In February 1993, Apple shipped its ten millionth Macintosh, a Color Classic.

Mac Models Timeline (continued)

"I think they'll make refrigerators first."

*International Data Corporation researcher **Aaron Goldberg**, when asked in 1984 if Apple will ever offer an IBM-compatible product*

It took ten years before Apple began shipping the Quadra 610 DOS Compatible, a full-featured Mac capable of running MS-DOS and Windows. Turnabout is fair play: In July 1995, IBM announced that it would manufacture Mac clones for Radius at its plant in Charlotte, North Carolina.

Apple shipped over one million Power Macs and PowerPC upgrades by the end of 1994, three months before the company's one-year goal.

Apple's first new Macs of 1995 were marginally faster versions of the Power Macs introduced less than a year before.

1994

Performa 560

Mac LC 550, LC 575; Performa 575, 577, 578; Quadra 610 DOS Compatible

Power Mac 6100/60, 7100/66, 8100/80

Workgroup Server 6150, 8150, 9150

PowerBook 520, 520c, 540, 540c; PowerBook Duo 280, 280c, Duo Dock II

Mac LC 630, Performa 630, 635CD, 636CD, 637CD, 638CD; PowerBook 150, Quadra 630

Performa 6110 series

Performa 6110CD, 6112CD, 6115CD, 6117CD, 6118CD; Power Mac 475, 575, 605, 630, 8100/110

Installed base: 16,400,000

1995

Power Mac 6100/66, 7100/80, 8100/100

Power Mac 8115/110

Mac LC 580, 630 DOS Compatible; Performa 588CD, Power Mac 580, 5200/75 LC; Workgroup Server 6150/66, 8150/110, 9150/120

Performa 5200CD, 5210CD, 5220CD, 580CD, 6200CD, 630CD DOS Compatible, 640CD DOS Compatible; PowerBook 550c, Duo Dock Plus; Power Mac 6200/75, 9500/120, 9500/132

Performa 5215CD, 6116CD, 6216CD, 6218CD, 6220CD, 6230CD, 631CD

Performa 6210CD, 6300CD, 5300CD; Power Mac 9515/132

Performa 6205CD, 6214CD; Power Mac 7200/75, 7200/90, 7500/100, 8500/120, 5300/100 LC; PowerBook 500 with PowerPC, 190/66, 190cs/66, 5300/100, 5300c/100, 5300ce/117, 5300cs/100, Duo 2300c/100

Performa 5320CD

Installed base: 20,900,000

Mac Models Timeline (continued)

1996

Performa 6290CD; Power Mac 7215/90, 8515/120

Performa 6310CD;
Network Server 500/132, 700/150;
Workgroup Server 7250/120, 8550/132

Performa 5260CD, 5270CD, 5400CD, 5410CD, 5420CD, 6320CD;
Power Mac 5260/100, 5400/120, 7200/120, 7600/120, 8200/100,
8200/120, 8500/132, 8500/150, 9500/150

Performa 6260CD, Power Mac 6300/120

Performa 5400/160, 5400/180, 6400/180, 6400/200;
Power Mac 7600/132, 8500/180, 9500/180MP, 9500/200

Network Server 700/200, Workgroup Server 8550/200

Performa 5260/120, 6360; PowerBook 1400c/117, 1400c/133,
1400cs/117; Power Mac 5260/120, 5400/180, 6400/200

Performa 5280, 5430, 5440, 6410, 6420;
Power Mac 4400/160

Installed base: 24,880,552

1997

PowerBook 3400c/180, 3400c/200, 3400c/240;
Power Mac 4400/200, 5400/200, 5500/225, 6500/225,
6500/250, 7220/200, 7300/166, 7300/180, 7300/200,
7600/200, 8600/200, 9600/200, 9600/200MP, 9600/233

PowerBook 1400cs/133,
2400c/180

Power Mac 4400/200 PC
Compatible, 6500/275,
6500/300, 7220/200 PC
Compatible, 7300/180 PC
Compatible;
Workgroup Server 7350/180,
9650/233

Power Mac 8600/300, 9600/300, 9600/350

Power Mac 8600/250, 6500/300 Home Edition,
6500/275 Home Edition, and 6500/275 Small Business Edition

PowerBook 1400cs/166

PowerBook G3/250, 3400/250; Power Mac 7600/200,
9600/350, G3/233 desktop, G3/266 desktop, G3/266 minitower

Installed base: 27,762,300

**Apple unleashed the super-fast PowerPC G3-
based Macs on November 10, 1997.**

Mac Models Timeline (continued)

1998

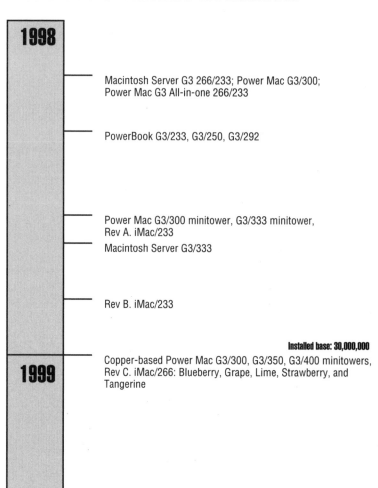

Macintosh Server G3 266/233; Power Mac G3/300; Power Mac G3 All-in-one 266/233

PowerBook G3/233, G3/250, G3/292

Power Mac G3/300 minitower, G3/333 minitower, Rev A. iMac/233

Macintosh Server G3/333

Rev B. iMac/233

Installed base: 30,000,000

Copper-based Power Mac G3/300, G3/350, G3/400 minitowers, Rev C. iMac/266: Blueberry, Grape, Lime, Strawberry, and Tangerine

1999

Apple designed the $1,299 iMac as the Internet-age "computer for the rest of us." Like the original NeXT Computer, the iMac features a radical industrial design and lacks a built-in floppy disk drive.

Apple extended the see-through design language of the iMac with the revised minitower Power Mac G3 released at Macworld Expo in San Francisco.

Why 1985 Wasn't Like 1984

In late 1984, Apple didn't have a stunning new product up its sleeve like it had the year before with Macintosh, so it tried to manufacture some excitement over The Macintosh Office, which was essentially the concept of connecting a group of Macs to a LaserWriter and sharing information using a device called a file server. There was only one small problem: The file server, a key component, was nowhere near ready to ship. To his credit, Jean-Louis Gassée, then general manager of Apple France, refused to foist this charade upon his country, not-so-secretly referring to it as "The Macintosh Orifice." Although Apple would not ship a file server until 1987, that didn't stop it from promoting The Macintosh Office in the United States in 1985.

Referring to the lack of a server, Jean-Louis Gassée derided The Macintosh Office by calling it "The Macintosh Orifice."

The Macintosh Office connected Macs with LaserWriters and a non-existent file server.

Trying to recreate the magic of the phenomenal *1984* commercial (see "The Greatest Commercial That Almost Never Aired," page 87), Apple again turned to the creative team at its advertising agency to whip up something great for the upcoming Super Bowl XIX. Chiat/Day wanted to hire Ridley Scott, who directed *1984*, but he wasn't available, so his brother Tony was hired instead.

The result was a dark, 60-second commercial called *Lemmings,* in which long lines of blindfolded businesspeople, each with one hand upon the shoulder of the person ahead and briefcase in the other hand, trudge off the edge of a cliff like lemmings into the sea. Finally, the last man in the first line, presumably a Macintosh convert, lifts his blindfold and stops at the brink instead of plunging to his death.

Director Tony Scott reportedly found fault with the clouds over England and flew to Sweden to find just the right clouds to include in the commercial's background.

Lemmings **likened DOS users to mindless rodents committing mass suicide.**

Copywriter Steve Hayden warned Apple it risked biting "the karmic weenie."

Needless to say, *Lemmings* wasn't your typical commercial. It was thought-provoking, but it lacked the liberating appeal of *1984*. In fact, John Sculley hated it, and in a repeat of the prior year, ordered Chiat/Day to sell back the $1 million Super Bowl slot to ABC, which it managed to do. The creative team at Chiat/Day mounted an intense lobbying effort to get Sculley to reverse his decision, reminding him that Apple disliked *1984*, and that turned out to be a triumph.

Even though he was convinced he had done good work, copywriter Steve Hayden cautioned Apple, "You're going to bite the karmic weenie if you run *Lemmings* and can't deliver The [Macintosh] Office." Sculley left the decision up to marketing manager Mike Murray, who crossed his fingers and went for broke.

If you go to the bathroom during the fourth quarter, you'll be sorry.

This simple newspaper ad piqued viewers' curiosity and raised expectations for Apple's *Lemmings* commercial.

Chiat/Day was able to repurchase one minute of air time at a reduced price of $900,000 (what a bargain!), and the commercial ran in the fourth quarter of Super Bowl XIX on January 20, 1985. Although the San Francisco 49ers were well on their way to crushing the Miami Dolphins 38 to 16, much of the country remained glued to the television because Apple had placed teaser newspaper advertisements warning, "If you go to the bathroom during the fourth quarter, you'll be sorry." In retrospect, it was Apple that was sorry.

Steve Jobs and John Sculley had front row seats for the disaster as they were both watching the Super Bowl in person at Stanford Stadium. For this event, Apple had filled the notoriously uncomfortable wooden stands with soft, logo-emblazoned cushions and set up a huge stadium screen. To prime the audience of 90,000, Apple ran *1984* on the screen to an enthusiastic response before the game started. But when *Lemmings* ran at half time, the crowd sat in stunned silence. Not a good sign.

The commercial was supposed to convince the television audience of 43 million that The Macintosh Office offered liberation from the traditional, accepted ways of doing business (i.e., buying IBM PCs), but it managed instead to insult the very people it was trying to win over. By most accounts, *Lemmings* failed. Miserably.

Responding to all of the negative fallout, Murray suggested running a public apology in *The Wall Street Journal*. Creative director Jay Chiat threatened that if Murray placed such an ad, Chiat/Day would buy the opposite page and apologize for the apology. Murray quickly dropped the idea.

"This is the beginning of The Macintosh Office. I say beginning because this isn't going to be the 100 days of The Macintosh Office. It's going to take us two years to earn our way into the office."

Steve Jobs, *at the January 23, 1985 shareholder meeting (Was he inadvertently admitting that the file server was two years from completion?)*

The Macintosh Office wasn't a complete failure. It introduced AppleTalk networking, and by May 1985, Apple had sold over 2,500 LaserWriter printers at a cost of $6,995 each.

It's easy to look back and blame the *Lemmings* commercial for Apple's subsequent market troubles, but "you can't write a check with advertising that the product can't cash," emphasizes Hayden. "The fact that the file server was an empty plastic box might have something to do with the failure of The Macintosh Office." True enough. Imagine for a moment, that *Lemmings*, not *1984*, was used to introduce Macintosh. The commercial might have been redeemed because Apple could back it up with an extraordinary breakthrough product. Unfortunately, that was not the case with The Macintosh Office, and *Lemmings* was a sign that Apple was out of touch, if not out of control.

Big Bad Blunders

Like most companies, Apple trumpets its successes in widely circulated press releases and buries its mistakes in small-type footnotes, but for your reading enjoyment, I've exhumed a handful of boneheaded blunders that Apple probably wishes it had cremated.

Test Drive a Macintosh

John Sculley made a name for himself at Pepsi-Cola USA by coming up with the wildly successful "Pepsi Challenge," in which blindfolded consumers professed their preference for Pepsi over Coca-Cola. His reputation as a master of event marketing was enhanced with the critical acclaim lavished on Apple's *1984* commercial, which aired during Super Bowl XVIII. After the media frenzy surrounding the Mac's introduction began to fade, reality set in at Apple. After spending $15 million on a 100-day advertising blitz, Mac sales tapered off dramatically to roughly 20,000 units a month.

For the Mac's next big promotional push, Sculley fell back on his "Pepsi Challenge" ploy and conceived the "Test Drive a Macintosh" campaign. Sculley was so convinced of the superiority of the Mac that he figured all Apple had to do was get the computer into the hands of consumers and they too would fall in love with it. So Apple spent more than $2.5 million to buy all 40 pages of advertising in a special November 1984 election issue of *Newsweek* magazine. On November 8, 1984, Sculley remarked to the *San Francisco Chronicle*, "It's unclear whether Apple has an advertising insert in *Newsweek* or whether *Newsweek* has an insert in an Apple brochure." The issue's final, fold-out ad launched the innovative "Test Drive a Macintosh" promotion.

The way the program worked was that anyone with a credit card could walk into an Apple dealer, fill out some forms and take home a Mac for a 24-hour trial. At first it appeared Sculley had worked his marketing magic yet again. About 200,000 people participated in the program, eagerly lugging brand new Macs home for a day. Even *Advertising Age* magazine was impressed, naming "Test Drive a Macintosh" one of the ten best promotions of 1984.

Most who participated in Apple's "Test Drive" turned out to be tire-kickers, not buyers.

Apple may have been able to fool the outside world, but in Cupertino they realized the "Test Drive" program was more like a car wreck. Apple's dealers hated the program. They didn't have enough Macs to sell to earnest buyers, let alone lend out overnight to tire-kickers, and they resented the burdensome paperwork during their peak end-of-year sales season. Apple had wagered that program participants would become so enamored of their new toys that they'd decide to buy them outright instead of return them after 24 hours. Apple lost that bet as the vast majority of the loaner Macs were returned slightly worse for wear.

Lotus Jazz

Following its impressive introduction, the Mac sold well to early adopters, but the machine failed to gain acceptance in the all-important business market. Apple had introduced the Mac 512K in September, but there were still too few serious business applications. When Lotus Development Corporation (www.lotus.com) announced Jazz on November 12, 1984, Apple was anxious to find a "killer application" to help boost sagging Mac sales. Jazz looked like the answer to Apple's prayers since it came from Lotus, then the dominant force in the PC spreadsheet market with its Lotus 1-2-3. Scheduled for shipment in March 1985, Jazz was a $595 integrated software package comparable to the company's Symphony package for IBM PCs, including a word processor, spreadsheet, database manager, graphics editor, and telecommunications program.

Making a personal appearance at the November introduction, John Sculley declared Jazz, "strategically significant for Apple. This is a very important day for, obviously, Lotus—but also for Apple and the industry." When Mitchell Kapor, Lotus chairman, predicted that Jazz would be bought by about half of the Mac 512K buyers, Sculley corrected, "I would guess it would be quite a bit higher."

Jazz didn't get out the door until August 1985, and it failed to take the Mac market by storm. It required the top-of-the-line Mac 512K and a second floppy drive, which few users had. It lacked the macros, power, and speed that made Lotus 1-2-3 and Symphony hits on the PC. In addition, its word processor crapped out after only 17 pages of text had been entered. No wonder people accused Lotus of trying to do the hustle with Jazz. It was discontinued in June 1988.

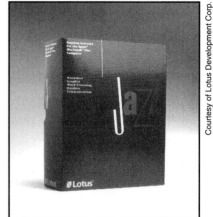

Courtesy of Lotus Development Corp.

Despite high expectations, Lotus Jazz failed to help the Mac crack the business market.

Macintosh Portable

Back in the early days of the personal computer industry, Steve Jobs was fond of deriding mainframes by saying, "Never trust a computer you can't lift." Jef Raskin took this idea to heart and originally specified that the Macintosh be an all-in-one portable computer. When Jobs took over the project, the industrial design focus shifted from portability to a reduced footprint, but he reminded the team to think of the desktop Mac as an interim step along the way to creating a "Mac in a book" by 1986. The only concession to portability in the first Mac was a recessed handle on top that allowed users to carry the 16.7-pound computer around with one hand.

"Our ultimate goal is to put Macintosh in a book, to make it the size of the notebook that's on your lap," product marketing manager Barbara Koalkin told *USA Today* just four months after the Mac's introduction. "We'd like to do that without sacrificing any of the features because we believe you need a nice display, you need a mouse, you need a certain amount of memory, you need a disk. What we're trying to figure out is how you get that into a very small package. That's not going to happen any time soon because the technology just isn't there." In fact, it took more than five years before Apple released its first "laptop" computer. Perhaps it should have waited a little longer.

In April 1985, Jobs failed to convince Apple's board of directors to build a battery-operated BookMac, as he called it, around a newly introduced flat panel display. By September, Jobs was gone and the idea languished in the labs until the fall of 1986, when Jean-Louis

"[Smaller portables] are OK if you're a reporter and trying to take notes on the run. But for the average person, they're really not that useful, and there's not all that software for them, either. By the time you get your software done, a new one comes out with a slightly bigger display and your software is obsolete. So nobody is writing any software for them. Wait till we do it—the power of a Macintosh in something the size of a book!"

Steve Jobs, *speaking in a 1985* Playboy *interview*

The Macintosh Portable offered many innovative features, such as a full-size keyboard, trackball (replaced by an optional numeric keypad above), and hard disk, but it will always be remembered for its weight.

> "At a certain point, everyone knew the Mac Portable was not destined for greatness. There is an odor that emanates from such a project. People tend to distance themselves from that odor."
>
> *Industrial designer **Jim Stewart***

Gassée initiated the Laguna project. "Our goal was to recreate the Mac SE in a portable measuring 8.5 by 11 by 1.5 inches, weighing about six pounds," says Terry Christensen, who had just managed product design on the Mac SE. "But having no experience with portables, we didn't know where to begin." That didn't stop Apple.

September 20, 1989, marked the unveiling of the $5,799 Macintosh Portable. At the time, Apple's 1989 annual report proudly noted that "in the fourth quarter … we introduced a product the world had been waiting for: the innovative, no-compromise Macintosh Portable." The key phrase here is "no compromise." Jobs had inculcated the Mac team with a reverence for perfectionism, and Gassée continued the tradition by indulging his engineers' egos, giving them free rein to design everything from scratch rather than buy industry-standard parts. The result was a product with many innovative features that was virtually unsuitable for its intended purpose.

The Mac Portable came with a 68000 running at 16MHz, 1MB of static RAM expandable to 4MB, and a 1.4MB floppy drive. Performance-wise, it was roughly equivalent to the Mac SE, which had been released more than two years earlier at less than half the price. Why did it cost so much? The Mac Portable was loaded with features unheard of in PC notebooks of that era. It had a full-sized keyboard, a trackball that could be mounted on either side to accommodate both right- and left-handed users, sound output, and an optional internal 40MB Conner hard disk.

Another novel feature was the screen. Gassée insisted on an expensive active-matrix screen, where each pixel is controlled by its own transistor, resulting in a crisp monochrome display with no ghost images or submarine effect common on cheaper passive-matrix displays. To compound matters, he originally specified a liquid crystal display (LCD) with 640 by 480 pixels, despite the fact that nobody was then manufacturing LCDs that large. The screen was ultimately reduced to 640 by 400 pixels, and Sharp built a factory dedicated to its manufacture. The Mac Portable ended up with the largest and clearest screen of any portable on the market, but it wasn't perfect. Sharp had trouble manufacturing a defect-free large active-matrix display, so Apple simply declared that a Mac Portable was within specifications if it had six or fewer dead pixels.

But the biggest problem with the Mac Portable was its weight. Marketing insisted on a predictable, long-life battery, so instead of using the same nickel-cadmium cells common in the PC market, Apple went with lead-acid batteries, the same type used in automobiles.

These batteries ran up to 12 hours on a charge, but were bulky and heavy. Really heavy. The Mac Portable weighed 15.8 pounds, almost the same weight as the original Mac—at a time when competing laptops weighed less than 10 pounds—leading industry pundits to deride it as the Mac Luggable. It was so massive that it didn't fit on airline tray tables, and even when balanced on one's knees, the Portable was hard to use in flight since its screen was almost unreadable in anything less than direct overhead light. It wasn't until February 11, 1991, that Apple introduced a revised Portable with backlighting. Given all its problems, the Mac Portable sold reasonably well, thanks to the pent-up demand of Mac users.

Like the original Mac, the Portable had more than 60 signatures of the product design team etched in the case underneath the keyboard.

PowerBook 5300

Following the Portable disaster, Apple finally got it right in October 1991 with its lightweight PowerBooks, which sold more than 400,000 units in their first year, contributing more than $1 billion in revenues. By November 1993, Apple had sold more than one million PowerBooks, but Apple didn't maintain its competitive lead, and the PowerBook line began to lag the desktop Macs in performance. The first Power Macs shipped in March 1994, but the faithful had to wait until August 25, 1995, before they could buy a notebook with a PowerPC. The PowerBook 5300 was developed under the code name Anvil, an apt description if ever there was one. It had so many problems that it significantly weighed down Apple's financial results.

The PowerBook 5300, Apple's first PowerPC-based laptop, was beset by a world of woes.

Apple had just shipped 1,000 PowerBook 5300s to eager dealers around the country when two early-production units caught fire, one at an Apple programmer's house and another at Apple's factory in Singapore. It turns out their Sony-manufactured lithium-ion (LiIon) batteries overheated while charging on AC power and exploded due to pressure inside the cells. Fortunately, nobody was hurt, but Apple's reputation went up in smoke as the national media portrayed the event as yet another example of Apple's decline. On September 14, Apple recalled all PowerBook 5300s, claiming that only 100 had by then made it into the hands of customers. Less than two weeks after the recall, Apple replaced the LiIon batteries with nickel-metal-hydride (NiMH) batteries originally intended for the PowerBook 190. The replacement NiMH batteries had 26 watt-hours of capacity, compared to 36 watt-hours for the original LiIon batteries, prompting Apple to lower the prices across the line by about $100 per model.

In a supreme bit of irony, the Sony factory responsible for producing the defective LiIon batteries in Koriyama, Japan, was itself eventually destroyed by fire.

Bursting batteries weren't the PowerBook 5300's only problem. The plastic case was prone to cracking, the power plug was too thin and

"We screwed up, clearly."
*Apple COO **Marco Landi**, on the troublesome PowerBook 5300*

often snapped off, and the power supply didn't produce sufficient current to run certain combinations of expansion-bay and PC Card accessories simultaneously. Also, the circuitry responsible for reducing power consumption during Sleep mode would shut down before completing its job, reducing the maximum nap from ten days to four. Some units locked up completely if the user pressed the Reset button and Power key together. On May 10, 1996, Apple halted production of the PowerBook 5300 and initiated another recall to replace motherboards for anyone affected by these problems. According to Dataquest, the recall helped drag down Apple's notebook revenues to $1 billion for 1996, from $1.5 billion the year before.

In the movie *Courage Under Fire*, Denzel Washington's character uses a PowerBook 5300 several times. The only problem is that the movie takes place right after the Gulf War in 1991, but the PowerBook 5300 wasn't released until August 1995. The only Mac "laptop" available in 1991 was the Mac Portable, a 15.8-pound behemoth that would have qualified Denzel for a Purple Heart if he had carried it around all the time.

On April 18, just weeks before the recall, Apple unveiled a $15 million tie-in with Paramount Pictures' *Mission: Impossible* film starring Tom Cruise. The promotion featured television and print advertisements, a special web site, and co-sponsorship of the movie's premiere. The choice of a film named *Mission: Impossible* seemed particularly ironic, since Apple had just reported its largest loss ever—$740 million for the second quarter—and some wags commented that newly installed CEO Gilbert F. Amelio was facing a task more daunting than any mission Mr. Phelps had ever accepted.

Tom Cruise, who is a Mac user in real life, uses a PowerBook 5300c in the movie, but Apple didn't have any control over the script because it signed on as a sponsor too late in the game. As a result, Cruise's character must put up with a clunky command-line interface rather than the Mac's graphical user interface. Even worse, when Cruise and cohorts plan to break into the CIA's computer system, the computer expert among them insists they need "Thinking Machines laptops." Never mind that Thinking Machines (www.think.com) has never made anything smaller than a supercomputer, much less a laptop. That's Hollywood for you. After ponying up $15 million, you can't even insist that your computer is the one requested in the script. To top it all off, the tie-in was generating demand for a product that dealers didn't have in stock anymore due to the recall—a situation that would last for four months.

Telecom Troubles

In many ways, the history of Apple consists of a long string of events in which the company failed to capitalize on emerging markets that it correctly identified years before its competitors. An excellent example is the trouble Apple has had with telecommunications.

Apple's entry into the online world began in 1984 as an effort to reduce the expense of supporting the company's worldwide network of dealers. An Apple II demo of an online system called Apple Shared Knowledge was developed, but John Ebbs, Apple's head of support and formerly a senior executive at General Electric, convinced management to showcase the Mac's value to corporations by using it to deploy the pricing and product database. His idea was to marry the corporate timeshare capability of General Electric Information Services Co. (which ran a consumer service called GEnie), with the ease of use of a Mac.

In July 1985, AppleLink debuted. It was the first online service to feature easy-to-use graphics, windows, and icons instead of a command-line text interface. Its extension of the desktop metaphor into the online world was as revolutionary as the Macintosh itself. While originally intended as a bulletproof dealer reference/support system, within weeks of its launch it became the de facto email system for Apple and its dealers. Although it bore Apple's name, it was actually maintained and operated as a joint effort of Apple and GE. As it was released to external customers over the years, users were

On August 28, 1991, the first true email message from space was sent by the crew of the space shuttle STS-43 Atlantis using a Mac Portable and specially configured AppleLink software. The shuttle crew's message: "Hello Earth! Greetings from the STS-43 Crew. This is the first AppleLink from space. Having a GREAT time, wish you were here,...send cyro and RCS! Hasta la vista, baby,...we'll be back!"

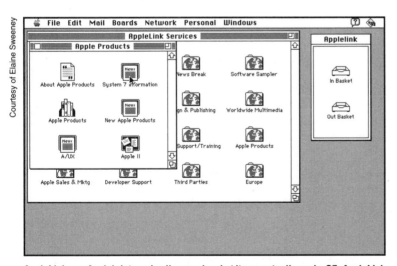

AppleLink was Apple's internal online service, but it was actually run by GE. AppleLink successfully used the Mac's desktop metaphor to make telecommunications simple.

charged from $10 to $100 per hour, depending on the service they received and their country of residence. Before long, Apple was paying over $30 million a year to GE, although a study demonstrated that use of the service saved Apple at least $100 million annually in reduced costs (paper, personnel, productivity, telephone, travel, etc.).

AppleLink was considered a resounding success, and it occurred to Apple that perhaps it should offer a similar version aimed at reducing consumer support expenses. At the time, a small firm called Quantum Computer Services was running QuantumLink, an online service for Commodore computer users. Apple dallied with the idea of buying Quantum outright for several million dollars, but instead decided to work with them to build a graphical service in the mold of the internal AppleLink, aimed initially at Apple II users but designed with the Macintosh in mind. Code-named Project Samuel, it was a joint venture with Apple providing its interface expertise, marketing muscle, funding, and logo. For its part, Quantum would build and operate the system.

At the AppleFest held in Boston on May 20, 1988, AppleLink— Personal Edition was introduced. For $6 per hour nonprime time, and $15 per hour prime time, subscribers could access Apple-specific resources such as a reference library, software center, and company store. Plus there were general services such as entertainment, business

Courtesy of Trevor Griffiths and Elaine Sweeney

AppleLink—Personal Edition came out first on the Apple II and was abandoned before the Mac version shipped.

services, online shopping, and education. Before the Macintosh version was released, Apple and Quantum began quarrelling over the future direction of the service, and Apple underwent another in a long series of reorganizations. Under pressure to eliminate what the new leadership felt were extraneous business commitments, Apple pulled its support for AppleLink—Personal Edition, but compensated Quantum by providing funding to complete the Mac beta and bring it to market without the Apple logo. In October 1991, Quantum renamed itself America Online and opened up its service to everyone, not just those using Apple computers.

Meanwhile, the GE-operated AppleLink remained in heavy use by approximately 14,000 Apple employees and contractors, as well as 20,000 dealers and developers around the world. Despite receiving $8 million per year from outside users, Apple was still losing money providing them access to the system. Apple put Peter Friedman in charge of managing the division in an attempt to reduce its costs and to formulate a plan for getting into the online services business. By 1992, the cost of employee use of AppleLink had been reduced by several million dollars a year, and the outside business turned a small profit on $25 million in revenue from 50,000 external users. However, it still remained closed to the general public, and Apple continued to write enormous checks to GE. Apple decided to kill two birds with one stone by building a new service that would be open to consumers and ultimately replace the costly AppleLink.

After talking to dozens of vendors, Apple turned to its old partner, America Online (formerly Quantum). In December 1992, Apple essentially agreed to pay a royalty based on usage for the Macintosh code that it had funded and co-developed for the aborted AppleLink—Personal Edition. Apple guaranteed America Online a minimum of $15 million in royalties over five years and agreed to pay $2.5 million to bring the system up to Apple's specifications. Since replacing AppleLink would save Apple $30 million a year in expenses, it seemed like a good investment. Nonetheless, Apple's chief counsel, Albert A. Eisenstat, shrewdly concluded that the deal would give AOL the funding and visibility it needed to be successful with a competitive service while Apple would

On November 9, 1995, Apple exercised its right to buy 2 million shares of restricted AOL stock at a cost of $12.5 million, representing 5.1 percent of the company. At the time, the fair market value was $161.5 million. To protect itself from market volatility, Apple entered into a derivative transaction that locked in a minimum price of $40 per share and allowed it to participate in an upside gain of up to $120 per share. The stock split shortly thereafter, and according to a former Apple executive, the company sold its shares in the third quarter of 1996 at a profit of about $39 million. If only Apple could have held off for two years; those shares became worth ten times as much on the strength of AOL's market performance.

probably botch the execution of its own system. So Eisenstat insisted that Apple acquire warrants that allowed it to buy a substantial stake in AOL at an attractive price. That way Apple could at least profit from AOL's success.

The Apple Online Services group and AOL spent 1993 working together on the new service. AOL adapted its technology to Apple's specifications, and the software was installed in Apple's new data center in Napa, California. Apple added its own modifications to the software, changed the overall look of the design, and assembled content from a few hundred third-party companies. All of this took longer than expected because Apple was then attempting to sell itself to AT&T. The merger talks were distracting to the Apple Online Services group and disconcerting to AOL, since it was negotiating with many players, including AT&T, in an attempt to build its own company. The merger fell through at the end of April, but the two companies continued to discuss a joint online venture until November, when Apple pulled out, fearing AT&T's dominance.

The Apple-AOL deal didn't bear fruit until January 5, 1994, when Apple announced that its new online service, named eWorld, would be operational by that spring. On June 20, eWorld officially opened its electronic gates to Mac users only, with the NewtonMail messaging service to follow. Apple promised Windows support in 1995, but that fell victim to budget cutting when 80 percent completed. eWorld had a strong sense of community and a friendly, colorful, graphical user interface that used the metaphor of a town square, with activities centered around familiar buildings.

The strange bell-shaped inhabitants of eWorld were called ePeople.

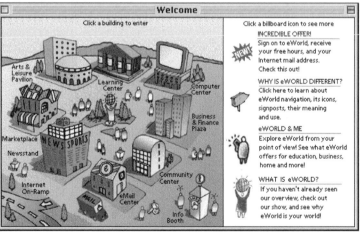

Courtesy of Raymond Kam

Like AOL upon which it was based, eWorld had a friendly, colorful, graphical user interface. Cleo Huggins was the art director for eWorld, and Mark Drury the illustrator.

Unfortunately, eWorld was slow to catch on for a variety of reasons. By mid-1994, the Internet was beginning its meteoric rise, and there were already several other proprietary online services such as America Online, CompuServe, Delphi, and Prodigy. Due to a lack of a cohesive strategy, it wasn't until late 1995 that the eWorld client software was included with every computer sold. In the meantime, AppleLink came installed on PowerBooks, and client software for some of Apple's online competitors was bundled on desktop Macs, while eWorld was left out. Another problem was the pricing. A monthly subscription set you back $8.95, which included just two free hours of evening or weekend use, with subsequent hours priced at $4.95 on the evenings or weekends, or $7.90 per hour from 6 AM to 6 PM weekdays. Apple intentionally kept the price high to moderate demand, but failed to adjust it downward when the demand never materialized.

By its first birthday, eWorld had signed up only 90,000 subscribers. Christopher Escher, director of marketing for eWorld, announced, "Our memberships have been doubling approximately every six months. We feel that's a pretty successful growth rate." To beef up the service, in June 1995, Apple added limited Internet support to eWorld 1.1 (code-named Golden Gate) and began forcing its employees to use eWorld instead of AppleLink. By September, eWorld had 115,000 members, compared to AOL's 3.5 million. With the rise of the Internet, it became clear that eWorld wouldn't make it as a proprietary online service, so in October 1995, Apple announced its intention to transition eWorld into an Internet-based system, and employees would move directly to an access-secured corporate intranet under a plan code-named DeLink.

When Gil Amelio took over Apple in February 1996, he rhetorically asked *The Wall Street Journal*, "Does the world really need another computer [online] service?" If eWorld was any indication, apparently

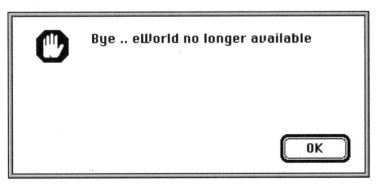

At midnight on March 31, 1996, the sun set permanently on eWorld.

"If it's necessary to shoot one of the lead buffaloes in order to send a message to the rest of the herd, you'd better be prepared to do it."

*Apple CEO **Gil Amelio**, explaining his decision to kill eWorld*

not. After one and one-half years of operation, eWorld boasted only 147,500 subscribers. On March 1, 1996, Apple announced that the sun would set permanently on eWorld at the end of the month. "The best way to structure [Apple's Internet] presence is with a portfolio of Web sites and services for particular customer groups, not a general online service like eWorld," explained Diane Keith, Apple's director of Internet productions. All eWorld subscribers were offered $15 off the Apple Internet Connection Kit and 20 free hours of connect time on AOL. Exactly one year after shutting down eWorld, operation DeLink concluded on March 31, 1997, with the termination of GE's AppleLink.

The Remarkable Rise and Fabulous Fall of John Sculley

If you're a Macintosh true believer, you probably remember John Sculley as the man who ripped the heart out of Apple when he dethroned its folk-hero founder, Steve Jobs, in 1985. If you're an investor, you probably remember him as the shrewd businessman who guided and grew Apple through many difficult years only to suffer the same fate he had visited upon Jobs. Neither depiction is entirely fair, nor entirely false. Sculley's ten-year reign at Apple was filled with promise and enthusiasm, intrigue and betrayal, recovery and triumph, anguish and irony.

When Mike Markkula came out of his comfortable early retirement to join Apple in January 1977, he had hoped to bow out gracefully after a few years of helping the young company grow with his seed money, managerial experience, and industry contacts. However, in a corporate power shift in March 1981, Markkula reluctantly assumed the role of president from the first man to hold that position, Mike Scott, and Jobs took Markkula's place as chairman of the board of directors. Markkula was back in the thick of it, but only temporarily.

The search for a new chief executive officer began not long after Markkula was thrust into the presidency at Apple. Jobs wanted someone, unlike Scott, whom he could manipulate, and the board hoped to find an experienced executive who could manage Apple's phenomenal growth. Apple tried unsuccessfully to recruit Don Estridge, the leader of the team that released the IBM PC on August 12, 1981. As IBM's VP of worldwide manufacturing, Estridge was making $250,000 a year in salary and bonuses. To entice Estridge to switch teams, Apple offered him considerably more money and a generous bundle of stock options. Estridge, however, remained "true blue" to IBM and turned down Apple's lucrative offer, but another candidate found the goodies too tempting to pass up. Apple finally found its man in John Sculley, the highly regarded president of Pepsi-Cola USA, the beverage subsidiary of PepsiCo.

"Think of Silicon Valley as Florence in the Renaissance. It's the place where anybody who is excited about doing something to change the world wants to be."
Heidrick & Struggles headhunter **Gerry Roche**, *urging Sculley to accept Apple's offer*

Among the people approached to become Apple's CEO was Admiral Bobby Ray Inman, deputy director of the CIA until June 1982. But Inman rightly concluded, "They needed someone with a marketing background and I didn't have it."

Sculley was once married to the stepdaughter of Pepsi's chairman, Donald Kendall.

> ## "Do you want to spend the rest of your life selling sugared water or do you want a chance to change the world?"
>
> **Steve Jobs**, *trying to convince Sculley to quit Pepsi and join Apple*

When he moved to California in 1983, Sculley purchased a $1.9 million, 63-year old, five-bedroom English Tudor house at 1224 Cañada Road in the tony community of Woodside. Sculley renamed it the Blackburn Valley Morgan compound; Blackburn being a Sculley family name and Morgan the type of horse his third wife Leezy (Lee Adams) liked to raise.

> ## "Some naysayers claim the partnership will never last—that intense, mercurial Jobs, who owns nearly 12 percent of Apple stock (worth almost $200 million at current prices), will drive intense, focused Sculley back East."
>
> (Fortune, *February 20, 1984*)

> ## "Apple has one leader, Steve and me."
>
> **John Sculley**, *at a private dinner celebrating his first year at Apple*

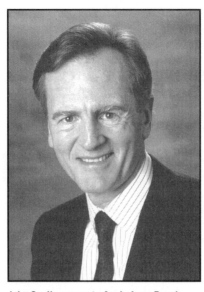

John Sculley came to Apple from Pepsi.

After 18 months of wooing, 44-year-old Sculley was named president and CEO of Apple on April 8, 1983. Sculley likes to tell people that what attracted him to Apple was the intellectual challenge of changing the world, but something as banal as money may have had a tiny little bit to do with his decision to hop from one coast to the other. To lure him away from his $500,000-a-year job at Pepsi, Apple offered him $1 million in annual pay (half salary, half bonus), a $1 million signing bonus, a $1 million golden parachute clause, options on 350,000 shares of Apple stock, and the difference in cost to buy a home in California equivalent to the one he owned in Connecticut.

For a while, things were going great for Sculley. He got on board just in time to ride the euphoric wave that was the Macintosh introduction, and he got along famously with Jobs, no small accomplishment. Sculley and Jobs shared a symbiotic professional relationship. Sculley viewed himself as Jobs' marketing and management mentor, whereas Jobs was Sculley's technology tutor. During the good times of 1983 and 1984, the two were inseparable, often referred to as "The Dynamic Duo" in the business press. But the good times didn't last.

Following the successful introduction of the Macintosh in January 1984, Apple was feeling confident. Jobs and Sculley went for broke and built up a massive inventory for the Christmas season, but the demand never materialized and Apple found itself sitting on a pile of unsold computers (forecasting demand continues to flummox Apple to this day). Tensions ran high at Apple because the company was facing serious trouble for the first time in its history. In the past, whatever mistakes Apple made (such as the Apple III and Lisa) were more than offset by the success of the Apple II, which had an installed base of 2.3 million. Things were different now, because the entire industry had suffered a slump and the Apple II wasn't strong enough to carry the company by itself. Apple would soon announce its first quarterly loss ever and be forced to lay off one-fifth of its employees.

"The Dynamic Duo," Steve Jobs and John Sculley at the Mac's introduction in 1984.

"I've made a lot of decisions in my life, but never one that changed my life more, never one that I felt better about, than coming to Apple. It isn't working for a company; it's a chance to work with people who were part of shaping history."

John Sculley, *upon his one-year anniversary at Apple*

When times get tough, the tough get going, and it became apparent to the tough-minded executives at Apple that Jobs was more of a liability than an asset. Not content to restrict himself to the role of product visionary of the Macintosh division, Jobs was playing manager, meddling in areas of the company over which he had no jurisdiction. Step on enough toes, and they'll soon be kicking your ass, which is exactly what happened to Jobs. During a marathon board meeting that started on April 10, 1985, and continued for several hours the next day, Sculley threatened to resign if the board didn't back him on his decision to remove Jobs as executive VP and general manager of the Macintosh division. The board agreed to strip Jobs of any operating role in the company, but allowed him to remain chairman. Sculley, who genuinely liked Jobs, didn't act right away, hoping to make a smooth transition. Mistake. Big mistake.

"One thing that impressed me about Apple was that while the popular image was of two young boys starting a company, it was actually backed by one of the most sophisticated, experienced boards of directors you could find."

John Sculley

Less than a month later, on the eve of a trip to China where he would speak to the vice premier about using computers in education, Sculley was tipped off by Jean-Louis Gassée, VP of product development, that Jobs planned to overthrow him during his absence. "I was the one who told Sculley what the [other executive committee members] should have told him, because I was the last one approached [by Jobs]. Let the record be clear on that. You destroy the company if you have [a coup], and this company is more important than any of us," said Gassée years later. Sculley immediately canceled the trip and convened an emergency meeting of the company's executive staff the very next day, May 24. When Sculley confronted Jobs with the coup rumor, Jobs lashed back, "I think you're bad for Apple and I think you're the wrong person to run this company."

"Steve was nothing short of exciting. He was arrogant, outrageous, intense, demanding—a perfectionist. He was also immature, fragile, sensitive, vulnerable. He was dynamic, visionary, charismatic, yet often stubborn, uncompromising, and downright impossible."

John Sculley, *demonstrating his mastery of adjectives*

> "I had given Steve greater power than he had ever had and I had created a monster."
>
> **John Sculley**

> "[Jobs] has the ability to make people around him believe in his perception of reality. It's a combination of very fast comeback, catch phrases, and the occasional, very original insight, which he throws in to keep you off balance."
>
> *Former manager of Mac software engineering* **Guy L. Tribble III**

Stung by Jobs' vicious attack, Sculley asked each executive to choose sides. One by one they fell in line behind Sculley and Jobs stalked out of the room close to tears. Even with this clear show of support, Sculley contemplated resigning, but changed his mind after a good night's rest. Two days after the meeting, Jobs had the temerity to suggest that Sculley become chairman and that he be appointed president and chief executive officer. Sorry, Charlie, but Sculley didn't play that game. On May 31, a week after the explosive executive meeting, Sculley signed the paperwork that stripped Jobs of all operational responsibilities. He retained the figurehead title of chairman and was put in charge of "global thinking" in a remote office dubbed Siberia. Jobs, the founder, had been hoist on his own petard, Sculley the outsider.

Just as he vowed to exact his revenge after Scott had taken the Lisa away from him, Jobs began thinking of ways to get back at Sculley and Apple. On September 12, Jobs told the board of directors that he and a few "low level" employees planned to start an unnamed company that would address the needs of higher education, and he asked if Apple would be interested in licensing Macintosh software to him. He assured the board that his new venture would complement Apple, not compete with it, but offered to resign as chairman nonetheless. The board refused to accept the resignation, asking him to defer the move for a week as it contemplated the possibility of buying as much as 10 percent of the new venture. At a 7:25 AM meeting the next day, Friday the 13th, Jobs presented Sculley with a list of the five employees he was taking with him: Susan Barnes (senior controller for U.S. sales and marketing), George Crow (engineering manager), Dan'l Lewin (higher education marketing manager), Rich Page (Apple Fellow), and Bud Tribble (manager of software engineering).

Sculley was incensed. These employees were privy to sensitive data on the Big Mac project Apple had under way (also known as 3M because it would have a 17-inch, million-pixel display, a million bytes of memory, and run a million instructions per second with a 68020 processor and Unix software). Feeling that Jobs had crossed over the line, the executive staff discussed the possibility of removing Jobs as chairman, but Jobs beat them to the punch. On September 17, Jobs officially resigned, but instead of quietly tendering his resignation to Markkula, he also sent copies to the press in an obvious attempt to provoke a sympathetic reaction from the public. The public responded all right, but not the way he imagined; the news of Jobs' departure sent Apple stock up a full point that day.

Steve Jobs' Resignation Letter

This is a verbatim copy of chairman Jobs' resignation letter sent to company vice chairman A.C. "Mike" Markkula:

September 17, 1985

Dear Mike:

This morning's papers carried suggestions that Apple is considering removing me as Chairman. I don't know the source of these reports but they are both misleading to the public and unfair to me.

You will recall that at last Thursday's Board meeting I stated I had decided to start a new venture and I tendered my resignation as Chairman.

The Board declined to accept my resignation and asked me to defer it for a week. I agreed to do so in light of the encouragement the Board offered with regard to the proposed new venture and the indications that Apple would invest in it. On Friday, after I told John Sculley who would be joining me, he confirmed Apple's willingness to discuss areas of possible collaboration between Apple and my new venture.

Subsequently the Company appears to be adopting a hostile posture toward me and the new venture. Accordingly, I must insist upon the immediate acceptance of my resignation. I would hope that in any public statement it feels it must issue, the company will make it clear that the decision to resign as Chairman was mine.

I find myself both saddened and perplexed by the management's conduct in this matter which seems to me contrary to Apple's best interest. Those interests remain a matter of deep concern to me, both because of my past association with Apple and the substantial investment I retain in it.

I continue to hope that calmer voices within the Company may yet be heard. Some Company representatives have said they fear I will use proprietary Apple technology in my new venture. There is no basis for any such concern. If that concern is the real source of Apple's hostility to the venture, I can allay it.

As you know, the company's recent reorganization left me with no work to do and no access even to regular management reports. I am but 30 and want still to contribute and achieve.

After what we have accomplished together, I would wish our parting to be both amicable and dignified.

Yours sincerely,

Steven Jobs

Steven P. Jobs.

"Our minds are sort of like electrochemical computers. Your thoughts construct patterns like scaffolding in your mind. You are really etching chemical patterns. In most cases, people get stuck in those patterns, just like grooves in a record, and they never get out of them. It's a rare person who etches grooves that are other than a specific way of looking at things, a specific way of questioning things. It's rare that you see an artist in his 30s or 40s able to really contribute something amazing."

Steve Jobs

At the time he left Apple, Jobs owned roughly 6.5 million shares of stock, or about 11.3 percent of the company.

"I feel like somebody just punched me in the stomach and knocked all my wind out. I'm only 30 years old and I want to have a chance to continue creating things. I know I've got at least one more great computer in me. And Apple is not going to give me a chance to do that."

Steve Jobs, *on being stripped of an operating role at Apple*

> "It is hard to think that a $2 billion company with 4,300-plus people couldn't compete with six people in blue jeans."
>
> **Steve Jobs**, *on Apple's suit following his resignation*

> "[Sculley] took a bunch of computer hackers who run around in sandals and jeans and married them to Wall Street. It takes a smart human being to marry cultures like that."
>
> Outlook on Mobile Computing *editor*
> **Andrew Seybold**

Jobs' resignation didn't appease Apple. On September 23, the company filed a suit against Jobs and Page, enjoining them from using any proprietary information and charging Jobs with dereliction of his duties as chairman. The suit was ludicrous. Before his resignation, Jobs was considered an incompetent manager with little technical skill, but once he departed he suddenly became a major threat to the well-being of Apple? Realizing the suit only gave Jobs credibility, Apple quietly settled out of court in January 1986.

With Jobs out of the way, Sculley led Apple through its most prosperous times, helping grow the business from $600 million in net sales when he joined in 1983 to almost $8 billion a decade later. During his tenure, the Mac's installed base reached over 12 million units. Along the way, he picked up an interest in politics and stumped for Bill Clinton, who was rumored to have eliminated Sculley as his running mate only because he was twice divorced. After the 1992 election, Sculley was asked to join Clinton's new cabinet as deputy commerce secretary, but he declined. He also turned down top jobs at American Express and IBM, both of which were facing hard times. He'd soon regret not jumping at those opportunities.

In 1990, Sculley anointed himself Apple's chief technology officer, despite his lack of a formal technological background. Many Apple engineers scoffed at the notion, considering this the supreme act of hubris. "He was a total poseur," opined Andy Hertzfeld, software wizard. Just as Jobs commandeered the Mac project after being ousted from the Lisa project, Sculley wanted to prove himself. "He had this absolute passionate need to put his name on things," said Jean-Louis Gassée. Ultimately, Sculley saw the Newton project in Apple's labs and decided it would be his baby. Sculley championed "personal digital assistants"at the Consumer Electronics Show in Las Vegas in January 1992 and released the Newton MessagePad at the Macworld Expo in Boston on August 3, 1993.

Step back a moment to the end of 1992. Apple had sold more computers than any other vendor worldwide, it was the most profitable personal computer company, and it had a cash reserve of over $2 billion. Nonetheless, Sculley feared that Apple couldn't survive without merging with a larger company. He was tired of fighting an uphill battle and wanted to resign, but Apple's board asked him to stick around long enough to help sell the company (see "From Diesel to Doctor," page 183). Apple's earnings per share peaked at $4.33 in fiscal year 1992, only to collapse to 73¢ per share the following year on deteriorating gross margins inflicted by fierce price competition. Many critics felt that Sculley had been too busy dabbling in politics and promoting his pet product—the much-maligned Newton MessagePad—to focus effectively on the Mac. The board of directors lost faith in Sculley, whose heart obviously was no longer in the job. On June 18, 1993, Sculley stepped down as CEO and was replaced by Michael H. Spindler (then president, COO, and board member). Like Jobs in 1985, Sculley retained the title of chairman and was supposed to focus on emerging new business opportunities for Apple and was instructed not to talk about anything except the Newton. Like Jobs, he found the figurehead role odious and began planning his exit during a two-month sabbatical and vacation.

Michael H. Spindler replaced John Sculley as Apple's CEO in June 1993, but Sculley would stick around as chairman for four more months.

Sculley longed to move back to the East Coast to rejoin his wife. On October 1, 1993, at his four-acre estate in Greenwich, Connecticut, Sculley held a five-hour meeting with Peter Caserta, president of Spectrum Information Technologies of Manhasset, New York. Caserta demonstrated his company's AXCELL cellular modem working with the Newton. Sculley was so impressed with the technology and the portfolio of patents held by Spectrum that he failed to adequately investigate Caserta's shady past when offered the reins of the $100-million, 38-person company.

On October 15, the day after Apple posted a 97 percent drop in earnings for its fourth quarter, Sculley gladly played the sacrificial lamb, resigning his position as Apple's chairman and taking with him $1 million in severance pay, a one-year consulting fee of $750,000, a commitment from Apple to buy his $4 million Woodside mansion and $2 million Lear 55 jet, and $2.4 million of unearned stock options.

> "I've had some wonderful years at Pepsi, an extraordinary journey at Apple, and now I am ready to head off to new challenges. I'm tremendously grateful for the support of so many phenomenal Apple people. I wish everyone involved with Apple great success in the years ahead. I'll be out there cheering you all on."
>
> *John Sculley*, upon resigning

"He rushed into [Spectrum]. It was exactly the way he did things when he was at Apple. If John saw something, whether it was virtual reality or reality, he went for it. At that time at Apple there was this huge safety net, so you got to make mistakes and try things and learn things, and on the whole it was positive."

Be CEO **Jean-Louis Gassée**

"Now that Sculley's consulting with Kodak, they're going to have trouble making film."

Oracle CEO **Lawrence Ellison**

Total take: just over $10 million. Just three days later, Sculley shocked the business world with his announcement that he was joining Spectrum as chairman and CEO at a salary of $1 million with options to purchase 18 million shares (20 percent of the firm's outstanding common stock). It wasn't his compensation that raised eyebrows, it was the company he was joining.

Spectrum was embroiled in a class-action lawsuit by shareholders pertaining to inflated revenue projections made by Caserta in May, and the Securities and Exchange Commission was investigating charges of stock manipulation. Furthermore, Spectrum engaged in aggressive accounting practices that made it look much more profitable than it really was. Sculley claims he didn't know the full story when he accepted his position at Spectrum, but he was smart enough to realize that he had stepped in it but good. He began looking for an escape hatch, and on February 7, 1994, he resigned from Spectrum and filed a $10 million suit against Caserta, claiming he failed to reveal the SEC probe and Spectrum's accounting practices in an attempt to dupe Sculley into joining the firm so that Caserta could dump his stock at inflated prices. Spectrum promptly turned around and sued Sculley for $300 million, charging him with breach of contract, mismanagement, and theft of trade secrets. In March, both parties withdrew their lawsuits.

Although one might assume that Sculley's reputation in the business community had been irreparably soiled, it appears he has a more resilient Teflon coating than Ronald Reagan. On June 24, 1994, Eastman Kodak's newly hired chairman George Fisher announced that the firm had retained Sculley with a quarter-time contract as a "marketing advisor to assist Kodak in building its digital imaging and brand marketing strategies." Ironically, Sculley had been widely rumored as a candidate for chairman and CEO of Eastman Kodak, but he chose Spectrum instead.

In 1995, Sculley founded a New York-based private investment and strategic advisory firm with his brothers Arthur and David. Sculley Brothers LLC (www.sculley.com) views itself as a "venture catalyst" firm focused on the financial services, communications, and media/entertainment industries. One of its early investments was Live Picture (www.livepicture.com), a privately held publisher of Internet imaging software based in Soquel, California. Not content to make a passive investment, in February 1995, Sculley was named acting CEO of Live Picture. He has since relinquished the role of CEO, but remains the chairman of the board at Live Picture.

John Sculley Predicts ...

When interviewed in the September 1987 issue of *Playboy* by noted computer journalist Danny Goodman, John Sculley was riding high in the world of corporate executives and didn't mind offering his views on the future:

In the next 20 years ... the Soviets will land a manned mission on Mars.

The Soviets never even landed a man on the moon, and the U.S.S.R. dissolved itself in 1992.

And that is the same time that it's been estimated that the value of the Japanese stock exchange will exceed the value of all the American stock exchanges.

The Japanese stock exchange has a lot of catching up to do to offset the "Asian contagion" of 1997.

Optical-disk media are going to revolutionize the way personal computers are used.

The AppleCD SC ($1,199) shipped in March 1988, and today CD-ROMs are a mainstay in the computer industry.

We won't recognize computers in two or three years, I believe, because they will allow us to access information, whether it's pictorial, graphic, sound, or text, that we couldn't have even imagined a few years ago. No longer will it be crude stick figures, but we'll see rich, full-color animations.

Apple released QuickTime on June 3, 1991, and has firmly established itself as the leader in multimedia.

[Artificial intelligence] will change the personal computer from an information machine to a knowledge system where most of the hard work will be done invisibly by software agents that wander through data bases and extract information that's relevant to the individual user.

On August 3, 1993, Apple introduced the hand-held Newton MessagePad, which featured, among other things, built-in intelligence for managing routine tasks.

The appearance of the computer will change. It won't even resemble the form we have become accustomed to. We'll either wear it on our wrist or carry it in our pockets. It'll use radio signals to access information or to send information back to a network.

The Newton MessagePad was the first Apple device with the ability to exchange information using infrared technology, and now most PowerBooks share this capability.

It will be difficult to tell where the telephone ends and the computer begins.

Today you can't pick up a newspaper or turn on the television without hearing about the Internet, but back in 1987 few outside the scientific and educational communities had ever heard of it, much less foreseen its tremendous potential.

Sculley Timeline

1983
- Lisa and Apple IIe introduced
- Sculley joins Apple
- Apple II installed base = 1,000,000

Apple III+ introduced

1984
- Lisa 2 and Macintosh introduced
- Mac 512K introduced
- "Test Drive a Mac" promotion launched
- Mac XL introduced

1985
- Lisa discontinued; Jobs kicked upstairs

Sculley authorized to strip Jobs of operating role

- Apple files suit against Jobs after he resigns
- Microsoft ships Windows 1.01; licenses Mac technology
- Apple drops suit against Jobs; Mac Plus introduced

1986
- Mac 512Ke introduced
- Apple IIGS introduced

1987
- Mac II and Mac SE introduced
- Newton project starts under Sakoman

1988
- Microsoft ships Windows 2.03
- Apple sues Microsoft and HP
- AppleLink—Personal Edition introduced
- Jobs introduces NeXT Computer

Apple IIc Plus and Mac IIx introduced

1989
- Mac SE/30 introduced
- Mac IIcx introduced
- Mac Portable and Mac IIci introduced

Remaining Lisas buried; Jobs ships NEXTSTEP 1.0

Sculley Timeline (continued)

1990
- Spindler promoted to COO and executive VP of Apple
- High-end Mac IIfx introduced
- Windows 3.0 released
- Apple spins off General Magic
- Low-end Macs introduced (Classic, IIsi, LC)
- Gassée resigns from Apple

1991
- Spindler elected to board of directors
- Sculley backs Pocket Newt
- System 7 released
- Sculley demos Pink for IBM
- Court reconsiders originality of Apple's GUI
- First PowerBooks and Quadra introduced; IBM partnership announced; PowerPC, Taligent, Kaleida projects begin

1992
- Microsoft releases Windows 3.1; court holds most Windows elements covered by '85 agreement
- First Performas introduced
- Apple pays AOL for code for eWorld

1993
- NeXT discontinues hardware line
- AT&T merger discussions break down
- Sculley replaced by Spindler as CEO
- MessagePad introduced; Windows suit dismissed
- Sculley resigns from Apple, joins Spectrum
- Apple petitions Supreme Court

1994
- Sculley resigns from Spectrum, each files suit against other
- First Power Macs ship
- Suits dropped
- Sculley retained as consultant for Eastman Kodak; eWorld introduced
- Amelio joins Apple's board of directors

1995
- Kaleida ships ScriptX
- Sculley joins Live Picture; Supreme Court rejects Apple's appeal
- MessagePad 120 announced
- Microsoft ships Windows 95
- Kaleida folded
- Newton 2.0 ships; Taligent folded

1996
- Spindler replaced by Amelio as CEO
- eWorld discontinued
- Apple buys NeXT; Jobs returns

"Apple has been a somewhat dysfunctional world, arrogant when it was most successful and wonderfully innovative when its back was up against the wall."

Former Apple CEO John Sculley

EVOLUTION OF THE APPLE MACINTOSH

EVOLUTION OF APPLE MANAGEMENT

Windows:
What Went Wrong?

Microsoft and its boyish, multi-billionaire chairman, William Henry Gates III, are much maligned in the Macintosh community. Many Mac fanatics view Gates as the anti-Christ, stuffing inferior products down the throats of the world's computer users in an all-out effort to rule the industry and crush the Mac. Sure, Gates wants it all (he already has a darn big chunk of it), but he is absolutely not a Mac hater. In fact, he's probably the biggest fan of the Macintosh way of computing. Gates' transformation from benevolent co-conspirator to reviled competitor, and how Apple itself is really to blame for the success of Windows, is a fascinating tale.

Steve Jobs realized that the Mac would need a full complement of useful applications to be successful, and the most important third-party developer of all was Microsoft. Jobs suspected that Microsoft would take what it learned writing Mac software to write similar applications that would run on IBM PCs. Jobs' fear of Microsoft was well founded but misdirected. On January 22, 1982, Jobs forced Gates to agree that Microsoft would not "undertake in any way to sell, lease, license, publish or otherwise distribute … any financial modeling, business graphics or data base program which utilizes a mouse or tracking ball for any computer not manufactured by Apple." Unbelievably, nothing in the agreement precluded Microsoft from writing an operating system that would compete with the Mac. That would prove to be a disasterous oversight.

At Microsoft, Jeff Harbors gave the Macintosh the code name Sand, in reference to Steve Jobs' grandiose vision of Apple's Mac factory consuming raw sand at one end of the highly automated line, turning it into silicon, and eventually churning out finished computers at the other end. Serendipitously, the code name also stood for Steve's Amazing New Device.

In return for Gates' promise to develop mouse-based applications exclusively for the Mac until 12 months after its introduction (or January 1, 1983, whichever came first), Jobs provided Microsoft with precious Mac prototypes. True to its word, Microsoft began the most extensive Mac software development effort outside of Apple, but it also began work on Windows for the IBM PC and its clones. Gates was simply hedging his bets. Although he had amassed a fortune with the command-line interface of MS-DOS, he, like Jobs, realized

"We bet the company on Windows and we deserve to benefit. It was a risk that's paid off immensely. In retrospect, committing to the graphics interface seems so obvious that now it's hard to keep a straight face."

Microsoft CEO **Bill Gates**, *in a July 1994* Playboy *interview*

"If Macintosh isn't a success, then the market is left to the PC. But we're super-enthusiastic. If Apple can meet its production goals, we expect half of Microsoft's retail sales in 1984 to be Macintosh-related."

Bill Gates

that the future of the industry was in graphical user interfaces. Since Apple was writing its own Mac operating system, Gates wanted to make sure Microsoft got a piece of the action on the PC.

Eager to steal Jobs' thunder, Gates announced Windows at the Helmsley Palace Hotel in New York on November 10, 1983, and predicted that by the end of 1984, Windows would be used on more than 90 percent of all IBM PC-compatible computers. Just a few months later, when Apple introduced the Mac, Gates stood proudly as a staunch supporter of the Cupertino upstarts and announced the immediate availability of MultiPlan and Microsoft BASIC. Microsoft had invested heavily in its Mac software division and was eager to reap the rewards of being the first to market with many of the major applications that would follow in the months ahead.

Although Gates publicly expressed high hopes for the Macintosh, privately Microsoft's Windows project steamed ahead at full speed. The difficult task of slapping a graphical user interface on top of the text-based MS-DOS was compounded by fear of being sued if the end result looked too much like the Mac. A few weeks before releasing Windows 1.01 in 1985, Microsoft was genuinely concerned that Apple was going to sue over interface similarities between Windows and the Mac, so Gates bluffed Apple CEO John Sculley with an ultimatum: Call off the lawyers or Microsoft will stop development on Word and Excel for Macintosh.

This was a crucial period for Apple. The Mac was selling only 20,000 units a month, far below the initial forecasts of 100,000 units a month. Despite revenues that were ten times that of Microsoft, Apple desperately needed its continued support, and Gates knew it. However, Apple's top brass was convinced there was no way Microsoft would walk away from the Mac applications market, which it was already dominating. They urged Sculley to stand tough, but instead, he blinked. On October 24, 1985, four days before Gates was to turn 30 years old, Sculley handed him the best birthday present ever: Apple would allow Microsoft to use some Mac technology in Windows, and in turn Microsoft would hold off shipping a Windows version of Excel for a while, giving the Mac a chance to secure a foothold in the business market.

Microsoft shipped Windows on November 20, and two days later during Fall COMDEX (a huge industry trade show) in Las Vegas, Gates and Sculley signed a confidential, three-page agreement that granted Microsoft a "non-exclusive, worldwide, royalty-free, perpetual, nontransferable license to use these derivative works in

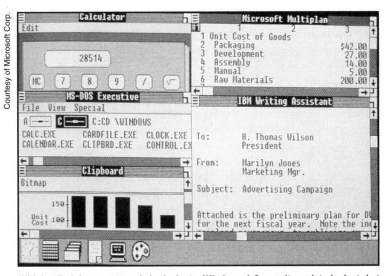

Courtesy of Microsoft Corp.

With its tiled documents and clunky fonts, Windows 1.0 wasn't much to look at, but it was far better than MS-DOS and close enough to the Mac to make Apple nervous.

"Hey, Steve, just because you broke into Xerox's house before I did and took the TV doesn't mean I can't go in later and take the stereo."

Bill Gates, *in response to Jobs complaining about how much Windows looks like the Mac*

present and future software programs, and to license them to and through third parties for use in their software programs." In exchange, Apple got Microsoft's commitment to upgrade Word for Macintosh, delay Excel for Windows until October 1, 1986, plus an acknowledgment that "the visual displays in [Excel, Windows, Word, and MultiPlan] are derivative works of the visual displays generated by Apple's Lisa and Macintosh graphic user interface programs." In other words, Microsoft got Apple's crown jewels and Apple got shafted. Not since British Prime Minister Neville Chamberlain appeased Adolf Hitler with the Munich Pact of 1938 has the world seen such a fine demonstration of negotiation skills.

"I don't know what is going to happen to Windows, or to VisiOn, but IBM's windowing package will be the standard. We hear it is not that great, but it will be the standard."

Steve Jobs, *betting on the wrong horse in April 1984*

Courtesy of Corbis

Separated at birth? Apple's John Sculley (left) and Britain's Neville Chamberlain.

"We didn't realize we'd signed an agreement that would jeopardize our rights in the future. Our lawyers weren't good enough. We never had any intention of giving Microsoft the rights on anything more than version 1.0."

John Sculley, *commenting on the Microsoft agreement in 1996*

As any computer industry executive will tell you, the software business is an annuities game where you sell a product once and continue to reap revenue from periodic upgrades. Upgrading the buggy Word was inevitable because it was in Microsoft's financial interest to do so. Furthermore, Gates knew that Microsoft wouldn't be able to ship Excel for Windows before the postponement date, so the stipulation was moot. In fact, it didn't ship until October 1987. Finally, what's the harm of acknowledging the Mac's influence on Windows in a confidential document?

Ironically, after Apple successfully sued Franklin Computer Corporation in 1983 for copying its read-only memory code in order to sell Apple II clones, Gates himself lauded the outcome in an opinion piece for *The New York Times* business section: "Imagine the disincentive to software development if after months of work another company could come along and copy your work and market it under its own name … Without legal restraints on such copying, companies like Apple could not afford to advance the state of the art."

The first version of Windows didn't really catch on, but Microsoft is nothing if not persistent. Once it sets its sights on something, it keeps cranking away at it, doggedly making minor revisions and alterations. Gates loved the Mac and was slowly but surely fashioning Windows in its image. In January 1988, Microsoft released Windows 2.03, which incorporated Mac-like icons and threw aside the old tiled windows in favor of overlapping windows. The result was too close for comfort as far as Apple was concerned, and on March 17 (Saint Patrick's Day), 1988, Apple responded by filing an 11-page suit in federal court in San Jose, accusing Microsoft of infringing Apple's copyrights by producing computer programs that imitate the Lisa/Mac audiovisual works. Also named as a defendant in the suit was Hewlett-Packard, whose NewWave ran on top of Windows. Apple would eventually seek $5.5 billion in damages.

"That's not what a Mac does. I want Mac on the PC, I want Mac on the PC."
Bill Gates,
arguing in favor of overlapping, not tiled, windows for Microsoft Windows

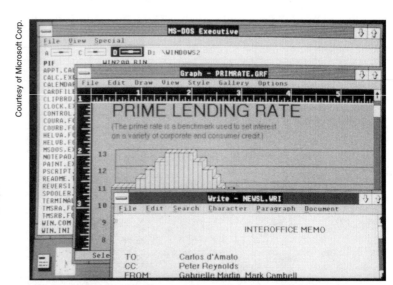

Courtesy of Microsoft Corp.

With its overlapping documents, Windows 2.03 was more Mac-like than before. Apple didn't find the imitation flattering and initiated a "look-and-feel" lawsuit seeking $5.5 billion in damages from Microsoft and partner Hewlett-Packard.

Microsoft countersued, claiming that its 1985 agreement with Apple gave it the right to use the contested features in Windows, but Apple maintained that the agreement applied to only the first version of Windows. The suit had the desired effect of instilling fear, uncertainty, and doubt in the Windows development community. As Borland's Philippe Kahn stated, it was like "waking up and finding out that your partner might have AIDS." On July 25, 1989, U.S. District Judge William W. Schwarzer ruled that all but 10 of the 189 contested visual displays in Windows 2.03 were covered by the 1985 licensing agreement. A confident Microsoft steadfastly continued updating Windows, releasing version 3.0 on May 22, 1990, at the City Center Theater in New York.

Over time the court ruled that the 1985 agreement wasn't a complete defense for Microsoft, acknowledged the originality of Apple's copyrighted works, added Windows 3.0 to the complaint, and dismissed many of the counterclaims. But on August 14, 1991, the tide turned when the court reconsidered the originality of Apple's audiovisual display. On April 14, 1992, U.S. District Judge Vaughn R. Walker issued a four-minute oral ruling that substantially narrowed the scope of the issues when it held that most of the Windows and NewWave interface elements were either covered by the 1985 license or could not be protected under copyright law. Finally the whole enchilada was decided in Microsoft's favor on August 24, 1993, when the court dismissed Apple's action. In September 1994, Apple filed an appeal with the U.S. Court of Appeals for the Ninth Circuit, but that court upheld the original judgment. As a last resort, on December 19, Apple filed a petition, called a writ of certiorari, with the U.S. Supreme Court, asking the justices to review the case. On February 21, 1995, the court refused to hear the case, putting an end to the seven-year, $10 million legal battle.

"When we were developing the Macintosh we kept in mind a famous quote of Picasso: 'Good artists copy, great artists steal.' What do I think of the suit? I personally don't understand it … Can I copyright gravity? No."

NeXT CEO **Steve Jobs**

Apple maintained the 1985 agreement applied to Windows 1.0 only, but Microsoft interpreted it as covering subsequent upgrades. Emboldened by a series of favorable court decisions, Microsoft continued making Windows increasingly Mac-like with every release.

> "Apple says, 'Hey, Win 3.1 is crummy and it always was crummy.' And we say, 'No, it just turned crummy. It was really great til Thursday.'"
>
> **Bill Gates**, *after shipping Windows 95*

> "Windows 95 is the best thing to happen to Apple in a long time because it hit us like a 2-by-4 right between the eyes."
>
> *Apple evangelist* **Guy Kawasaki**

Microsoft reportedly paid the Rolling Stones $12 million for the use of their song *Start Me Up* in the Windows 95 introductory advertising campaign.

> "Win 95 is the most overhyped product in the history of the PC industry; even more than the Newton."
>
> *Apple's director of Mac platform marketing* **Michael Mace**

The ruling was a mere technicality at that point because a much-improved Windows 3.1 had by then come to dominate the personal computer marketplace, with Apple's Mac share hovering around 15 percent. Even that small fraction of the market was slipping from Apple's grasp by the time Microsoft introduced Windows 95 (code-named Chicago) on August 24, 1995.

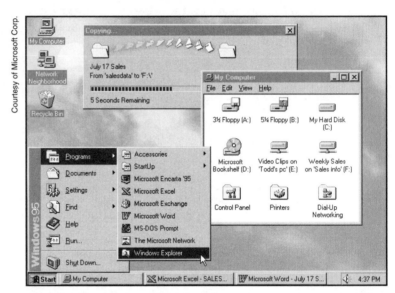

Courtesy of Microsoft Corp.

Just seven months after the U.S. Supreme Court refused to consider Apple's appeal, Microsoft released Windows 95, which to the casual observer has a user interface that is indistinguishable from that of the Macintosh operating system.

The $200-million launch of Windows 95 was a media event like no other for a computer product. It was front-page news, led the evening newscasts on every network, and had people lining up at midnight to buy the shrink-wrapped package from retailers who hosted late-night launch parties. Apple responded by placing a two-page spread in *The Wall Street Journal* that spelled out in huge block letters: "C:\ONGRTLNS.W95" with a little Apple logo below. The ad, created by MWW/Savitt, was in the same smug vein as the "Welcome, IBM, seriously" ad that Apple ran years before when IBM released its PC (see "The Strangest Bedfellow of All," page 45), and it was about as effective in stopping the Wintel onslaught as the previous ad was in deterring buyers of the IBM PC. Retailers sold more than three million copies of Windows 95 in its first five weeks on the market alone, whereas Apple sold only 4.5 million Macs during the entire year, the company's high-water mark as far as unit sales are concerned.

The full damage of the 1985 agreement remains difficult to assess. Had Apple held its ground, Microsoft may not have grown as powerful as it has. Now, more than a dozen years after Sculley caved in to Gates' demands, a weakened Apple must compete with hundreds of vendors selling Intel-based PC clones running Microsoft's Windows 95, Windows 98, and Windows NT, each more Mac-like than ever.

"Fifty years from now, history books are going to say Bill Gates built the computer. Apple will be forgotten."

Mac Finder co-author **Steve Capps**, *now a Microsoft employee*

"The trouble with Apple is it succeeded beyond its wildest dreams. We succeeded so well, we got everyone else to dream the same dream. The rest of the world became just like it. The trouble is, the dream didn't evolve. Apple stopped creating."

Steve Jobs

"DOS computers manufactured by companies such as IBM, Compaq, Tandy, and millions of others are by far the most popular, with about 70 million machines in use wordwide. Macintosh fans, on the other hand, may note that cockroaches are far more numerous than humans, and that numbers alone do not denote a higher life form."

New York Times, *November 26, 1991*

"Windows."

Jean-Louis Gassée, *providing a technically incorrect response to the question "What contest, held via Usenet, is dedicated to examples of weird, obscure, bizarre, and really bad programming?" posed by Bill Gates during the Spring 1993 Computer Bowl*

Windows Timeline

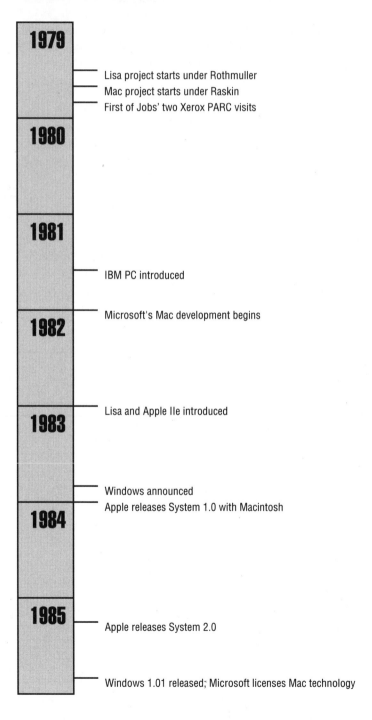

1979

Lisa project starts under Rothmuller
Mac project starts under Raskin
First of Jobs' two Xerox PARC visits

1980

1981

IBM PC introduced

Microsoft's Mac development begins

1982

Lisa and Apple IIe introduced

1983

Windows announced
Apple releases System 1.0 with Macintosh

1984

Apple releases System 2.0

1985

Windows 1.01 released; Microsoft licenses Mac technology

Windows Timeline (continued)

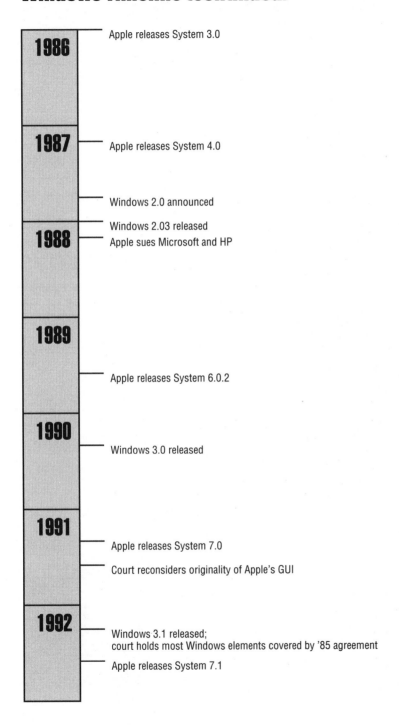

1986 — Apple releases System 3.0

1987 — Apple releases System 4.0

Windows 2.0 announced

Windows 2.03 released
1988 — Apple sues Microsoft and HP

1989

Apple releases System 6.0.2

1990

Windows 3.0 released

1991

Apple releases System 7.0

Court reconsiders originality of Apple's GUI

1992 — Windows 3.1 released;
court holds most Windows elements covered by '85 agreement

Apple releases System 7.1

"The day I left Apple we had a 10-year lead over Microsoft. In the technology business a 10-year lead is really hard to come by … Apple had that with the graphical user interface. The problem at Apple was that they stopped innovating. If you look at the Mac that ships today, it's 25 percent different than the day I left. And that's not enough for 10 years and billions of dollars in R&D. It wasn't that Microsoft was so brilliant or clever in copying the Mac, it's that the Mac was a sitting duck for ten years. That's Apple's problem: their differentiation evaporated."

Steve Jobs

"Windows [3.1] is like a Mac in the same way that a transvestite is like a real woman. It's 95 percent the same, and actually what some people would prefer, but not really the same for those who care about small differences."

PC Magazine *columnist* **John Dvorak**

Windows Timeline (continued)

1993

Windows NT 3.1 released

Apple suit dismissed;
Apple files appeal

Apple petitions U.S. Supreme Court

1994

"One of the reasons I think Microsoft took ten years to copy the Mac is 'cause they didn't really get it at its core."

Steve Jobs

Apple releases System 7.5

1995

U.S. Supreme Court refuses to hear Apple's appeal

Windows 95 released

1996

"We are being flim-flammed by Bill Gates and his partners. Look at Windows 95. That's a lot of flimflam, you know … The Windows thing isn't bought by women. I bet if you look at the sales figures, it's 80 percent men. Crazy young men or crazy older men who love toys."

*Science fiction author **Ray Bradbury***

Apple releases System 7.6

1997

Apple releases Mac OS 8.0

Apple releases Mac OS 8.1

1998

Windows 98 released

"The Mac has been dead in the water since 1985 in terms of its user interface. And Windows is still a sort of caricature of the Mac. Windows 95 doesn't really get it. The user interface is not very good."

Steve Jobs

1999

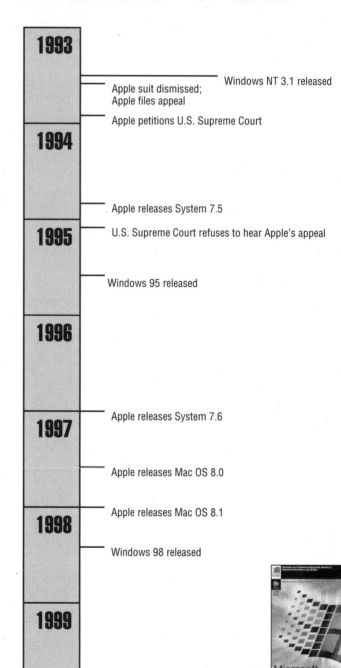

Courtesy of Microsoft Corp.

The Fallen Apple

In many ways, the story of Newton is very similar to that of Macintosh. Like the Mac before it, the Newton was created largely to satisfy the desire of its designers to own a revolutionary device that only they could conceive. As with the Mac, Newton development began as a small, ill-defined project and grew into a division that some hoped—and many feared—would change the face of Apple forever. The Newton relied heavily on unproven technology and was targeted at new markets, in much the same way that the Mac popularized many computing innovations in an effort to become "the computer for the rest of us." And just as declining Mac sales played a part in Steve Jobs' ouster, so did disappointing market reaction to the Newton help seal John Sculley's fate. Proving that it failed to learn from the Mac experience, Apple was slow to address Newton's initial shortcomings, allowing competitors' derivative devices to dominate the personal digital assistant (PDA) market it had created and ultimately forcing a weakened Apple to discontinue Newton in disgrace.

Just as the Macintosh started with one man, Jef Raskin, the Newton was the brainchild of hardware engineer Steve Sakoman. After helping create and launch the Mac Plus, Mac SE, and Mac II, by March 1987 Sakoman was feeling a bit burned out and was entertaining the idea of leaving Apple to start his own company. He wanted to do something new and exciting, not churn out endless variations of the Macintosh. When he discussed his plans with senior VP of R&D Jean-Louis Gassée, Sakoman was enticed to stay at Apple with the promise that he could start a small Special Projects group researching wireless networking and cursive handwriting recognition. Sakoman was intrigued, but insisted that he would do so only if Gassée promised that his "skunk works" would retain a startup mentality free from corporate interference and marketing's meddling. Gassée agreed, and Sakoman set out to investigate what it would take to create a new breed of pen-based, mobile, personal information devices.

> "In five years or less, computers will probably be capable of recognizing handwriting. We will have taken one step forward in understanding the mystery of shapes recognition. No one knows today what intellectual operation or algorithm allows us to reliably recognize a face, a voice, someone's handwriting. There are complex shapes that we can describe fairly completely but without being able to recognize them definitely."
>
> *Senior VP of R&D*
> **Jean-Louis Gassée**, *writing in 1985*

143

"I suspect Newton is used as a name because the device can easily be dropped (and probably as easily broken) thus confirming certain precepts of gravitation developed by Isaac Newton."

Industry columnist **John C. Dvorak**

Steve Capps, a veteran of the original Mac team, was instrumental in the early development of the Newton project.

As an Apple Fellow working in the Newton group, Steve Capps tooled around Cupertino in a red Honda Civic SI bearing the vanity plate "NOOTOON."

Every project at Apple needs a code name, so Sakoman choose Newton for his new undertaking, in part because the original Apple logo depicted the 17th-century English scientist sitting beneath an apple tree, but mainly because he believed that "Newton shook up people's ideas about the way things are." Sakoman's plan was to come up with something so radically different from personal computers that it would have a revolutionary effect on the industry, in much the same way that the Macintosh redefined computing three years prior.

By late 1987, Sakoman had staked out his turf in an old chip company's building on Bubb Road in Cupertino and had begun assembling a small team of engineers. He snared his first superstar engineer when he convinced Steve Capps to return to Apple and join the nascent Newton team that November. The flamboyant Capps, who favors shorts and checkerboard-patterned Vans tennis shoes, had left Apple in 1985 to build his own music software company and had just invented the Jaminator, the ultimate air guitar/synthesizer. He had co-written the Mac's Finder with Bruce Horn and knew what it was like to be involved in the startup phase of a promising project. Capps was concerned that the Newton would end up just another expensive yuppie toy, but Sakoman assured him that wouldn't happen.

Sakoman originally envisioned a small, lightweight computer and communicator that organized ideas and information at a cost of $2,495, the same as the original Mac. Unencumbered by management oversight, the engineers kept upping the ante, and as Capps feared, the resulting feature creep turned the product into "a monster in a box." The Newton group was an engineer's dream: you could research whatever you wanted without pressure to produce an actual product that might some day turn a profit. If a new technology seemed like it was cool, it found its way into the specification. The device grew to a slate code-named Figaro, which measured 8.5 by 11 inches, had a touch-sensitive, active-matrix screen, a pen for handwriting recognition data input, a hard disk, plus an infrared port for beaming data across vast distances. Estimated cost: $6,000 to $8,000.

By 1989, the Newton group was generating ferment on the Apple campus. Just as the Apple II division resented the coddling of the Macintosh development team back when the Apple II was carrying the company, now it was the Mac team that felt slighted. The Mac was Apple's bread and butter, yet resources were being poured into the Newton team and they had little to show for it. The Newton's secrecy contributed to the paranoia, since few outside the group really understood what they were working on. Critics feared that the Newton would compete with the Macintosh Portable, which was to be released September 20, 1989. As far as many people at Apple were concerned, the Figaro mock-up created by outside industrial designer Giorgetto Giugiaro was just a portable computer with a pen for an input device. Despite Gassée's initial promises, Sakoman found himself increasingly having to defend Newton at the corporate level, probably because Gassée's star had begun to fade.

Gassée had been named president of Apple Products in August 1988, placing him just below Sculley in the corporate hierarchy. With their relationship growing increasingly combative over issues such as licensing (Gassée hated the idea), Sculley essentially demoted Gassée when Michael H. Spindler was named COO on January 29, 1990. The worldwide manufacturing and marketing units that previously reported to Gassée were placed under Spindler. Whatever power to protect the Newton group Gassée once had was fading fast, and Sakoman eventually tired of fighting for its existence. In protest over how Gassée had been treated, Sakoman resigned from Apple on March 2, 1990, the same day Gassée announced he too would leave by September 30.

After leaving Apple, Sakoman and Gassée co-founded Be, Inc. (see "The Copland Crisis," page 225).

With its leader suddenly gone, the Newton group's continued existence was called into question. On the night of March 11, HyperCard creator Bill Atkinson invited Capps, Sculley, Marc Porat, Andy Hertzfeld, and Susan Kare to a meeting at his home to discuss forming a new company. Porat had spent the last year in Apple's Advanced Technology Group (ATG) trying to determine the company's future direction. He favored weaning Apple from its sole reliance on the Mac by developing a new smart agent network service with telecommunication companies that could be accessed using a small hand-held device. These ideas were embodied in projects code-named Paradigm and Pocket Crystal. Capps asked Sculley what it would mean to Newton if these projects were chosen as Apple's new direction. Sculley admitted he didn't quite understand what Newton was and told Capps to put together a Newton prototype that he could show at the next board of directors meeting in April.

Intrigued by what Capps had told him, Sculley dispatched Larry Tesler, who came from Xerox PARC to help design the Lisa interface and was then VP of ATG, to check out Newton and see if there was anything of value that could be utilized elsewhere at Apple if the group was disbanded. At Sculley's urging, the Newton team had quickly created a hardware mock-up with a display driven by a Mac. Through HyperCard stacks that simulated what the Newton eventually would be capable of doing, it was possible for outsiders to see the potential that the Newton team had intuitively understood all along. Tesler was blown away by Newton and begged Sculley to let him take Sakoman's place as the new project leader.

When Capps showed Sculley the prototype, he was as enthusiastic as Tesler. Just as Jobs saw the nascent Mac project as his ticket to prove something to the Lisa team that had kicked him out, Sculley saw in the Newton prototype a chance to prove his technical merit since it could be the steppingstone toward the Knowledge Navigator, which he had described in his 1987 autobiography, *Odyssey*. "Individuals could use it to drive through libraries, museums, databases, or institutional archives," wrote Sculley. A concept video created later demonstrated how the portable Knowledge Navigator could use voice recognition, wireless communications, and active assistants to effortlessly gather and organize information. The industry press derided the Knowledge Navigator as blue-sky dreaming since the enabling technologies didn't yet exist, but Sculley remained convinced of its merits, and the Newton prototype reaffirmed his belief.

Courtesy of Rick English

Sculley saw in the nascent Newton project the embodiment of many of the ideas he had proposed years before with his Knowledge Navigator concept.

Most importantly, Sculley realized Apple needed a new breakthrough product to make up for the Mac's declining margins and the increased competition Apple would face when Microsoft released Windows 3.0 in May 1990. Sculley envisioned a day when various digital media would converge and figured the Newton provided an opportunity to make money on hardware, software licenses, and related telecommunication services. With the board's approval, Sculley gave the Newton his full support, a price point, and a deadline. The product should be ready for sale at $1,500 on April 2, 1992. The Newton team now had just two years to go from prototype to product.

Larry Tesler took over the Newton project after Steve Sakoman left Apple. He favored developing the larger Newton Plus.

Sculley put Tesler in charge of the Newton team in May 1990. Now armed with a mandate, the engineers drew up plans for three different Newtons: a small hand-held device, a mid-sized unit, and a large tablet. Tesler and the old guard favored staying the course with the product plan called Newton Plus, which was similar to the Figaro design: a large (9 by 12 inch) tablet with pen-based handwriting recognition and a brand-new high-level programming language. The mid-sized (6 by 9 inch) Newton had few supporters, but many of the younger engineers, including Capps, thought the hand-held (4.5 by 7 inch) Pocket Newt, as it was called, was the way to go. The Pocket Newt's strongest advocate was Michael Tchao, the product marketing manager who had just been assigned to the Newton group. He had helped launch the ill-fated Mac Portable the previous September and was anxious to avoid repeating the mistakes that culminated in that "no compromise" behemoth. Tchao desperately tried convincing Tesler that the group should focus its efforts on the much smaller, less-expensive device that would appeal to the mass market of computer-phobic consumers. Tesler, the consummate engineer, strongly opposed the Pocket Newt idea, reasoning that it was foolish to start from scratch with an underpowered hand-held device when the Newton Plus was backed by four years of work and Figaro concepts had already been created. Sure, the Newton Plus would cost $5,000, but only after proving the concept could Apple follow up with a scaled-down model, reasoned Tesler. Tchao, Capps, and Michael Culbert continued fiddling with Pocket Newt as an underground project while the rest of the team focused on Newton Plus.

While work on the Newton hardware and software progressed in Cupertino, a small ATG team in Cambridge, Massachusetts—in cooperation with researchers from Harlequin Group Plc, Carnegie Mellon University, and elsewhere—was toiling in secrecy on a revolutionary programming language for Newton. The language would combine the efficiency of C++ with the simplicity of Smalltalk.

According to Sculley, it had "a very small kernel, efficient garbage collection, and [was] ideally suited for communications services and products such as [personal digital assistants], set-top boxes, digital telephones, even next-generation PCs. It was intended to be a completely open and licensable object-oriented OS," much like Sun Microsystem's Java (then code-named Oak). Since the project was considered so top secret that the division wasn't even listed in the company directory, the language was code-named Ralph, after Ralph Ellison, author of *Invisible Man*. Led by Isaac R. "Ike" Nassi, director of Eastern U.S. Research for Apple Products, Ralph was eventually renamed Dylan, for dynamic language, a decision that would result in a lawsuit from singer Bob Dylan (see "Trademark Tiffs," page 207).

> "[Sculley] did me a great favor: He hired me, promoted me, and let me go with enough money to start my own company."
> ***Jean-Louis Gassée***, *who got a severance package worth $1.7 million*

General Magic

The coming months were not easy ones for the Newton group. In July 1990, Apple announced that it was spinning off Porat's Paradigm and Pocket Crystal projects as General Magic (www.genmagic.com), lead by Mac superstars Atkinson and Hertzfeld, who both tried unsuccessfully to recruit Capps. The Newton team couldn't understand why Apple was suddenly supporting what it viewed as a competitor. Things looked even bleaker when their supporter, Gassée, made good on his promise to resign on September 30.

Engineering was also in for a major shake-up. The Newton team had been designing its product around a little-known chip from AT&T that was optimized for running code written in C, not Apple's new Ralph language. Apple had already helped finance the design of the chip to the tune of $1 million when AT&T asked for another $1 million to help finish the chip's development. After conducting an assessment of low-cost RISC (reduced instruction set computing) processors, Tesler concluded that AT&T's chip carried inherent price/performance disadvantages. As a result, on September 8, Tesler dumped the AT&T chip for the ARM 610 from Advanced Reduced Instruction Set Chip Machines (also known as ARM Ltd.) of Cambridge, England. A few months later, Apple acquired 43 percent of ARM and placed Tesler on its

Newton engineer Mike Culbert, a J.R.R. Tolkien fan in his youth, gave the AT&T chip its code name: Hobbit. Remarkably, AT&T decided to use Hobbit as the shipping name for the chip even after the Newton group dumped it in favor of the ARM 610.

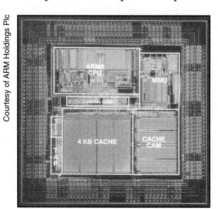

Courtesy of ARM Holdings Plc

Tesler's decision to switch to the RISC-based ARM 610 created a lot of extra work.

board of directors as Apple's representative. The chip switch meant that most of the code completed to date had to be rewritten to work on the RISC-based ARM 610 processor.

Increasingly distressed at the direction the Newton project was taking under Tesler, Tchao decided to risk his job by going over his boss' head. On February 10, 1991, aboard Mike Markkula's private Falcon 900 jet headed to Tokyo's Macworld Expo, Tchao made an impassioned pitch to Sculley. He protested that the ambitious Newton Plus was too large, too expensive, and too complicated to be completed on time. Instead, he advocated focusing on Pocket Newt, which was smaller, cheaper, and more feasible. The ballsy gambit worked. Sculley gave Tchao's plan his blessing and directed Tesler to concentrate on Pocket Newt, which came to be known as Junior. The Newton Plus (renamed Senior) project continued in diminished form with the understanding that it would resume in earnest after Junior was released.

Sculley's original deadline was little more than a year away, and much work remained. Apple was attempting to create an entirely new class of consumer products using an untested RISC chip, groundbreaking handwriting recognition software, and a completely new programming language. On top of all these obstacles, the Newton represented a new business model for Apple. Traditionally Apple had been a maverick, going it alone with proprietary software and hardware. The mounting success of Microsoft's broadly licensed Windows had painfully demonstrated the inadequacies of Apple's approach. Apple had to learn how to negotiate licensing agreements if it was going to turn Newton into a new profit center. In September, Apple began formal negotiations with Sharp.

On January 7, 1992, during his keynote speech at the Winter Consumer Electronics Show (CES) in Las Vegas, Sculley rhapsodized about the "digital convergence" of the computer, communication, and content industries and the need for a new type of device, which he dubbed the personal digital assistant. Based upon research performed by Harvard University and Doug Solomon at Apple, he projected that this would comprise a $3 trillion market by the beginning of the 21st century. Although Sculley would later insist he meant he was talking about the size of the entire digital convergence market, many in the audience that day interpreted his remarks as meaning that PDAs would be generating $3 trillion in sales within ten years. Apple's wildly successful October introduction of the PowerBook line lent Sculley's prediction considerable credibility and made Apple's competitors nervous. If Sculley was right, the market would be huge, and nobody wanted to be left out.

On March 17, 1998, shortly after Apple ceased Newton development, ARM Holdings Plc (www.arm.com) announced plans for an initial public offering in which Apple would sell part of its 37.4 percent of the outstanding stock. Apple made $23.4 million in pretax profit when it sold 18.9 percent of its stake during the April 16 IPO.

By the end of 1991, a team of Apple engineers spearheaded by Paul Mercer had developed a working $400 hand-held device, code-named Swatch, based upon the Mac OS. Tesler was furious, but Sculley was intrigued. Mercer's mistake was lining up Sony as the manufacturer at a time when Apple was negotiating with Sony's competitor Sharp to produce the Newton. As a result, Swatch was shelved.

The Evolution of the Newton

Here are the specifications for all of the Newton devices shipped by Apple.

NAME	MessagePad	MessagePad 100	MessagePad 110	MessagePad 120
Code name	Junior	Wedge	Lindy	Gelato
Date	8/2/93	3/4/94	3/4/94	1/30/95
Price	$699	$499	$599	$599
INTERNAL				
CPU	ARM 610	ARM 610	ARM 610	ARM 610
Speed	20MHz	20MHz	20MHz	20MHz
ROM	4MB	4MB	4MB	4MB
RAM	640K	640K	1MB	1MB (max 2MB)
VIDEO				
Pixels	240 x 336	240 x 336	240 x 320	240 x 320
Backlighting	no	no	no	no
Gray-scale	b&w	b&w	b&w	b&w
Rotation	no	no	no	no
INPUT/OUTPUT				
Serial	one	one	one	one
InterConnect	no	no	no	no
Infrared	9600 baud	38.4kbps	38.4kbps	38.4kbps
PCMCIA slots	one Type II	one Type II	one Type II	one Type II
Keyboard	no	no	no	no
Microphone	no	no	no	no
PHYSICAL				
Lid	no	no	yes	yes
Length (inches)	7.25	7.25	8.00	8.00
Width (inches)	4.50	4.50	4.00	4.00
Height (inches)	0.75	0.75	1.20	1.20
Weight (pounds)	0.90	0.90	1.28	1.28
BATTERIES				
Type	4 AAA	4 AAA	4 AA	4 AA
Life	14 hours	14 hours	28 hours	28 hours
SOFTWARE				
Newton OS	1.0	1.2	1.3	1.3
Word list	na	13,000	13,000	13,000
Additional words	na	1,000	1,000	1,000
Deferred recognition	no	yes	yes	yes

NAME	MessagePad 130	MessagePad 2000	eMate 300	MessagePad 2100
Code name	na	Q	Project K, Shay	na
Date	3/14/96	3/24/97	2/17/97	10/20/97
Price	$799	$949	$800	$1,000
INTERNAL				
CPU	ARM 610	StrongARM SA-110	ARM 710a	StrongARM SA-110
Speed	20MHz	162MHz	25MHz	162MHz
ROM	8MB	8MB	8MB	8MB
RAM	2.5MB	5MB	3MB (max 5MB)	8MB
VIDEO				
Pixels	240 x 320	320 x 480	320 x 480	320 x 480
Backlighting	yes	yes	yes	yes
Gray-scale	b&w	16 grays	16 grays	16 grays
Rotation	yes	yes	yes	yes
INPUT/OUTPUT				
Serial	one	no	one	no
InterConnect	no	one	one	one
Infrared	38.4kbps	115kbps (IrDA)	115kbps (IrDA)	115kbps (IrDA)
PCMCIA slots	one Type II	two Type II	one Type III	two Type II
Keyboard	no	optional ($100)	built-in	optional ($100)
Microphone	no	yes	yes	yes
PHYSICAL				
Lid	yes	yes	yes	yes
Length (inches)	8.00	8.30	12.00	8.30
Width (inches)	4.00	4.70	11.40	4.70
Height (inches)	1.20	1.10	2.10	1.10
Weight (pounds)	1.28	1.40	4.00	1.40
BATTERIES				
Type	4 AA	4 AA	NiMH	4 AA
Life	28 hours	24 hours	28 hours	24 hours
SOFTWARE				
Newton OS	2.0	2.1	2.1	2.1
Word list	93,000	93,000	93,000	93,000
Additional words	1,000	1,000	1,000	1,000
Deferred recognition	yes	yes	yes	yes

Sculley's public predictions regarding the potential of the PDA market forced the Newton engineers to rush to market.

Sculley didn't reveal the Newton at the Winter CES, but planned to do so just four months later at the Summer CES in Chicago, the traditional venue for demonstrating products for the coming Christmas season. The only problem was that Newton wasn't close to being a finished product. Therefore the Newton project suddenly kicked into high gear. Marketing needed to create point-of-purchase displays, packaging, sales sheets ... the works. They didn't even have a name yet. Among the product names proposed for the Newton by outside consultants were BrainAmplifier, KnowPad, PowerEnabler, and ZippyPad. As marketing wrestled with these issues, the Industrial Design Group (IDG) worked feverishly to finalize the form factor and physical features of the hand-held device. Sculley insisted it be small enough to fit into his jacket pocket. When it looked as if there was no way they could shave another millimeter off the case, "we considered sneaking into Sculley's office and resewing his jacket pockets to make them a tiny bit larger," admitted IDG's Bob Brunner. Instead they barely succeeded in passing Sculley's "pocket test" by flattening some curves and reducing the wall thickness.

The excitement generated by the CES keynote helped Apple nail down the deal with Sharp, and in March the two companies announced a joint licensing and development agreement for the Newton. As the Newton's first licensee, Sharp would engineer and manufacturer the device for Apple and create a slightly modified version that Sharp would market as the Sharp ExpertPad. By April, the Newton team was finally able to get the software to run on a prototype of the hardware, but crashes were common. It was clear the original ship date was a pipe dream at this point. Sculley pushed the team to relentlessly squash the thousands of remaining bugs so that the Newton would at least be stable enough to demonstrate at the upcoming Summer CES. Capps and his crew spent many long days and sleepless nights trying to get Newton ready for its unveiling.

At 10 o'clock on the morning of May 29, the Park West nightclub in Chicago was packed with more than 600 journalists and computer industry insiders anxious for the first glimpse of the Newton. There was tremendous excitement in the room as Sculley took the stage and gushed that Newton "is not just about a product or even a technology. It is about nothing less than a revolution." Coming from the company that revolutionized the industry with the Macintosh, the skeptical press was prepared to believe that this wasn't an idle boast. The Newton was Apple's first major new product line since the Mac debuted eight years prior, and everyone was wondering if Apple could work its particular brand of magic again.

When Tchao took the stage to proudly demonstrate a hand-held Newton, it refused to turn on. Momentarily stunned by his baby's refusal to cooperate, Tchao deftly launched into a speech that explained how Newton allowed users to "capture, organize, and communicate." Not willing to risk another public failure, Capps followed with a demonstration using a Newton prototype on a card inside a Mac. The crowd seemed impressed, and when Tchao returned to the stage with a working prototype sporting fresh batteries, they were willing to forgive the earlier slip. The Newton looked hot and soon the buzz was that Apple had another potential winner on its hands. As it turns out, the favorable press was the worst thing that could have happened to Newton. It raised the public's expectations and competitors' eyebrows.

Apple had successfully demonstrated the Newton prototype, but there was still much work to be done before it could ship. Frightened competitors scrambled to begin developing PDAs of their own, lest they be left out of a lucrative new market. AT&T gave its Hobbit chip to GO for use in its slate-sized computer, and Casio announced plans to improve its popular B.O.S.S. pocket organizer with Tandy under the name Zoomer. Microsoft, never missing a chance to hedge its bets, announced its own WinPad device (this never shipped). Even General Magic, Apple's own spin-off, was providing its Magic Cap operating system for use on Motorola's wireless Envoy and Sony's MagicLink. The race to get a finished product to market was on.

> "In retrospect, Sculley's decision to preannounce Newton was a mistake, because it raised expectations higher than necessary and forced us to commit to a design several months before the product actually shipped."
> Apple industrial designer **Tim Parsey**

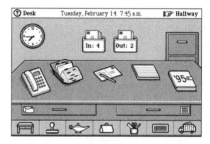

General Magic's operating system used a metaphor of familiar environments, like hallways, street scenes, and desks.

Courtesy of Lernout & Hauspie

As head of Apple's new Personal Interactive Electronics division, Gaston Bastiaens had grand plans and spent lavishly on Newton development.

The summer of 1992 brought yet another reorganization at Apple. The Newton group became part of the newly formed Personal Interactive Electronics (PIE) division led by VP and general manager, Gaston Bastiaens. The Belgian-born Bastiaens had come to Apple on July 15 from Philips Electronics in Eindhoven, Netherlands, where he had been director of the Consumer Electronics Division and general manager of the Interactive Media Systems Group, helping launch the Philips CD-Interactive player.

A year before the Newton was introduced, Apple knew its much-touted handwriting recognition software was troublesome.

By the fall, it was painfully obvious that major problems remained in Calligrapher, Newton's handwriting recognition software developed by Stephan Pachikov of ParaGraph (www.paragraph.com) in Moscow. His royalty agreement required 95 percent accuracy, but the code was nowhere near that good. As a result, Apple began backpedaling, subtly shifting the product's focus to communications instead of data capture. At the same time, development stopped cold on the Senior project. Since Junior didn't have the processing power or memory required by a sophisticated programming language such as Dylan, a replacement was needed. Yet again much of the software would have to be scrapped and rewritten, this time for the new C language used in Junior. The demanding workload was never greater and finally became too much to bear for one Newton team member.

Programmer Ko Isono worked on the software that controlled the display of text and graphics on the Newton. In May, upon returning from a trip to his native Japan, he announced to surprised co-workers that he had married. Like the rest of the team, Isono worked incredibly hard, and his Japanese wife was often left to herself in a land she did not know. On December 12, marital and professional stress prompted Isono to shut himself in the bedroom of his Fremont home, take out a pistol, and shoot himself to death. News of Isono's tragic suicide shocked the Newton team and destroyed morale. To numb the pain, many buried themselves even more deeply in their work.

By the time the Winter CES opened in Las Vegas on January 8, 1993, Bastiaens was able to demonstrate an alpha version of Newton. Although it made no public announcements regarding a new ship date, internally Apple was pushing to get Newton out the door on July 29. Weary of Apple's endless promises, the press became downright antagonistic at the CeBIT trade show held on March 25 in Hannover, Germany. It was there that a reporter badgered Bastiaens, asking, "Will it ever be available? Or is Apple just going to keep announcing that it will be available?" Bastiaens shot back, "I bet my wine cellar on this: The Newton will be available this summer [at a price] well below $1,000." He also shocked the Newton team by publicly announcing that Apple was freezing beta immediately, meaning if they weren't already in the code, no new features were going to make it into the product. From here on out, it was a sprint to the finish line, squashing bugs with every step.

As the Newton team tried to tie up its loose ends, things began unraveling elsewhere. Feeling that his role in the Newton group had diminished, Tesler returned to ATG as chief scientist on April 9. Then the shocking news came on June 3 that Casio and Tandy had beat the

Newton to market with their Zoomer PDA. Apple responded by pushing the Newton's launch date from July 29 to August 2. The board of directors was fed up. Despite Sculley's claims to have spent less than 2 percent of his time on the Newton, the board felt they could no longer afford to indulge him as Apple was preparing to announce its largest quarterly loss ever, $188.3 million for the third quarter of 1993. On June 18, the board forced Sculley to step down as CEO and replaced him with Spindler (then president, COO, and board member). To put the best face on things, Sculley was allowed to remain as chairman. The only good news to come out of Cupertino that summer was Sculley's June 23 announcement at Digital World '93 that "In the last week, our first Newton PDA entered its final testing phase before manufacturing. This product is on track, on schedule, and on its way to revolutionizing the way people capture, organize, and communicate information." On June 27, Apple managed to ship the Newton "golden master" software to Sharp allowing manufacturing to begin, a full year behind its original schedule.

Courtesy of ARM Holdings Plc

The original Newton MessagePad was a stylish black tablet that offered much more than just handwriting recognition.

In comparison to the Mac's 1984 introduction, the Newton's debut during Macworld Expo on August 2, 1993, was fairly low key. After six and one-half years of development, Sculley and Bastiaens seemed more exhausted than excited when they took the stage at the Boston Symphony Hall and announced that the first Newton was finally shipping. Dubbed the MessagePad, the solid black plastic device measured 4.5 inches wide by 7.25 inches long and weighed under a pound. The pressure-sensitive monochrome LCD had a resolution of 240 by 336 pixels. Inside was a 20MHz ARM 610 processor supported by a 4MB ROM and 640K of RAM. A LocalTalk port allowed for connecting other serial devices, and the single PCMCIA Type II card slot could accept additional memory, an optional Wireless Messaging Card, or a modem. There was also an infrared transceiver that "beamed" data to other Newtons at 9600 baud over a distance of one meter. All this could be powered by four 6-volt AAA alkaline batteries for up to 14 hours.

9:40 Tue 3/5 ◆ **Business**

☑ **Thu 2/15** ▭ ✉

☐ ○ **Budget**

☐ ○ **Kay email**

☐ ○ **motherboard**

 replacement

☐ ○ **equipment lease**

☐ ○ **license proposal**

☑ ○ **letter about order**

☑ ○ **Southern prop**

Names Dates Extras Undo Find Assist

The Newton came with a handful of built-in features for managing common daily tasks.

Newton Awards

"Products of the Year," *Fortune*
"Most Promising Portable," *PC LapTop Computers*
"Technical Excellence: Design," *PC Magazine*
"Award of Excellence," *Byte*
"Product of the Week," *PC Week*

Apple tried stressing the MessagePad's communications and organizational features. With optional cards, the MessagePad could receive pages and exchange faxes as well as email, plus it came with the ability to organize names, dates, phone numbers, and so on in a fileless "data soup." But the one feature that overshadowed all others was handwriting recognition. Apple said that you could write "Lunch with Bob tomorrow" on the screen with the provided stylus and the MessagePad would interpret your scrawl into uniform text. Then the intelligence would kick in, scheduling a meeting on the calendar tomorrow at noon, with the contact listed as the last-accessed person named Bob. When it worked, it was wonderfully impressive. Unfortunately, handwriting recognition remained less than perfect, often resulting in peculiar interpretations of the words on screen. Apple promised that accuracy would improve over time as Newton learned its user's handwriting idiosyncrasies, but that did little to curtail the firestorm of public ridicule, which reached its height with Garry B. Trudeau mocking the Newton in a series of *Doonesbury* cartoons that ran the week of August 23.

Despite its handwriting problems, the Newton MessagePad picked up a number of prestigious industry awards. Apple sold 50,000 Newtons in its first ten weeks on the market. Not bad when you consider it took 73 days for Apple to sell that many Macs, but it was a far cry from the blockbuster success Apple needed to decrease its reliance on the Mac. After the spurt of sales to early adopters and loyal Apple advocates, sales slowed significantly (to 7,500 units per month), just as they had for the Mac, and for many of the same reasons. Pundits applauded the Newton's unique and innovative features but attacked its unreliable handwriting recognition and high price of $699.

Despite never actually having used a MessagePad, cartoonist Garry B. Trudeau skewered a Newton lookalike in a series of *Doonesbury* strips that ran within a month of its release. A long-time Mac fan, Trudeau never intended the strip to be a review of the Newton, but rather saw it as a satire of "guys and their toys."

Also, compelling third-party programs were lacking, in large part because Apple hadn't seeded developers with the Newton Toolkit until the previous May at the Worldwide Developers Conference. In addition, although Apple promoted the Newton as a communications device, the modem and pager cards weren't available immediately, and the NewtonMail service didn't become fully operational until January 1994.

Newton's lukewarm reception sealed the fates of both Sculley and Bastiaens at Apple. Since handing over operational control to Spindler on June 18, Sculley focused on getting Newton out the door. Now he had little to do as chairman except plan his own exit, which he formally announced on October 15. Three days later, he revealed he was joining Spectrum Information Technologies, a tiny cellular phone company based in Manhasset, New York. Apple had just posted a 97 percent drop in earnings for its fourth quarter, so few were sorry to see Sculley go. Nor were many tears shed when Bastiaens quit in April 1994.

As was the case with the Mac, Apple was slow to address Newton's shortcomings primarily because the team was burned out from working so hard for so long. The first improvement came on March 4, 1994, with the introduction of the MessagePad 100 and 110. The MessagePad 100 was essentially the original Newton updated with the same ROM used in the 110. It was created by taking the existing MessagePads in inventory, disassembling them by hand, then unsoldering and updating the ROM. To distinguish these enhanced units from the originals, they were silk-screened with the model name MessagePad 100. The MessagePad 110 (code-named Lindy, the brand name of a pen) was a new unit altogether. It was manufactured in Taiwan by Inventec, not Sharp, and featured a revised industrial design consisting of a removable lid that protected the screen, the size of which had shrunk to 240 by 320 pixels. Battery life almost doubled with the switch to AA cells, and Apple now offered an optional Charging Station (code-named Crib). The new lid and batteries made the MessagePad 110 a little bit heavier, but nobody complained because, in addition to the extra weight, the unit featured 1MB of RAM, essentially tripling the memory available to the user.

Apple released the next member of the Newton family—the MessagePad 120 (code-named Gelato because it was available in two flavors: 1MB and 2MB)—in Germany in October 1994, but U.S. customers had to wait until January 30, 1995. By then Newton users could choose from over 100 commercial applications from third-party developers and StarCore, Apple's Newton software publishing and distribution arm. In addition to several applications, the MessagePad

> ## "Newton has set the whole category of PDAs back by two years."
> *Microsoft CEO* **Bill Gates**

Gaston Bastiaens left Apple in March 1994, started his own firm, worked briefly at Quarterdeck, and in October 1996, he became CEO and president of Lernout & Hauspie Speech Products (www.lhs.com) in Burlington, Massachusetts.

The evolutionary MessagePad 120 came bundled with Palm Computing's Graffiti.

120 came bundled with Graffiti, Palm Computing's popular data-entry software that was more accurate than Newton's original handwriting recognition. The 1.3 update to the Newton's OS improved its ability to erase PCMCIA flash cards and remember user preferences. Also, notification windows could remain open when the MessagePad went to sleep, and the phone dialing routines could handle asterisk and pound sign characters. "Overall, the MessagePad 120 represents the continued commitment to and evolution of Apple's Newton-based hardware products and is a response to customer feedback," said Shane Robison, VP and general manager of PIE.

The clouds of criticism that hung over the Newton project since its introduction didn't part until Apple unveiled the Newton 2.0 operating system (code-named Dante because it took its creators to the seventh level of hell, as in Dante Alighieri's *Inferno*) in November 1995 at the Fall COMDEX, where it received *Byte*'s coveted "Best of COMDEX" award. Initially available in December as a $109 upgrade for the MessagePad 120 (support for other models followed in the first half of 1996), Newton 2.0 was the first truly substantial improvement to the beleaguered PDA. The new operating system provided better organizational and communications capabilities, as well as the ability to synchronize data with Windows and Mac OS applications. A screen rotation feature enabled users to change the view from portrait to landscape mode. By far the most welcome new feature was the revised handwriting recognizer for printed words (initially developed by ATG for use on the Mac under the code names Rosetta and Mondello) and an improved cursive recognizer from ParaGraph, both of which were highly accurate. "Newton 2.0 marks what could become the turning point for the platform," said Kimball Brown, VP of mobile computing at Dataquest. "The new capabilities in Newton 2.0 are vastly improved over the previous version, providing new ways for developers to add functionality for customers."

Just as things started to look up for the Newton at the end of 1995, the situation at Apple was deteriorating rapidly, with rumors of a corporate takeover running rampant throughout Silicon Valley. After an embarrassing and demoralizing appearance at the company's shareholder meeting, Spindler was replaced as chairman and CEO by Gilbert F. Amelio on February 5, 1996. Amelio had a reputation as a no-nonsense turnaround artist and many expected that one of his first moves would be to ax the money-losing Newton group so that the firm could focus on saving the Macintosh market. Ken Dulaney, an analyst at The Gartner Group Inc., estimated that by early 1996, Apple had spent almost half a billion dollars developing and

To show there were no hard feelings over the *Doonesbury* series many took as a pan of the original Newton, Steve Capps' wife, Marie D'Amico, an Apple lawyer, wrote to Garry Trudeau and convinced him to draw a special panel for use as an Easter egg in Newton 2.0 on the MessagePad 120. To invoke it, write *egg freckles* then tap Assist.

Prior to being replaced by Amelio, Spindler had instructed Sandy Benett, acting VP of the Newton Systems Group, to line up an outside investor or buyer for the division.

promoting Newton with little possibility of turning a profit. So it came as a surprise on February 16, when Amelio publicly announced, "We will almost certainly keep Newton." Just months earlier Spindler had instructed Sandy Benett, acting VP of the Newton Systems Group, to seek outside investors. Now Amelio considered Newton "one of Apple's crown jewels," and was determined to make it sparkle.

Less than a month later, on March 14, in Hannover, Germany, Apple announced the MessagePad 130 at CeBIT, the largest computer trade show in the world. The $799 device was the first Newton to offer backlighting for on-demand use and a new durable, non-glare screen for viewing and entering information in any lighting condition. It also came with 512K more system memory for better performance with new Internet solutions and improved multitasking. "As pioneers in the PDA market, we're listening closely to the market to ensure that we deliver products that meet our customers' needs," said Benett. "The MessagePad 130 is the result of this feedback and proof that Apple continues to forge ahead in the evolution of its own Newton-based products."

Apple had long ago abandoned the dream of selling millions of Newtons to the unwashed masses as a general-purpose consumer electronics "organizer plus" and was now targeting mobile professionals and specialized vertical markets. Analysts accused Apple of repeating the mistakes it made with the Mac: It had fallen in love with its own technology and decided to keep prices high as it sold to the niche market of well-heeled professionals. Apple justified its approach by explaining that the Newton was a fully functional computer with the power to replace a laptop. In contrast, Palm Computing was about to enter the market with its Pilot 1000 ($299) and Pilot 5000 ($369), two low-cost devices designed from the ground up to work with desktop computers, not replace them.

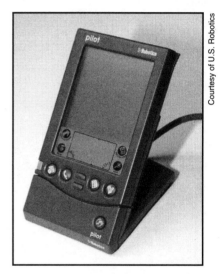

Courtesy of U.S. Robotics

Founded in 1992 by Jeff Hawkins and bought by modem-maker U.S. Robotics in September 1995, Palm Computing (www.palm.com) entered the PDA market with the Pilot 1000 and Pilot 5000 in April 1996. Instead of attempting to match the Newton feature for feature, Palm created a smaller, less-expensive "connected organizer" that acted as an accessory to a desktop computer using one-button HotSync technology, an approach that resonated strongly with consumers. In March 1997, the PalmPilot Personal and Professional editions shipped, followed by the Palm III ($399) in April 1998. By the first half of 1998, Palm had captured 41.4 percent of the PDA market, according to International Data Corp.(www.idc.com).

The MessagePad 2000 was notably faster than its predecessors thanks to its 160MHz StrongARM processor.

The backlit MessagePad 130 was a welcome addition to the Newton family, but it wasn't until October 28 that Apple unveiled hardware as compelling as the Newton 2.0 operating system. On that day, Apple unveiled the MessagePad 2000 (code-named Q), which it called "the first in a new generation of hand-held, mobile Internet computers." Built for life on the road, the 1.4-pound device was a complete mobile computer for the business professional, with a full range of personal productivity and desktop connectivity applications. When it shipped on March 24, 1997, the $949 MessagePad 2000 came bundled with Dates (calendar), Notepad (to-do list), Names (contact manager), faxing, EnRoute i-NET (email client), Newton Connection Utilities, NetHopper (web browser), NewtonWorks (word processor), QuickFigure Pro (spreadsheet, $50 extra), and even built-in audio recording capability to take voice notes or record a meeting—up to an hour on one 4MB PC memory card. The new model borrowed the backlit, rotating screen of the MessagePad 130 and added 16 levels of gray for improved graphics. The biggest news wasn't what you saw, but what you felt immediately when using the MessagePad 2000: It was amazingly fast, thanks to the 160MHz StrongARM processor. "The StrongARM processor makes a real difference," said Benett, VP of the Newton Systems Group. "Applications of all kinds run noticeably faster and more efficiently than with a conventional device. Handwriting is translated almost instantaneously into digitized text, and you can switch between applications and share data quickly and seamlessly."

Introduced alongside the MessagePad 2000 was the $800 eMate 300 (code-named Project K, Schoolbook, and Shay), a Newton distinguished by its translucent green, ABS-plastic enclosure in the shape of a clamshell with a handle, protecting a built-in keyboard. Apple was afraid that demand for the eMate 300 would outstrip supply, so it decided to restrict sales to the education market initially. As these new devices garnered positive press, Newton sales picked up and it appeared Apple had finally delivered products worthy of the initial PDA promise. "The MessagePad 2000 is a hot ticket item," said Steve Elms, president of Newton Source, a chain of specialty stores with outlets in Los Angeles, New York, and San Francisco. "We can't keep them on our shelves." Declining to release exact figures, Benett revealed that Newton sales were about three times what they had been the previous quarter, well above projections. Apple may have been blowing out its own internal numbers, but the marketplace was demonstrating a decisive preference for less-expensive, less-capable devices. Palm had just introduced the PalmPilot Personal ($299) and Professional ($399) and was on its way to selling one million units within 18 months.

Although it looked like a futuristic PowerBook, the eMate 300 was essentially a Newton with a built-in keyboard.

On the product front, Apple was finally hitting on all cylinders with Newton, but behind the scenes, management had been trying to sell the division to raise cash and focus on the Macintosh. According to Amelio, "keeping the Newton alive had been costing Apple some $15 million a quarter … but now, with the MessagePad 2000, Newton was breaking even and poised to be a money-earner for the company." At the Seybold conference held in New York that April, chief technology officer Ellen M. Hancock admitted that Apple was looking for an investment partner for the Newton Systems Group. It was rumored that Apple had approached Acorn Computer Group, Ericsson, Oracle, Samsung, Sony, Sun Microsystems, and UMAX. Amelio was secretly willing to accept as little as $50 million, but each potential buyer decided to pass for one reason or another.

"Do I think the Newton is offering distinctly superior user value? No."
*Apple COO **Marco Landi***

Having failed to find a buyer, on May 22 Apple announced it was spinning off Newton as a wholly owned subsidiary called Newton Inc. to support, sell, and market the MessagePad 2000. The spin-off also assumed ownership of the eMate 300, although Apple reserved for itself the exclusive license. "Over the past year, we have seen the Newton Systems Group launch compelling products based on the Newton operating system," said Amelio. "We believe that the time is right to establish the group as a focused entity. This decision allows the new subsidiary to pursue its business and create the marketing and operating strategies it needs to succeed." Approximately 130 Apple employees were transferred to the new enterprise led by COO Benett (the CEO position was vacant and would remain so).

Apple CFO Fred Anderson said Cupertino would fund Newton Inc.'s initial operations but hoped to eventually find outside investors or take the company public within two years. In a surprising announcement, he predicted Newton Inc. would be profitable within 12 months. "We expect significant growth and profit in Newton's first year," said Anderson. While Apple declined to provide market figures, analysts put the installed base for Newton OS 2.0-based units at roughly 150,000. The company reportedly had sold more than 10,000 MessagePad 2000s in the first six weeks after the product's introduction in March and expected to sell 50,000 to 75,000 units in 1997. "We don't have to be wildly more successful than today" to become profitable, Benett affirmed.

On August 6, Benett proudly announced "Newton Inc. is now completely autonomous from Apple. We have our own board of directors, financial model, and business plan focused on the development of products and licensable technologies to meet the computing and communications needs of today's corporate mobile

Almost immediately after Newton Inc. was spun out of Apple, complete with a new logo, Jobs pulled it back inside.

users." Newton Inc. sported a new corporate logo and was in the process of relocating to old Apple offices in Santa Clara, California. It looked like Newton was finally going to get a chance to prove itself unencumbered by Cupertino politics. Then the unthinkable happened: Apple announced it was not spinning off Newton after all.

The plan to form Newton Inc. was hatched under Amelio, but following Amelio's July 9 resignation, Steve Jobs had been running the company, and apparently this was just one of many of Amelio's decisions with which he didn't agree. On September 4, Newton Inc. executives met with Jobs, who told them not to bother moving into their new digs. Five days later, Apple announced it would pull the Newton subsidiary back in and create a division for the eMate 300, calling it "a major strategic opportunity" and promising to expand its availability beyond the education channels to which it had been previously restricted. Although he seemed to focus on the eMate 300, Jobs publicly insisted, "We are not dumping the MessagePad."

The $1,000 MessagePad 2100 was the last Newton device Apple ever shipped.

As if to demonstrate that Jobs could be taken at his word, Apple launched the $1,000 MessagePad 2100 on October 20. The 2100 was the first Newton to support an Ethernet card, providing much faster connections with networks. Electronic mail and Internet browsing were easier thanks to AllPen Software's NetHopper 3.2 graphical web browser and Newton Internet Enabler 2.0, Apple's TCP/IP software that provided Internet and intranet connections plus AppleTalk and Ethernet support. The biggest improvement was the 4MB of RAM (up from 1MB in the MessagePad 2000) and a related increase in the system heap that allowed users to comfortably run multiple programs without being forced to reset. The MessagePad 2100 was ready to go when Apple pulled the Newton group back in, so instead of proving Apple's commitment to the MessagePad, its release simply showed that Apple was prudently attempting to recoup some of its development costs.

By the end of 1997, all Newton work had ceased at Apple, and many of the division's key employees had jumped to competitor 3Com's

Palm Computing subsidiary—maker of the popular PalmPilot—or been transferred to Apple's portable products division, rumored to be working on PDAs based upon a scaled-down version of the Mac OS, much in the fashion that Microsoft developed its Windows CE operating system specifically for hand-held computers. Responding to the rumor on December 29, an Apple spokesperson told CNET NEWS.COM, "We are satisfied with the success of the Newton group." The eMate is doing well and the "MessagePad is doing well too—units are on backorder." But numbers compiled by Dataquest told a different story. According to the San Jose-based research firm, Apple sold 63,000 MessagePads in 1996, down from 88,000 the year before. Indications were that Apple had managed to sell only 43,000 units in the first half of 1997, with sales tapering off drastically as rumors circulated that Apple was developing a Mac OS-based eMate.

On February 27, 1998, just weeks after reorganizing Claris into a stand-alone subsidiary called FileMaker Inc., Apple announced it would discontinue further development of the Newton OS and devices and that it did not anticipate extending the current licensing program. Although some speculated it was Jobs' way of getting back at Sculley for forcing him out of Apple in 1985, he explained, "This decision is consistent with our strategy to focus all of our software development resources on extending the Macintosh operating system. To realize our ambitious plans we must focus all of our efforts in one direction." Apple stressed its long-term commitment to affordable mobile computing and hoped its Newton customers and developers would make the transition to Mac OS-based products, which were promised for early 1999. Apple vowed to provide support for existing Newton users and said it would continue to market and sell its current inventory of MessagePad 2100 and eMate 300 devices, though initially it inexplicably refused to lower prices. It's not known if any large customers took advantage of Apple's offer to place purchase orders for 1,000 or more MessagePad 2100 or eMate units.

When Newton Inc. was spun off six months earlier, it had 130 employees, but by the time the ax fell in February, only 30 remained in the group. Apple finally admitted what many had speculated, that it had moved most employees to a hardware R&D group focusing on a new Mac OS-based low-end portable. Apple decided not to sell the Newton unit because it failed to find anyone willing to pay enough to offset the investment Apple had made in the technology, and it didn't want to lose key engineers. CFO Anderson said Apple wouldn't take a charge against earnings and in fact expected to save a "few million dollars" quarterly from shutting down the unit, which, he noted, "has not been historically profitable."

After three years of development, Microsoft announced its Windows CE 1.0 operating system for handheld PCs on November 17, 1996. According to Redmond, the suffix in Windows CE doesn't represent a single concept, but rather implies a number of design precepts, including "Compact, Connectable, Compatible, and Companion."

"Steve Jobs is running the company like a little dictator. He didn't like Newton because it was Sculley's idea, so he killed it."

Newton developer **Edward Martin**

"Focus is all about saying no. To get back on a growth track we have to be focused on that mission. Newton, although it is a great technology, did not fit that mission."

Apple CFO **Fred Anderson**

"Whether or not the product succeeded, we helped set up a category. We set that whole form factor. You have to be bold to make bold jumps. When you succeed, you're everybody's favorite hero, and when you fail, you're everybody's goat."

*Newton lead engineer **Steve Capps**, who moved on to Microsoft after leaving Apple in June 1996*

Almost 11 years after the Newton project was initiated, and after spending an estimated half-billion dollars on its development and marketing, Apple had managed to sell only 150,000 to 300,000 Newton devices during four and a half years on the market. The profitless product became a lightning rod for criticism, pushed one engineer to suicide, and proved the undoing of a high-profile CEO and numerous vice presidents. It will probably go down in history as yet another Apple failure in the tradition of the Lisa and Mac Portable, but it is important to remember that out of those disasters came the Macintosh and PowerBook successes. Even if Apple is unable to redeem itself with a successful product based upon its Newton experience, it deserves credit for pioneering the PDA market.

Newton Timeline

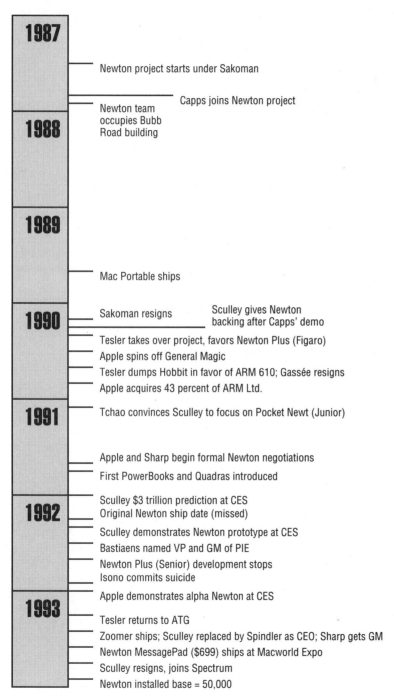

1987

Newton project starts under Sakoman

Capps joins Newton project

Newton team occupies Bubb Road building

1988

1989

Mac Portable ships

1990

Sakoman resigns

Sculley gives Newton backing after Capps' demo

Tesler takes over project, favors Newton Plus (Figaro)

Apple spins off General Magic

Tesler dumps Hobbit in favor of ARM 610; Gassée resigns

Apple acquires 43 percent of ARM Ltd.

1991

Tchao convinces Sculley to focus on Pocket Newt (Junior)

Apple and Sharp begin formal Newton negotiations

First PowerBooks and Quadras introduced

1992

Sculley $3 trillion prediction at CES

Original Newton ship date (missed)

Sculley demonstrates Newton prototype at CES

Bastiaens named VP and GM of PIE

Newton Plus (Senior) development stops

Isono commits suicide

Apple demonstrates alpha Newton at CES

1993

Tesler returns to ATG

Zoomer ships; Sculley replaced by Spindler as CEO; Sharp gets GM

Newton MessagePad ($699) ships at Macworld Expo

Sculley resigns, joins Spectrum

Newton installed base = 50,000

c a p p s
W a l t e r
A n d y
m a r t i n
J o h n
m i c h a e l
M i k e
L a r r y
E r n i e
s h i f t e h

To invoke an Easter egg displaying a list of the developers, write *About Newton* then tap Assist.

The MessagePad 130 was the first Newton to come with a backlit screen.

Newton Timeline (continued)

1994
- NewtonMail service becomes operational
- First Power Macs ship; Bastiaens leaves Apple
- Bob Dylan sues Apple over Dylan (née Ralph)

1995
- MessagePad 120 ($599) announced
- Apple offers rebates up to $100 to stimulate Newton sales

1996
- Newton 2.0 announced
- Newton 2.0 ($109) ships
- Spindler replaced by Amelio as CEO
- MessagePad 130 ($799) ships; USR ships PalmPilot 1000 ($299) and 5000 ($369)

1997
- eMate 300, MessagePad 2000, and Newton 2.1 announced
- Microsoft ships Windows CE 1.0
- Apple buys NeXT; Jobs returns
- eMate 300 ($700), MessagePad 2000 ($949) ship; 3Com ships PalmPilot ($299)
- Apple announces Newton spin-off — Newton Inc. officially spun off
- Apple pulls Newton Inc. back in; Microsoft ships Windows CE 2.0
- MessagePad 2100 ($1,000) ships

1998
- Apple discontinues Newton development; Newton installed base = 150,000 to 300,000; Windows CE Handheld PC installed base = 500,000

1999

2000

"The Newton in 1998 looks remarkably unchanged from the Newton in 1993, with the exception that the handwriting now works and the screen is readable. Why wasn't it miniaturized; cost reduced; why didn't [Apple] learn from the great success of the PalmPilot that simple tasks like data synchronization with your desktop PC are really useful; etc.?"

Former Apple CEO **John Sculley**

Jobs After Apple:
To NeXT and Beyond

After being stripped of all operational responsibilities on May 31, 1985, Jobs had little to do at Apple, so he began canvassing the country's colleges asking them to describe their ideal university computer. In early September, Jobs had lunch with Paul Berg, Nobel laureate and Stanford University biochemist. When Berg complained of the difficulty of performing "wet-lab" research on gene splicing, Jobs suggested simulating the experiments on a computer. Berg was supposedly so enthusiastic about the idea that Jobs realized he was onto something big. Within weeks Jobs decided to launch a startup with five other Apple employees: Susan Barnes (senior controller for U.S. sales and marketing), George Crow (engineering manager), Dan'l Lewin (higher education marketing manager), Rich Page (Apple Fellow), and Guy "Bud"- Tribble (manager of software engineering).

When Jobs announced his plans to Apple's board of directors, it initially expressed an interest in investing in the new venture, Next Inc. (later changed to NeXT Computer, Inc.), but the board went ballistic when Jobs revealed the names of the five employees who would be joining him. Jobs resigned as Apple chairman, and Apple sued him for dereliction of duties. Apple eventually dropped the suit in January 1986, when Jobs agreed to a six-month moratorium on hiring Apple employees. Curiously, Apple insisted on a non-compete clause that required any computers created by Jobs' new company to be more powerful than any of Apple's offerings.

Jobs was way off base when he originally predicted that NeXT would produce a machine by the spring of 1987. As it turned out, it wasn't until October 12, 1988, that Jobs unveiled the NeXT Computer to an eager crowd of 4,500 assembled at Louise M. Davies Symphony Hall in San Francisco. Even that was premature, because the final version of the NEXTSTEP operating system (originally called NeXTstep) didn't ship until September 18, 1989. Jobs, however, didn't see the NeXT Computer as late. He insisted it was "five years ahead of its time."

At the time he left Apple, Jobs owned roughly 6.5 million shares of stock, or about 11.3 percent of the company. Over the course of the year, Jobs began liquidating his massive holdings at what would prove to be fire-sale prices. According to Securities and Exchange Commission records, Jobs dumped 4.028 million shares in 1985 for $70.5 million. By February 1986, Jobs claimed to have sold all but one share, so that he would still receive Apple's annual reports. Assuming this is true and that he managed to sell at the highest price realized by February, the most he could have grossed was $135 million. As it turns out, Jobs couldn't have picked a worse time to sell his Apple stock.

To be sure, Jobs needed some seed money to buy Pixar and fund NeXT, but he could have made do with the proceeds from selling a small fraction of his Apple position (Pixar cost $10 million and Jobs' initial investment in NeXT was just $7 million). Jobs' assertion that he was selling because he had lost faith in Apple's executives was certainly valid. However, had he held on until the 2-for-1 split in April 1987, he would have owned 13 million shares, worth $952 million when the stock reached its all-time high of $73.25 on April 12, 1991. Including dividends, Jobs left over $836 million on the table when he cashed out of Apple.

"Develop for it? I'll piss on it."

Bill Gates, *Microsoft chairman, in response to* InfoWorld's *Peggy Watt asking if Microsoft would develop applications for the NeXT Computer*

The NeXT Computer won glowing reviews, but poor market acceptance.

For the first four months of its life, NeXT operated out of Jobs' Woodside mansion at 460 Mountain Home Road (the iron-gated entrance is actually on Robles Drive). The first formal offices were in the Stanford University Industrial Park in Palo Alto, not far from Xerox PARC. The company eventually moved to an office complex in Redwood City, where it remained until Apple purchased it in 1996.

The specifications certainly were impressive: 25MHz Motorola 68030 processor, 8MB of main memory expandable to 16MB, 250MB Canon optical disc drive, Motorola 68882 math coprocessor, and Motorola 56001 digital signal processor to drive real-time sound, array processing, modem, fax, and encryption functions. All this was housed in a cube 12 inches on each side, with a 17-inch Sony monochrome monitor, keyboard, and mouse. The NeXT Computer ran a Unix 4.3-based Mach operating system and featured a powerful object-oriented development environment. Also included on disc was the complete works of Shakespeare, a dictionary, a thesaurus, a book of quotations, the documentation, WriteNow, Mathematica, a relational database server, an artificial intelligence language, a C compiler, a personal information manager, and graphical electronic mail with integrated voice capabilities.

NeXT announced that it would sell the entire package direct to colleges and universities, which would in turn resell them to students and faculty for $6,500. At the time, Apple's top-of-the-line computer was the Mac IIx, with a 16MHz 68030 and a suggested retail price of $7,769 for a stripped-down model.

When describing the NeXT Computer, the press never failed to make a big deal about the unique black matte finish of the 12-inch cube, calling it a bold new look. Actually, Jobs had his hand in designing

The Money Trail

NeXT began life in 1985 with a $7 million stake from Jobs, but was operating at a ferocious burn rate that would leave it penniless by the end of 1986. Rather than dig into his own pockets again, Jobs distributed a prospectus throughout the venture capital community, which he had spurned when NeXT was founded. Now Jobs was only too willing to accept their investments. He sought $3 million for a 10 percent stake in NeXT, giving the productless, revenueless NeXT a ludicrous $30 million valuation. Not surprisingly, there were no takers.

As luck would have it, H. Ross Perot was watching television one night in November 1986 when he came across John Nathan's *The Entrepreneurs*, a documentary in which NeXT was featured. Perot was so fascinated by the young startup that he called Jobs the following day and casually remarked, "If you ever need an investor, call me." Not wanting to appear too eager, Jobs waited a week before inviting Perot to come take a look at his firm and meet its employees. Instead of focusing on the hard numbers, which would never stand up to due diligence, Jobs insisted Perot consider the intangibles. The approach appealed to Perot, who essentially opened his checkbook and asked Jobs how much he wanted.

Apparently Jobs was running a very special sale that day just for Texas billionaires. Jobs demanded $20 million for 16 percent of NeXT, giving the firm an unbelievable valuation of $125 million. In February 1987, Perot accepted without blinking and became the company's largest investor and a board member. "Do the math," said one venture capitalist, "and you have to assume that Perot is investing more out of emotion than prudence." Perot justified the price by responding, "I'm investing in quality."

Perot got a bargain compared to Canon. In June 1989, the Japanese conglomerate paid $100 million for a 16.67 percent share of NeXT, giving the company an implicit value of $600 million. By the time NeXT dropped its hardware in February 1993, Perot had trimmed his stake to 11 percent, leaving Canon with its 16.67 percent and Jobs as the majority shareholder with 46 percent of outstanding shares.

In 1994, NeXT reported its first yearly profit of $1.03 million on revenues of $49.6 million. By September 1995, Jobs claimed NeXT was consistently profitable. The following year, Goldman, Sachs & Company tried to take NeXT public, but the IPO never got off the ground. Just as well, since Apple would soon come knocking on the door with checkbook in hand (see "The Copland Crisis," page 225).

> "He told me that we're going to hit one out of the ball park."
>
> **Steve Jobs**, *after future presidential candidate Ross Perot invested in NeXT*

Nobody has ever accused Steve Jobs of frugality. When it came to choosing a logo for his new company, Jobs spared no expense. He met with four noted designers, but none was deemed worthy. Ultimately, Jobs decided he wanted 71-year-old Yale professor Paul Rand to design the NeXT logo. Widely considered the grand master of American graphic arts, Rand had previously designed logos for such business institutions as ABC, IBM, UPS, and Westinghouse. In fact, it was Rand who, in the 1960s, convinced International Business Machines to drop its full name and use only initials. Rand continued to consult for IBM, so initially he declined to work for Jobs, citing a conflict of interest. Amazingly enough, Jobs convinced IBM vice chairman Paul Rizzo to release Rand of his obligation.

Perhaps Rand had heard about how mercurial Jobs could be, because before accepting the commission, he insisted on being paid $100,000 in advance to create only one design, and he would be under no obligation to revise his work if it failed to please Jobs. Jobs accepted the terms and in June 1986, Rand produced a logo reminiscent of a child's wooden block tilted at a precise 28° angle, bearing the letters of the company, each in a different color, perhaps inspired by artist Robert Indiana's *Love* painting that was popularized by a 1973 postage stamp.

The bizarre capitalization of the company's name was Rand's idea, who explained that the lower-case *e* would stand out and could represent "education, excellence, expertise, exceptional, excitement, e = mc2."

another black computer years ago. In the summer of 1981, Apple produced a special version of the Apple II for the audio-visual equipment manufacturer, Bell & Howell. It was distinguished from the standard Apple II by extra audio and video connectors on the back panel and its all-black plastic housing. Also interesting is that the same industrial design firm—Hartmut Esslinger's frogdesign (www.frogdesign.com)—responsible for the big, black NeXT Computer was also responsible for the sleek "Snow White" Apple IIc introduced in 1984.

Like the Macintosh before it, the NeXT Computer took longer than expected to develop, was more expensive than originally hoped for, used a non-standard disk drive, and did not have a color display. Nonetheless, the initial press reaction was enormously favorable. Stewart Alsop, editor of *P.C. Letter*, predicted that NeXT would sell 25,000 machines in 18 months. Michael Murphy, editor of *California Technology Stock Letter*, went one better in predicting that NeXT would sell 50,000 machines in two years. Louise Kohl, executive editor at *MacUser*, predicted, "This machine will replace sex."

When all the hoopla of the introduction faded, it became apparent that higher education just didn't see things the same way as the fawning press. The NeXT Computer didn't deliver what the educators had asked for. It was too expensive to be a personal computer and too underpowered to be a workstation, leading NeXT's marketing staff to invent the term "personal workstation" so that it could claim to be a leader in a market segment that heretofore didn't exist.

As soon as it became apparent that NeXT wasn't going to be successful selling only to higher education, it struck a deal with Businessland, giving the nation's largest computer retailer the rights to sell 100,000 machines in three years. At the March 1989 announcement, Businessland's chairman, president, and CEO David Norman boldly predicted, "NeXT revenues will be as much over the next twelve months as Compaq was over the last twelve months. Compaq business was about $150 million."

Considering that Businessland would sell the computer for $9,995 with absolutely no discounting, Norman's boast worked out to roughly 10,000 machines, plus peripherals, in the coming year. While that may not seem like an unrealistic goal, consider that toward the end of 1988, NeXT was selling a pathetic 400 machines a month at the educator's price of $6,500. Oblivious to the clear signals the marketplace was sending, NeXT's head of manufacturing was ramping up the factory to produce 120,000 computers annually.

Humbled by the underwhelming response to the NeXT Computer, Jobs and company set about addressing some of the major complaints about its speed, price, lack of color, hard drives, and floppies. On September 18, 1990, NeXT introduced four new workstations based on the brand-new, 25MHz Motorola 68040 processor. The $4,995 NeXTstation, or "slab," was shaped like a pizza box and contained a 2.88MB, 3.5-inch floppy disk drive, a 105MB hard disk, 8MB of memory expandable to 32MB, and a monochrome monitor.

Courtesy of NeXT Computer, Inc.

The NeXTstation addressed many of the faults of its predecessor, but still failed to find a market.

"We knew we'd either be the last hardware company that made it or the first that didn't, and we were the first that didn't."

Steve Jobs, *on NeXT's aborted computer efforts*

The $7,995 NeXTstation Color came with a 16-inch MegaPixel Trinitron monitor capable of displaying 4,096 colors, a sound box, and memory expandable from 12MB to 32MB. The $7,995 NeXTcube, housed in a case similar to the original NeXT Computer, came standard with the same display, memory, and disk configuration as the NeXTstation, but since it was designed to be a network server, it offered more expansion possibilities in those areas. For an additional $3,995, users

> "We also need an alternative to Microsoft in the systems-software area. And the only hope we have for that, in my opinion, is NeXT."
>
> ***Steve Jobs***

> "I think Ross would be an excellent president. I think he's got a real chance and I'm helping him every way I can."
>
> ***Steve Jobs***, *commenting on Perot's failed 1992 bid for the U.S. presidency*

> "In my 20 years in this industry, I have never seen a revolution as profound as [object-oriented programming]. You can build software literally 5 to 10 times faster, and that software is much more reliable, much easier to maintain and much more powerful."
>
> ***Steve Jobs***

> "All software will be written using this object technology someday. No question about it."
>
> ***Steve Jobs***

could add the 32-bit NeXTdimension video board giving the NeXTcube 16.7 million colors in Display PostScript. In comparison, the best Apple had to offer at the time was the $8,969 Mac IIfx with a 40MHz 68030.

To outward appearances, NeXT was on a roll, but looks were deceiving. The '040-based machines didn't ship for months after their introduction due to a shortage of the new processors from Motorola. Furthermore, the NeXTdimension's compression chip was abandoned by its third-party developer, leaving an empty socket on the board and a bad taste in the mouths of true believers who had spent almost $12,000 for the high-end color system. In April 1991, one of the founders, Susan Barnes, called it quits. Then on May 14, NeXT was forced to terminate its March 1989 sales agreement with Businessland because the retailer closed its outlets. To make matters worse, the firm's highly respected outside investor, H. Ross Perot, resigned from the board of directors in June, complaining that "I shouldn't have let you guys have all that money. Biggest mistake I made."

At the first NeXTWORLD Expo held in San Francisco on January 22, 1992, Jobs announced cheaper, faster, "Turbo" versions of the NeXTstation, NeXTstation Color, and NeXTcube, all built around the 33MHz Motorola 68040 processor. More significantly, he announced NEXTSTEP 3.0 and NEXTSTEP 486, a $995 version that would run on Intel 80486 processors simultaneously with Unix, MS-DOS, and

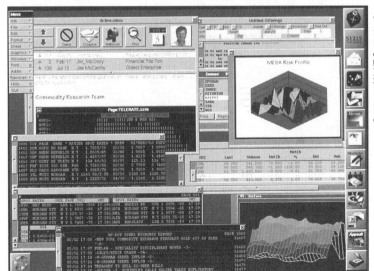

Courtesy of NeXT Computer, Inc.

By 1992, NeXT was pinning its hopes on its NEXTSTEP object-oriented operating system for Intel-based computers.

Windows. NEXTSTEP 3.0 was to ship in the second quarter of 1992, but didn't make it out the door until late September. NEXTSTEP 486 was originally promised for September, but didn't ship until May 1993. By then the name had changed to NEXTSTEP For Intel Processors, since it could run on both 486 and Pentium machines.

With $250 million down the tubes, Jobs realized he could never reproduce the magic necessary to create Silicon Valley's next Apple Computer, so he decided to shoot for becoming the next Microsoft. On February 10, 1993—"Black Tuesday"—NeXT laid off 280 of its 530 employees and announced it would sell the hardware side of its business to Canon so that it could focus on selling NEXTSTEP For Intel Processors as the premier object-oriented operating system for Intel-based computers.

Like an Erector set, object-oriented programming allows corporations to build large, complex custom applications using small, off-the-shelf objects, each designed to do specific tasks. While NEXTSTEP was widely considered to be a fabulous product, the market was not without competition. Microsoft's own object-oriented version of Windows NT (code-named Cairo) was released in 1994, and both IBM and Apple had high hopes for Pink, the operating system under development at their joint venture, Taligent. Pink never saw the light of day and dropped out of contention on December 19, 1995, when Taligent was absorbed into IBM as a wholly owned subsidiary. Windows NT, on the other hand, went on to great success in the enterprise market. The proprietary NEXTSTEP evolved into an open operating system called OPENSTEP, jointly developed with Sun Microsystems, but never found much acceptance outside of very small niche markets such as financial services. As a result, in the spring of 1996, NeXT began shifting its focus to an Internet development tool called WebObjects, which proved moderately successful.

Although his hardware failures had tarnished his image as Silicon Valley's golden boy, few people were willing to write off Jobs altogether, and many secretly wished he could pull off another miracle to match the Mac. Their wishes came true as 1996 drew to a close and Jobs orchestrated the redemption of NeXT with his triumphant return to Apple Computer (see "The Copland Crisis," page 225).

"You can have a good product with a lot of good philosophical thinking behind it—a lot of pureness—and still not sell. You gotta have some luck, too. The NeXT is a good machine that just didn't have the luck to make it successful."

Steve Wozniak

It took Apple only 73 days to sell 50,000 Macintosh computers. It took Jobs seven years to sell as many NeXT computers.

Alan Kay, then an Apple Fellow, first brought Pixar to Jobs' attention in 1984 when Lucas was trying to sell the division. In May 1985, Jobs tried to convince Apple's board of directors to purchase Pixar, but he found "no one else there was interested."

"We believe it's the biggest advance in animation since Walt Disney started it all with the release of *Snow White* 50 years ago."

Steve Jobs, *discussing* Toy Story

"The fact that [Jobs has] defied history, allowing lightning to strike twice—first with Apple and now at Pixar—really solidifies our view of him as a visionary."

Creative Strategies Consulting president **Tim Bajarin**

Pixar

On February 7, 1986, Steve Jobs paid $10 million for a majority interest in Pixar (www.pixar.com), the computer division of LucasFilm Ltd., the creator of *Star Wars* and other blockbuster movies. At the time of Jobs' purchase, Pixar had 43 employees, and while Jobs took the title of chairman, he did not draw a salary nor involve himself in the day-to-day affairs of the firm.

Pixar's main product in 1986 was a computer that processed 3D graphics at a speed of 40 million instructions per second. It was originally intended for sale to other computer makers for integration into their systems. At the time, president Edwin Catmull admitted the demand for the $120,000 machine among entertainment companies "is minuscule," yet Jobs believed, "image computing will explode during the next four years, just as supercomputing has become a commercial reality during the last several years."

Jobs asked Catmull to focus on developing technical products that could begin to generate revenue quickly. For many years, Pixar's main source of revenue was RenderMan, a program that allowed computer graphic artists to apply textures and colors to the surfaces of 3D objects. Running on Silicon Graphics workstations, RenderMan was used to create the dinosaurs for *Jurassic Park*. Pixar sold about 100,000 copies of RenderMan, but Jobs wanted Pixar to focus on developing content in the form of short films (*Tin Toy* won an Oscar in 1988) and television commercials (such as the animated Listerine spots).

In 1991, Pixar pitched Walt Disney Company on an hour-long computer-animated special. Disney shocked Pixar by asking for a full-length feature movie instead. On May 3, 1991, a deal was struck for three feature films, with Disney maintaining control over marketing and licensing, and Pixar creating the screenplays, for which it would receive a percentage of the box office gross revenues and video sales. Pixar wouldn't see a penny from merchandising, and that's where the real money comes from nowadays.

Jobs pumped at least $50 million into Pixar over the years. "If I knew in 1986 how much it was going to cost to keep Pixar going, I doubt if I would have bought the company," admits Jobs. He invested far more money in Pixar than NeXT. In late 1994, Jobs contemplated selling the profitless Pixar to Microsoft. Instead, Microsoft paid $6.5 million for a patent license, helping Pixar turn in its first profitable quarter. Although Pixar had accumulated a net deficit of $46.9 million by September 30, 1995, its fortunes were about to improve significantly.

Pixar's proprietary 3D animation technology made possible the first feature-length computer-generated film, Walt Disney Company's *Toy Story*. Pixar's 140 employees spent four years writing the screenplay, directing, staging, filming, editing, and producing *Toy Story* on 70 Silicon Graphics and 117 Sun Microsystems computers (total cost: $6 million in hardware), while Disney handled the financing, marketing, and distribution. *Toy Story* was released on November 22, 1995, and generated over $184 million in domestic box office revenues, making it the third most successful animated feature film ever, surpassed by only two other Disney titles: *The Lion King* and *Aladdin*.

Taking advantage of all the publicity surrounding the release of *Toy Story*, Pixar Animation Studios sold 6.9 million shares of stock to the public on November 29. Originally priced at $22 a share, Pixar (which trades on NASDAQ under the symbol PIXR) began trading at $47, hit a high of $49.50, and closed at $39 on volume of 4.8 million shares. Jobs' 30 million shares was suddenly worth an astonishing $1.17 billion on paper, more than the value of his Apple stock at any time during his tenure in Cupertino. The stock subsequently slid to a low of $12.25 during the third quarter of 1996, and peaked at $66 a share in July 1998, returning Jobs to the status of billionaire.

Following the success of *Toy Story*, Jobs renegotiated the deal with Disney so that Pixar could participate financially in the merchandising revenues. Initially Pixar's Interactive Division released CD-ROM games based upon the movie, but following the new deal with Disney, the consumer software division was dissolved on March 31, 1997, and its workers reassigned to work on *A Bug's Life*, which was released on November 25, 1998 to rave reviews and pulled in a record-setting $46.1 million over the five-day weekend, breaking the previous Thanksgiving weekend record of $45 million set by Disney's *101 Dalmations* (live-action) in 1996. *Toy Story 2*, the sequel to the 1995 blockbuster, was originally planned as a direct-to-video release, but Pixar and Disney reconsidered and expect it to be in theaters for the 1999 holiday season.

At 24 frames per second, a 77-minute animated feature film such as *Toy Story* requires approximately 110,000 individual frames.

"It's something between ironic and moronic that Jobs hit his biggest jackpot with the company where he is the least involved."

PC Letter *editor* **David Coursey**

NeXT Timeline

> "Without Jobs, Apple is just another Silicon Valley company, and without Apple, Jobs is just another Silicon Valley millionaire."
>
> *Technology journalist* **Nick Arnett**

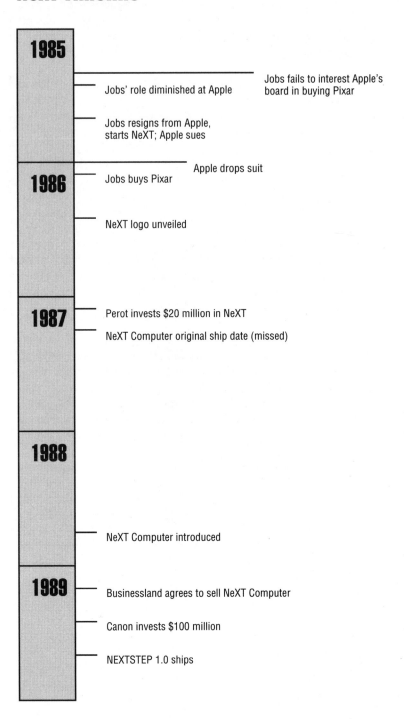

1985

Jobs' role diminished at Apple

Jobs fails to interest Apple's board in buying Pixar

Jobs resigns from Apple, starts NeXT; Apple sues

1986

Apple drops suit

Jobs buys Pixar

NeXT logo unveiled

1987

Perot invests $20 million in NeXT

NeXT Computer original ship date (missed)

1988

NeXT Computer introduced

1989

Businessland agrees to sell NeXT Computer

Canon invests $100 million

NEXTSTEP 1.0 ships

NeXT Timeline (continued)

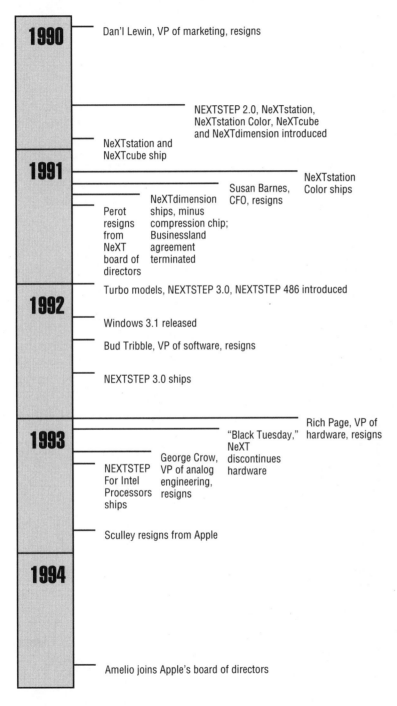

1990 — Dan'l Lewin, VP of marketing, resigns

— NEXTSTEP 2.0, NeXTstation, NeXTstation Color, NeXTcube and NeXTdimension introduced

NeXTstation and NeXTcube ship

1991 —

NeXTstation Color ships

Susan Barnes, CFO, resigns

NeXTdimension ships, minus compression chip; Businessland agreement terminated

Perot resigns from NeXT board of directors

1992 — Turbo models, NEXTSTEP 3.0, NEXTSTEP 486 introduced

Windows 3.1 released

Bud Tribble, VP of software, resigns

NEXTSTEP 3.0 ships

1993 —

Rich Page, VP of hardware, resigns

"Black Tuesday," NeXT discontinues hardware

George Crow, VP of analog engineering, resigns

NEXTSTEP For Intel Processors ships

Sculley resigns from Apple

1994 —

Amelio joins Apple's board of directors

After leaving NeXT, Dan'l Lewin worked at GO and KidSoft. As of 1998, he was president of Aurigin Systems (www.smartpatents.com), a startup selling software that enables organizations to uncover and use patent data for strategic business decisions.

> "Medicine will cure death and government will repeal taxes before Steve will fail. You can quote me."
>
> *Former Apple evangelist **Guy Kawasaki**, explaining to* NeXTWORLD *in the fall of 1991 why NeXT will eclipse Sun Microsystems as the dominant workstation manufacturer*

NeXT Timeline (continued)

> "There are a lot of people who do one incredible thing and then we never hear from them again. J. D. Salinger wrote *Catcher in the Rye*, but what else has he done?"
>
> *Former controller of the Mac division*
> **Deborah Coleman**, *on Jobs*

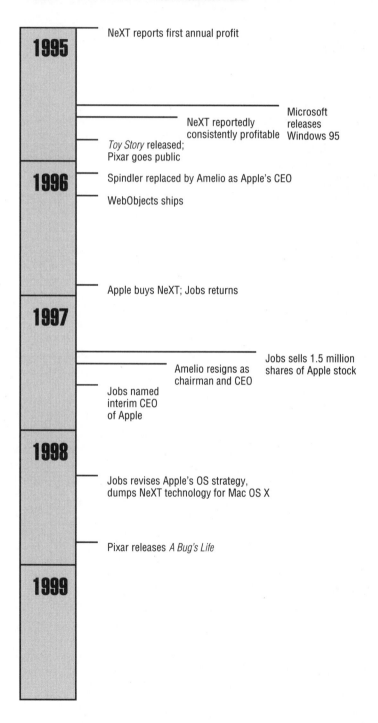

1995 — NeXT reports first annual profit

NeXT reportedly consistently profitable

Microsoft releases Windows 95

Toy Story released; Pixar goes public

1996 — Spindler replaced by Amelio as Apple's CEO

— WebObjects ships

— Apple buys NeXT; Jobs returns

1997

Jobs sells 1.5 million shares of Apple stock

Amelio resigns as chairman and CEO

Jobs named interim CEO of Apple

1998

— Jobs revises Apple's OS strategy, dumps NeXT technology for Mac OS X

— Pixar releases *A Bug's Life*

1999

The Star Trek Saga

The idea of porting the Mac OS to run on Intel processors wasn't new (Dan Eilers, Apple's director of strategic investment, first proposed the idea in 1985), but it gained a renewed sense of urgency after Apple shipped System 7 in May 1991 and it failed to make headway against Microsoft Windows 3.0. Ironically, it wasn't a determined Apple engineer or insightful executive who finally got the ball rolling. That honor goes to a company that few outside of the industry have ever heard of: Novell of Provo, Utah.

Networking giant Novell (www.novell.com) wanted to provide an alternative to Windows by creating a Mac-like interface for its DR-DOS that ran on Intel-based IBM PC clones, but feared getting sued by Apple (at the time, Apple's copyright infringement suit against Microsoft was still very much alive). Rather than risk an infestation of lawyers at its headquarters, Novell decided to find out if Apple was willing to work together on such a project. On Valentine's Day 1992, Darrell Miller, Novell's VP of strategic marketing, met with several Apple software managers to reveal his company's plan. Excited by the possibilities, the Apple contingent obtained CEO John Sculley's blessing, and the two companies immediately began working together on a project that came to be called Star Trek, because it would boldly go where no Mac had gone before: the Intel platform. When Bill Gates heard of Apple's plan to put the Mac OS on an Intel machine, he responded by saying it would be "like putting lipstick on a chicken."

A group of 4 engineers from Novell and 14 from Apple was put together by Gifford Calenda in suite 400 of a Novell marketing office called Regency One in Santa Clara, directly across the street from Intel's headquarters. That was no accident. Sculley had met with Intel CEO Andy Grove, who agreed to help the Star Trek project because, ever paranoid, he didn't want to be so dependent on Microsoft. Each Star Trek engineer was given an office with a Mac and a 486 PC clone donated by Intel.

On July 17, the Trekkie team was given until Halloween to come up with a working "proof of concept." As an indication of the importance

DR-DOS was created by Digital Research Inc., which had been sued by Apple in 1985 after it released GEM Desktop, an operating system that grafted a Mac-like interface onto PC clones. Too small to fight Apple, DRI settled the suit by altering its interface and was eventually acquired by Novell.

> ## "All the MBAs in the world can't convince us it's a good model."
> *Manager of Mac software architecture* **Roger Heinen**, *when asked in March 1992 about making System 7 run on Intel processors*

After working together on Star Trek and QuickTime, Fred Monroe and Fred Huxham eventually went on to form fredlabs inc. (www.fredlabs.com) in San Francisco. At the Macworld Expo in January 1997, fredlabs garnered considerable attention for its VirtualMac, which allowed users to run Mac applications within the BeOS running on a Power Mac.

Apple placed upon the project, each engineer would receive a bonus of between $16,000 and $25,000 if they succeeded. "We worked like dogs. It was some of the most fun I've had working," recalls team member Fred Monroe. Free of managerial meddling, the small team not only succeeded in getting the Mac's Finder to run on the PC clones, they also managed to get QuickTime and some of QuickDraw GX working, as well as the "Welcome to Macintosh" startup greeting. Having met their deadline, the Trekkies collected their bonuses and took off for a well-deserved vacation in Cancun, Mexico. In their minds, they had laid the groundwork for a product that could save Apple by allowing it to compete head-to-head with the inferior Microsoft Windows on its own turf: Intel-based computers.

Now it was up to team leader Chris DeRossi and Roger Heinen, VP of software engineering, to convince Apple's executive staff that Star Trek was worth pursuing. On December 4, they presented the Star Trek prototype to the assembled staff, many of whom couldn't believe their eyes. From all outward appearances, here was the fabled Mac OS running on an Intel computer; Star Trek had managed to penetrate deep behind enemy lines. Fred Forsyth, head of Apple's manufacturing business and hardware engineering, saw his career flash before his eyes. If Apple was successful in getting the Mac OS to run on Intel, demand for Apple's hardware would likely slump. Furthermore, the company was committed to moving the Macintosh to the PowerPC, and the Star Trek project was perceived to be a threat to that effort as well. How would it look to partners IBM and Motorola if Apple was porting the Mac OS to Intel processors at the same time it was collaborating on the PowerPC? Over these objections, Heinen was given the go-ahead to have his team attack the detail work to make Star Trek fully functional.

Armed with the executive staff's approval, Mark Gonzales, the project marketing manager, made the rounds of PC clone vendors to gauge their interest in bundling Star Trek on their systems. Most were intrigued, but argued that they couldn't afford to pay much for it because their contracts for Windows 3.1 forced them to pay a royalty to Microsoft for every computer shipped, regardless of what operating system it contained. (This anti-competitive practice eventually landed Microsoft in trouble with the Department of Justice.)

Worse than the clone-makers' tepid reception to Star Trek was Heinen's defection to Microsoft at the beginning of 1993. Without Heinen around to protect the Trekkies, in February the project was moved back onto Apple's campus at Bandley 5 and placed under the control of David C. Nagel, then head of the Advanced Technology

Star Trek was dealt a crippling blow when manager of Mac software architecture Roger Heinen left Apple for a position at Microsoft.

Group. The project ballooned from 18 people to 50, and most were forced to write detailed specifications and white papers instead of concentrating on writing code. Then COO Michael Spindler instituted a round of belt-tightening. After Nagel had allocated his budget to revising the OS for the PowerPC and updating System 7, there was not enough money left over to fund the completion of Star Trek, which was estimated to take 18 months and $20 million by some accounts. Nagel considered merging Star Trek with another project just getting under way. Code-named Raptor, it was an alternative to the Pink OS mired in the bickering at Taligent and was intended to run on any CPU, not just Intel or Motorola processors. However, the merger plan was deemed infeasible, and Star Trek disappeared into a black hole in June 1993. Work on Raptor would continue and eventually evolve into Copland, the long-promised, never-shipped sequel to Mac OS (see "The Copland Crisis," page 225).

Even if the engineers had managed to complete Star Trek, it wasn't as if suddenly every existing Mac application could run on Intel computers. Star Trek was designed to be source-level compatible, not binary compatible, with the Mac OS, meaning Mac applications would have to be recompiled by their developers to run on Intel processors. Those programs that directly addressed the Mac hardware would have to be rewritten. Needless to say, many software publishers were skeptical about the amount of work that would be necessary to port their products to PCs running Star Trek. Besides, a working demo of Star Trek isn't the same thing as a finished product. Remember, Apple engineers cobbled together pretty impressive proof-of-concept demos for Copland and Pink, too, but they never shipped either.

Just because Apple docked Star Trek doesn't mean you can't run Mac applications on other computers. In October 1995, Apple said that adapting the Mac OS for IBM's PowerPC Reference Platform (known as PReP) would be a technically daunting challenge and used that as an excuse to promote its variation, CHRP. That didn't stop Quix Computer (www.quix.ch), a company outside Lucerne, Switzerland, from succeeding in making the Mac OS work on PReP systems with just a half-dozen engineers. Despite the potential widespread demand for such a product, Apple refused to license the Mac OS to Quix, and as a result, Quix moved on to develop technologies for more receptive companies. Apple couldn't quash Executor as easily. A small company called ARDI (www.ardi.com) in Albuquerque, New Mexico, managed to reverse-engineer the Mac OS and Toolbox to create a version of System 7.0, called Executor, that can run on Intel 486, Pentium, and DEC's Alpha processors. Executor is far from a perfect port. It doesn't support serial port access (meaning AppleTalk and modems won't work), sound input/output is primitive, there are no provisions for internationalization, and neither extensions nor control panels can be used. Nonetheless, Executor runs many standard Mac programs on PCs. Imagine what it could do with Apple's support.

With no help from Apple, ARDI reverse-engineered the better part of the Mac OS, allowing PC users to run many Mac programs inside Executor.

In late 1997, many of the Star Trek engineers held a reunion in Cupertino following the expiration of their five-year non-disclosure agreements. Rumor has it that there's a new Star Trek NG (Next Generation) project involving an emulator that allows Mac OS applications to run on Intel hardware under Rhapsody. Only time will tell if Star Trek NG beams Apple back into the limelight or gets lost in space again.

From Diesel to Doctor

Although Michael H. Spindler joined Apple in September 1980 as marketing manager for European operations, the native of Berlin, Germany, didn't pop up on the radar screens of most Apple watchers until January 29, 1990, when he moved to Cupertino to assume the role of chief operating officer, taking over the worldwide manufacturing and marketing units that had previously reported to Jean-Louis Gassée. Nicknamed "The Diesel" because of his ability to attack complex problems head-on with no-nonsense management experience, Spindler was chugging down a career path that would take him to the highest executive office at Apple. In stark contrast to Steve Jobs and John Sculley, Spindler is a passionately private man who, according to one former executive, "did not get where he is by showing his butt in public." As a result, most people would be hard pressed to recall a single thing he accomplished while at the helm of Apple. That's a shame, because had he achieved his ultimate goal, its effect would have been more profound than anything anyone else at Apple had ever accomplished: The firm would have ceased to exist.

Almost since the moment he arrived in Cupertino, Michael Spindler tried to merge Apple with a variety of different corporations.

"This isn't anything new. Since 1986, we held serious discussions with DEC, Kodak, Sony, Sun, Compaq, IBM, and a few other companies I'd rather not name now. They were very thoughtful discussions. We considered everything from 'Let's trade technology' to 'Let's put the companies together' with each one of them."

*Chairman **Mike Markkula**, on 1996 merger speculation*

> "We used to have a joke that you don't sit in the first ten rows at a Spindler speech, because you might drown from all the sweat and spit."
>
> Apple sales manager **John Ziel**

Shortly after arriving in Cupertino, Spindler was instructed by CEO John Sculley to begin a secret search for a way to pair Apple's brand name and superior software with the market muscle and boardroom credibility of a larger company. Sculley felt that the Mac market would slowly erode and that Apple's only hope was to create new revenue streams from products such as the Newton and Pippin, but developing these products to the point of self-sufficiency would require the resources of a larger company.

Courtesy of Sun Microsystems

Sun Microsystems CEO Scott McNealy wanted to merge with Apple as far back as 1988.

Sun Microsystems, an up-and-coming workstation manufacturer, had been trying to merge with Apple since 1988, and by the fall of 1990, a deal was all but finalized when out of the blue, IBM president Jack Kuehler called Spindler and proposed working together on RISC (reduced instruction set computing) chips. Under the Sun deal, Spindler faced demotion when Sun CEO Scott G. McNealy took over as COO of the combined companies. Working with IBM, however, offered Spindler a way to save his high-powered job, so Apple left Sun at the altar.

Shortly after Spindler became president of Apple in November 1990, Sculley managed to convince IBM, the world's largest computer company, to partner with Apple and Motorola on the PowerPC chip, as well as on Taligent (to develop the Pink operating system) and Kaleida (to develop ScriptX multimedia tools). On July 3, 1991, Apple and IBM issued a preliminary press release but didn't consummate the deal until October 2, when executives signed the papers during a press conference at the Fairmont Hotel in San Francisco (see "The Strangest Bedfellow of All," page 45).

Although it had reached a historic alliance with its former archenemy, Apple was still anxious to merge. Throughout the summer of 1992, Apple was in serious talks with photography giant Eastman Kodak, but that deal fell apart over cultural differences. At the beginning of

1993, it looked like Apple had found the perfect partner in AT&T. Executives from both companies met frequently in hot and heavy discussions on how to combine the two firms, and it looked like a deal was imminent. But the merger collapsed at the end of April because AT&T was still smarting from its botched purchase of NCR and was preparing to snap up McCaw Cellular Communications for $11.5 billion.

While Apple was in discussions with AT&T, Sculley was also considering switching coasts to accept the position of CEO of IBM. It was the last straw for Apple's board. They felt that in spending so much time on the expensive Newton project and helping the Clinton campaign, Sculley had taken his eyes off the ball to the point where Apple was preparing to announce its largest quarterly loss to date. On June 18, 1993, Sculley was forced to step down as CEO and was replaced by Spindler. Before the year was out, Sculley would resign as chairman and leave Apple altogether.

Spindler got down to business by laying off 2,500 employees (16 percent of the workforce), canning many blue-sky projects, and cutting R&D costs by more than $100 million per year. The company turned in four quarters of strong growth and the stock doubled to more than $40 a share. He had successfully polished Apple so that it might once again be an attractive merger candidate, while managing the Mac's transition from Motorola's 68000 family of processors to the new RISC-based PowerPC developed jointly with IBM and Motorola.

From the consumer's point of view, Apple did a tremendous job making the transition as painless as possible by maintaining a high level of backward compatibility, but the real hero was a third-party Mac tools developer named Metrowerks (www.metrowerks.com). Apple had focused so much on producing the new generation of hardware and making the system software function seamlessly that creating PowerPC-native programming tools for developers wasn't a high priority (in fact, the task had been farmed out to Symantec under the code name Rainbow). Fortunately Metrowerks stepped into the breach with its amazingly fast CodeWarrior and kept many Mac developers from defecting to Windows.

Power Macs were introduced on March 14, 1994, at the Lincoln Center for the Performing Arts in New York, and Apple sold one million units in the first ten months. Ian W. Diery, then executive VP and general manager of the Personal Computer Division, vowed that Power Macs would always be cheaper than competing Wintel models, but he would be overruled by Apple's executive staff, which insisted

> ## "I am not available or interested in being CEO of IBM."
> ***John Sculley**, to* The Wall Street Journal *on March 11, 1993*

Courtesy of Motorola

Spindler deserves credit for managing the transition of the Mac from the 68000 family of CPUs to the new PowerPC.

on maintaining premium pricing to fund other projects at Apple. Spindler announced plans to double the Mac's market share in five years. Part of his strategy involved biting the bullet and finally allowing other vendors to clone the Mac (see "The Clone Quandary," page 193) as well as pushing more Mac models out the door to mass-market retailers faster than ever before. This shotgun approach to product development lead to quality control problems and consumer confusion, plus logistical and forecasting nightmares.

The successful introduction of Power Macs based upon the jointly developed PowerPC was proof that Apple and IBM could work together. In October 1994, executives from both companies holed up for two weeks at the Summerfield Suites Hotel near San Francisco International Airport to work on the terms of a merger. Things got ugly in November when Markkula, Spindler, and Joseph Anthony Graziano, Apple's chief financial officer, met with IBM CEO Louis V. Gerstner Jr. and his team at the Westin Hotel near Chicago's O'Hare International Airport to hammer out the details of a deal that would have been unthinkable a decade earlier: selling entreprenurial Apple to conservative IBM. After brief presentations by both sides, Gerstner pulled Spindler and Markkula aside and privately offered $40 a share for Apple (valuing the deal at about $4.5 billion), when the stock was trading around $35. The Apple contingent balked at the price. Spindler demanded golden parachutes for himself and other top Apple managers and held out for $60 a share, hoping to instigate a counteroffer. It never came. IBM left abruptly.

In 1989, Joseph A. Graziano was nicknamed "The Million Dollar Man" after Apple paid him a $1.5 million signing bonus to leave Sun Microsystems, where he had been CFO for two years. He had been Apple's CFO from 1981 to 1985, at which time he quit to spend time with his brother, Anthony, who was dying of cancer. When word of the signing bonus spread around Apple, employees began computing budgets and profits in a new unit of currency called the Graz. For example, if your budget got cut by $6 million, you'd say they slashed "four Grazs."

In addition to thinking IBM would come back to the table with a sweetened offer, Spindler made another huge miscalculation that September. During the planning meetings for fiscal 1995, he grossly underestimated sales growth. Even though the future looked promising—with a recovering domestic economy, strong demand for Power Macs, and Microsoft's delay in shipping a successor to Windows 3.0—Spindler's staff was haunted by the glut of PowerBooks left over from the previous year. Diery forecast a 15 percent growth rate. Graziano urged a more aggressive forecast designed to grab market share. Spindler sided with Diery, and the rest is history. During the holiday 1994 season, Apple couldn't meet demand for its machines because of parts supply problems. Apple was overwhelmed when actual demand grew at almost twice the predicted rate. To make matters even worse, Apple was whipsawed by changes in consumer preferences. The previous year consumers wanted low-end Macs. Now they were clamoring for high-end, high-margin Power Macs, but there were precious few to go around. Apple responded by cutting prices on Performas and later took an $80 million inventory writeoff.

"Our warehouses were clogged with Yugos when everyone wanted to buy Mercedes."

Apple's senior VP in charge of corporate marketing **Satjiv Chahil**

Following the disastrous holiday season, Apple began scrambling to find a large corporate suitor. In April 1995, Canon was said to be in talks with Apple, offering $54.50 a share (for total value of $6.5 billion) when Apple was trading around $35. Hoping to get more, Spindler went back to IBM in May claiming Gerstner had misunderstood his prior demands. Again IBM declined. By then it was in the process of acquiring Lotus Development Corporation for $3.52 billion, and demand had picked up for its high-margin mainframes. Anxious to find someone, anyone, willing to pay what he considered a fair price, Spindler approached Compaq, Hewlett-Packard, Philips, Sony, and Toshiba, but none of them was seriously interested in buying Apple. Spindler then initiated talks with Sun via its board member and legendary venture capitalist, L. John Doerr. Spindler was going through the motions because his brain knew a merger was in Apple's best interests, but in his heart he relished being the high-profile CEO of a *Fortune* 500 company and resisted trading that in to become a faceless VP at some larger firm.

As Spindler hawked Apple to one potential partner after another, things continued to deteriorate in Cupertino. In June, Apple's backorders reached $1 billion, representing 500,000 Macs. On August 24, Microsoft launched a $200-million blockbuster roll-out for Windows 95, the likes of which the computer world will never see again. In early September, two preproduction PowerBook 5300s caught fire, prompting an expensive and embarrassing recall (see "Big Bad Blunders," page 109). As if things weren't bad enough, a price war erupted in Japan, once Apple's most lucrative overseas market.

It looked like there wouldn't be anything worth selling if Apple didn't act fast. Graziano had enough of Spindler's indecisiveness. At a board meeting that started on October 2 in Austin, Texas, he urged Apple's directors to immediately sell the company or break it into separate hardware and software units that might be more attractive acquisition candidates (an idea Sculley had investigated during his final days in charge), claiming it was the only way Apple could survive. He laid the blame for Apple's ills at Spindler's feet. He argued that Spindler's new forecast of 30 percent Mac unit growth was unrealistic in the face of the Windows 95 tidal wave. Spindler was still half-heartedly entertaining offers where he could find them but seemed resigned to trying to service the remaining Mac market as an independent company. Spindler fought back and the board stood behind him. As Markkula told *The Wall Street Journal*, "The board has been very pleased with Michael's performance. He is the best thinker at Apple. He is truly a very brilliant man." Frustrated and disgusted at the board "sitting there with their thumbs up their asses," Graziano resigned.

> "I don't think preserving the legal entity that is Apple is as important as preserving our organization, philosophies, brand name, employees, customer base, and technology."
>
> ***Mike Markkula***

The flaming PowerBook 5300 was indicative of Apple's troubles during Spindler's watch.

> "Give us one strong quarter and all this will go away."
>
> ***Michael Spindler***, *to* The New York Times *on October 5, 1995*

"I've been to China and to the former Soviet Union, and I've seen what controlled economies are like. They suck. If Microsoft dominates the computer industry the way Bill [Gates] would like, our industry would suck too."

Sun CEO **Scott McNealy**

"You know, I've got a plan that could rescue Apple. I can't say any more than that it's the perfect product and the perfect strategy for Apple. But nobody there will listen to me."

NeXT and Pixar CEO **Steve Jobs**

By December 1995, a shared fear of Microsoft had driven Sun Microsystems' CEO Scott McNealy to meet with Apple's board at the St. Regis Hotel in New York, where they began nailing down the details of a stock-swap deal that would place McNealy in charge of the combined company. Ironically, five years before Apple had walked away from a deal to acquire Sun, and now the tables were turned, with the spurned McNealy on the verge of taking over Apple. It looked like Apple might be able to put a present under its shareholders' Christmas trees after all, but negotiations broke off when Apple warned of an impending $69 million quarterly loss.

The Sun deal may have slipped away, but there was still the possibility that Philips would come through. Talks with Philips had been running concurrently with the Sun negotiations, and the Dutch company had indicated a willingness to pay $36 a share. However, those hopes were dashed when Philips' board rejected the proposal by a single vote.

During the merger speculation surrounding Apple at the end of 1995, there was a very real possibility of the prodigal son returning to Cupertino. At the *Upside* Technology Summit held in Carefree, Arizona, on February 12, 1996, Oracle CEO Lawrence J. Ellison admitted that he and his best friend, Steve Jobs, contemplated making a bid for the company while the two were vacationing in Hawaii the previous December. "Steve and I talked about it at length," revealed Ellison. "Up to a week ago, we were seriously looking at buying Apple, but Steve and I couldn't exactly agree about the right way to do it … I felt I would be supporting him if he wanted to take his company back." At the time, Jobs' 30 million shares of Pixar stock were worth $600 million, and Ellison's 100 million shares of Oracle stock were worth $4.7 billion, so clearly they had the financing, but Jobs ultimately decided to drop the idea of attempting a hostile takeover.

At the shareholder meeting on January 23, 1996, an exhausted Spindler addressed a crowd of disgruntled investors and zealous business reporters who tasted blood in the water. He acknowledged that the company's Mac hardware licensing was behind schedule, but promised to fix that in the coming year. He explained that Apple was suffering from industry-wide demand that fell short of expectations and that consumers' appetite for low-end machines meant Apple had to adjust to still-lower margins. Extremely fierce price wars in Japan really hurt, since that market provided between 15 and 20 percent of Apple's overall revenues. Spindler also announced the firing of 1,300 employees (representing another 8 percent of the workforce in addition to the 20 percent laid off in 1995), and a reduction in the number of Mac models to reduce consumer confusion and cut costs.

Furthermore, he promised to change eWorld into an Internet-based service (see "Big Bad Blunders," page 109).

An embattled Spindler (left) had a hard time facing Apple's shareholders, despite assurances from Markkula that the board was happy with him as CEO.

> "His nickname is The Diesel; it should be The Train Wreck."
>
> Newsweek *columnist* **Steven Levy**

Spindler's synopsis of Apple's problems and his promised fixes did little to appease the assembled shareholders, some of whom called for him to resign. In a show of support, Markkula placed his hand on Spindler's back at a press conference after the meeting and said, "I like this guy. He's a very good person." The company even went so far as to issue a press release stating, "Apple's board of directors supports Michael Spindler and is working with management to meet Apple's challenges and return the company to financial health. Michael Spindler is in the office and is fully engaged in the business." The release went on to insist, "The company is not for sale. But certainly the company's board and management have been and remain aware of their obligations to maximize shareholder value."

Following the meeting, the board met to discuss Sun's latest merger offer. Sun proposed a stock swap, valuing Apple's shares at $23, far below its $31.625 closing price that day. The board knew the shareholders would never approve such a deal. The situation became even more bleak after news of the low-ball bid was leaked, along with reports that big Mac purchases were being delayed due to the turmoil, which would lead to slowing sales. Markkula called an emergency meeting of the board for January 31 at Manhattan's St. Regis Hotel. McNealy was invited to attend to personally pitch his merger proposal, but he stuck to his $23 offer and the board balked.

> "I have not heard any self-criticisms. You have mismanaged assets. You have wasted a valuable franchise, and you have brought a great company to its knees. Mr. Spindler, it's time for you to go!"
>
> Apple shareholder **Orin McCluskey**

Q. What do you get when you merge Sun and Apple?
A. Snapple.

Spindler, "The Diesel," was replaced by fellow board member Dr. Gilbert F. Amelio.

Since leaving Apple, Spindler has kept a low profile. He sits on the supervisory board of German publishing conglomerate Bertelsmann AG (www.bertelsmann.de).

The next order of business was to discuss the CEO situation. Spindler argued for more time, but the board refused. They ordered Spindler out of the executive office and off the board. Jürgen Hintz, a former marketing executive at Procter & Gamble, asked to be considered as CEO and was politely denied. Instead, without bothering to conduct a traditional executive search, they chose to replace Spindler with fellow board member Dr. Gilbert F. Amelio, chairman, president, and CEO of the world's fourth largest manufacturer of computer chips, National Semiconductor. In addition to CEO, Amelio was named chairman of the board, replacing Markkula, who would stay on as vice chairman. Apple's new leader flew back to the West Coast in Markkula's Falcon 900 to notify National Semiconductor executives of his plans. The following morning, National Semiconductor announced Amelio's resignation in a tersely worded press release. As if to demonstrate just how screwed up things were in Cupertino, it took Apple until late that evening, February 2, to confirm that Amelio had indeed replaced Spindler (see "The Doctor's Strong Medicine," page 215). The Diesel's reign of error was over.

According to statements filed with the SEC, Spindler was awarded $3.7 million in severance pay, more than two-and-a-half times his $1.42 million combined salary and bonus package for 1995. Apple also gave Spindler $50,000 for moving expenses, $150,000 to help pay off his Atherton home, and health insurance for two years.

"So it's time for me to go!" Spindler wrote in an email circulated company-wide. "Mistakes or misjudgments made? Oh yes—even plenty. Both in business and personal judgment terms. I take personal responsibility for things that didn't work and should have been worked. I tried to give it my best—both intellectually and physically in every corner of the world to carry this cause and its color. I tried to be as clear, honest and forthcoming in my communication with you. Those of you who—through all these long years—have helped me, supported me and even guided me—I thank you sincerely from the bottom of my soul for the friendship and being together. In fading away from the place which I loved and feared, I will become whole again—hopefully renew the father, husband and self I am."

Spindler Timeline

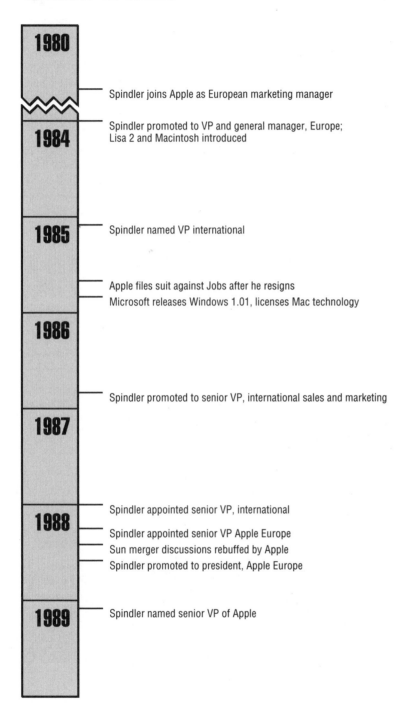

1980

Spindler joins Apple as European marketing manager

1984

Spindler promoted to VP and general manager, Europe;
Lisa 2 and Macintosh introduced

1985

Spindler named VP international

Apple files suit against Jobs after he resigns
Microsoft releases Windows 1.01, licenses Mac technology

1986

Spindler promoted to senior VP, international sales and marketing

1987

Spindler appointed senior VP, international

1988

Spindler appointed senior VP Apple Europe
Sun merger discussions rebuffed by Apple
Spindler promoted to president, Apple Europe

1989

Spindler named senior VP of Apple

Spindler Timeline (continued)

1990
- Spindler promoted to COO and executive VP of Apple, moves to Cupertino
- Microsoft releases Windows 3.0
- Gassée leaves Apple
- Spindler elected president
- Spindler elected to board of directors

1991
- Mac System 7.0 released
- IBM partnership announced; PowerPC, Taligent, Kaleida projects begin

1992
- Microsoft releases Windows 3.1

1993
- AT&T merger discussions break down
- Spindler replaces Sculley as CEO
- Sculley resigns from Apple

1994
- First Power Macs introduced
- IBM offers $40 a share; Spindler demands $60
- Amelio joins Apple's board of directors

1995
- Canon offers $54.50 a share (rejected)
- Backorders reach $1 billion
- Graziano resigns
- PowerBook 5300 recalled
- Microsoft releases Windows 95
- 1st clone license granted

1996
- Amelio replaces Spindler as CEO
- Sun offers $23 a share (rejected)

"Do you know this company was on the brink of bankruptcy in '85? The same thing in '88, '90, and '92. It will survive. It always has."
*Former Apple CEO **Michael Spindler***

The
Clone Quandary

Apple's greatest strategic mistake may have been its refusal to license the Macintosh hardware and operating system until it was too late. Many observers reason that when the Mac was introduced in 1984, it was so far superior to anything the competition offered that the only thing that held Apple back from domination of the personal computer industry was the company's stubborn policy of going it alone.

Macs rely heavily on Apple's proprietary read-only memory (ROM) and custom-designed chips called ASICs, short for Application-Specific Integrated Circuits. This prevents companies from producing Mac clones without Apple's blessing. Some vendors (such as Colby, Dynamac, and Outbound Systems, Inc.) have tried to get around this problem by building clones with motherboards into which users were expected to insert a ROM that came from a legitimate Mac and then obtain and install the necessary operating system. Needless to say, this was often more work that it was worth and never caught on. If you wanted to legally build a Mac clone, you had to get Apple's permission, and Apple simply refused to cooperate.

After Mac sales tapered off in late 1984, Apple faced a serious problem because management had essentially bet the future of the company on the new computer. One thing holding back sales was the perception that Apple was still an upstart company. As the sole source of Macs, it didn't represent a safe bet when it came to purchasing equipment. That's when the idea of licensing the Mac to others first began getting kicked around in the halls of Apple's Cupertino campus. If multiple vendors sold Macs, there would be more choice and buyers wouldn't be dependent upon a single source, reasoned supporters. Strangely enough, one of the strongest supporters of the licensing effort was none other than Microsoft CEO Bill Gates. On June 25, 1985, Gates sent a detailed memo to Apple CEO John Sculley and Apple Products president Jean-Louis Gassée, begging them to consider licensing the Mac OS to outsiders.

"If Apple had licensed the Mac OS when it first came out, Windows wouldn't exist today."

Robertson Stephens analyst
Jon van Bronkhorst

"When the Mac came out in 1984, we wrote letters to Sculley, and we told him who to go to at HP and who to go to at AT&T to license the machine because we'd really bet our future on the Mac. We stopped doing DOS application development and did all our work in the graphical environment, so we were very worried in 1985 when Mac sales slowed down actually from the first year and we were trying to make all these suggestions. It's probably too late to make a licensing program work."

Microsoft CEO **Bill Gates**, *during a January 30, 1996 speech*

Gates' Most Amazing Memo

To: John Sculley, Jean Louis Gassée
From: Bill Gates, Jeff Raikes
Date: June 25, 1985
Re: Apple Licensing of Mac Technology
cc: Jon Shirley

Background:

Apple's stated position in personal computers is innovative technology leader. This position implies that Apple must create a standard on new, advanced technology. They must establish a "revolutionary" architecture, which necessarily implies new development incompatible with existing architectures.

Apple must make Macintosh a standard. But no personal computer company, not even IBM, can create a standard without independent support. Even though Apple realized this, they have not been able to gain the independent support required to be perceived as a standard.

The significant investment (especially independent support) in a "standard personal computer" results in an incredible momentum for its architecture. Specifically, the IBM PC architecture continues to receive huge investment and gains additional momentum. (Though clearly the independent investment in the Apple II, and the resulting momentum, is another great example.) The investment in the IBM architecture includes development of differentiated compatibles, software and peripherals; user and sales channel education; and most importantly, attitudes and perceptions that are not easily changed.

Any deficiencies in the IBM architecture are quickly eliminated by independent support. Hardware deficiencies are remedied in two ways:

- expansion cards made possible because of access to the bus (e.g. the high resolution Hercules graphics card for monochrome monitors)
- manufacture of differentiated compatibles (e.g. the Compaq portable, or the faster DeskPro).

The closed architecture prevents similar independent investment in the Macintosh. The IBM architecture, when compared to the

Macintosh, probably has more than 100 times the engineering resources applied to it when investment of compatible manufacturers is included. The ratio becomes even greater when the manufacturers of expansion cards are included.

Conclusion:

As the independent investment in a "standard" architecture grows, so does the momentum for that architecture. The industry has reached the point where it is now impossible for Apple to create a standard out of their innovative technology without support from, and the resulting credibility of other personal computer manufacturers. Thus, Apple must open the Macintosh architecture to have the independent support required to gain momentum and establish a standard.

The Mac has not become a standard

The Macintosh has failed to attain the critical mass necessary for the technology to be considered a long term contender:

   a. Since there is no "competition" to Apple from "Mac-compatible" manufacturers, corporations consider it risky to be locked into the Mac, for reasons of price AND choice.

   b. Apple has reinforced the risky perception of the machine by being slow to come out with software and hardware improvements (e.g. hard disk, file server, bigger screen, better keyboard, larger memory, new ROM, operating software with improved performance). Furthermore, killing the Macintosh XL (Lisa) eliminated the alternative model that many businesses considered necessary.

   c. Recent negative publicity about Apple hinders the credibility of the Macintosh as a long term contender in the personal computer market.

   d. Independent software and hardware manufacturers reinforced the risky perception of the machine by being slow to come out with key software and peripheral products.

   e. Apple's small corporate account sales force has prevented it from having the presence, training, support, etc. that large companies would recognize and require.

   f. Nationalistic pressures in European countries often force foreign to consumers [*sic*] choose local manufacturers. Europeans have local suppliers of the IBM architecture, but not Apple. Apple will lose ground in Europe as was recently exhibited in France.

continued on next page…

"The computer was never the problem. The company's strategy was. Apple saw itself as a hardware company; in order to protect our hardware profits, we didn't license our operating system. We had the most beautiful operating system, but to get it you had to buy our hardware at twice the price. That was a mistake. What we should have done was calculate an appropriate price to license the operating system. We were also naïve to think that the best technology would prevail. It often doesn't."

Apple co-founder **Steve Wozniak**

"If we had licensed earlier, we would be the Microsoft of today."

*Apple executive VP **Ian W. Diery***

Recommendation:

Apple should license Macintosh technology to 3-5 significant manufacturers for the development of "Mac Compatibles":

United States manufacturers and contacts:

Ideal companies — in addition to credibility, they have large account sales forces that can establish the Mac architecture in larger companies:

- AT&T, James Edwards
- Wang, An Wang
- Digital Equipment Corporation, Ken Olsen
- Texas Instruments, Jerry Junkins
- Hewlett Packard, John Young

Other companies (but perhaps more realistic candidates):

- Xerox, Elliott James or Bob Adams
- Motorola, Murray A. Goldman
- Harris/Lanier, Wes Cantrell
- NBI, Thomas S. Kavanagh
- Burroughs, W. Michael Blumenthal and Stephen Weisenfeld
- Kodak
- 3M
- CPT

European manufacturers:

- Siemens
- Bull
- Olivetti
- Philips

Apple should license the Macintosh technology to US and European companies in a way that allows them to go to other companies for manufacturing. Sony, Kyocera, and Alps are good candidates for OEM manufacturing of Mac compatibles.

Microsoft is very willing to help Apple implement this strategy. We are familiar with the key manufacturers, their strategies and strengths. We also have a great deal of experience in OEMing system software.

Rationale:

1. The companies that license Mac technology would add credibility to the Macintosh architecture.
2. These companies would broaden the available product offerings through their "Mac-compatible" product lines:
   - they would each innovate and add features to the basic system: various memory configurations, video display

and keyboard alternatives, etc.
- Apple would lever the key partners' abilities to produce a wide variety of peripherals, much faster than Apple could develop the peripherals themselves.
  - customers would see competition and would have real price/performance choices
3. Apple will benefit from the distribution channels of these companies.
4. The perception of a significantly increased potential installed base will bring the independent hardware, software, and marketing support that the Macintosh needs.
5. Apple will gain significant, additional marketing support. Every time a Mac compatible manufacturer advertises, it is an advertisement for the Apple architecture.
6. Licensing Mac compatibles will enhance Apple's image as a technological innovator. Ironically, IBM is viewed as being a technological innovator. This is because compatible manufacturers are afraid to innovate too much and stray from the standard.

Having received no reply from Sculley and Gassée, Gates wrote a second letter on July 29, naming three other companies that would be receptive to licensing, and added, "I want to help in any way I can with the licensing. Please give me a call." Gates' overtures fell on deaf ears. Sculley didn't understand the specifics of how to go about licensing and Gassée refused to relinquish the Mac's lead to copycats.

Gates wasn't the only one pushing Apple to start a licensing program. Internally, VP William V. Campbell had persuaded a handful of marquee companies to request a license from Apple, among them AT&T and Sony. A few months after receiving Gates' memos, Sculley asked Dan Eilers, 30, then director of strategic investment at Apple, to make a pitch to the executive staff about licensing the OS. Eilers rightly believed that over time other vendors would copy the Mac's user interface, and Apple's advantage would erode. As that happened, Apple's market share would drop, and developers would be less willing to commit to the Mac, giving consumers less reason to buy the computer. Eilers argued that Apple should immediately port the Mac OS to Intel-based computers and develop an aggressive plan to license the Mac OS while it still enjoyed a significant advantage over the competition and it still had a chance of becoming the industry standard. Gassée was livid. He believed it was impossible to port the Mac OS to Intel hardware, feared licensing would rob Apple of revenue, and threatened that his engineers would leave if Apple

Courtesy of Be, Inc.

"I am aware that I am known as the Great Satan on licensing … I was never for or against licensing. I just did not see how it would make sense. But my approach was stupid. We were just fat cats living off a business that had no competition."

*Be CEO **Jean-Louis Gassée**, admitting he made a strategic mistake*

licensed the OS. Sculley caved in to Gassée's threats, and the idea was shelved.

Sculley didn't see, or refused to believe, what was obvious to so many others. Recalls Alan Kay, a Xerox PARC alum (see "From Xerox, With Love," page 51) and former Apple Fellow, "What I told Apple when I came in here was 'Now that you're selling the Macintosh, you're a software company, not a hardware company, because the thing that makes the Mac different from all other computers is nothing in the hardware, but it's in that ROM. And what you're selling is services, communication services between a human being and what the computer can do for them.' And, I said to them 'When you're in the software business you have to run on every platform, so you must put the Mac operating system on the PC and put it on Sun workstations and put it on everything else because that's what you do if you're in the software business, right?' Software people are always multi-platform, because you want to run on everything. And, that was a huge battle, probably the largest battle I lost here at Apple."

Courtesy of *MacAddict*

At the last minute in 1987, Apple backed out of a licensing deal with Apollo Computer.

In January 1987, Apple was set to sign a licensing deal with Apollo Computer of Chelmsford, Massachusetts, then the leading workstation vendor. The two companies had been working together since April 1986 to package Apple's Mac II and Apollo's Domain operating system as a low-end workstation. Apollo executives were set to board a plane for Silicon Valley to sign the contract committing them to buying 40,000 Mac IIs when Sculley backed out at the last moment because he felt that Apollo's star was fading in the ascent of rival Sun Microsystems. He was right. Sun went on to dominate the workstation market, and Apollo was eventually acquired by Hewlett-Packard.

By the time Apple sued Microsoft on March 17, 1988, for similarities between Windows and the Lisa / Mac audiovisual works, the issue of licensing was all but dead. "Apple's board was absolutely convinced we would win the suit," remembers Sculley. And the feeling was that pursuing licensing at that point would undermine the suit by fostering a perception of weakness. Besides, with the fortuitous success of the Macintosh in the desktop publishing industry—thanks to the combination of the LaserWriter and Aldus PageMaker—it looked like perhaps Apple had pursued the right strategy after all. Its market share remained a small fraction of the overall PC world, but its gross margins (averaging 51 percent from 1986 to 1990) were the envy of the industry. Eilers, however, remained convinced that such margins were unsustainable, and he was right. In a 112-page confidential document dated August 30, 1990, Eilers—then VP of strategy and corporate development—recommended making a "discontinuous jump." He proposed four options: licensing only the Mac OS, licensing both the OS and the hardware, creating a second Macintosh brand, or most radical of all, spinning off a small company code-named Macrosoft with the express purpose of porting the Mac OS to the Intel processor (see "The Star Trek Saga," page 179). They estimated it could be done in less than a year and that the Mac OS could grab 30 percent of the market within three years. This time it was COO Michael Spindler who urged Sculley to nix the ideas, saying, "It's too late to license. It doesn't matter anymore. The opportunity is past." The executive staff didn't share Eilers' sense of urgency and failed to take definitive action on any of his recommendations.

Courtesy of Motorola

Apple thought IBM would produce its own line of PowerPC-based Mac clones.

After partnering with IBM and Motorola on the PowerPC microprocessor in 1991, Apple was confident that IBM would eventually launch its own line of Mac clones to provide a larger market for the PowerPC chip, so Apple wasn't anxious to line up what it considered less-prestigious vendors. Besides, Spindler and Sculley secretly hoped to convince IBM to buy Apple and put them in charge of the combined companies' personal computer business.

Eilers eventually took over as CEO of Claris, Apple's software subsidiary, from Campbell in January 1991, but never let go of the licensing idea. Just a year later, he convinced Sculley to consider allowing Claris to manufacture and sell Mac clones via mail order, emulating the successful Dell Computer (www.dell.com) and essentially implementing his previous recommendation of creating a second Mac brand. By July 1992, Claris had developed working prototypes and was ready to roll, but the idea was shot down by Spindler, and again Sculley refused to overrule his subordinate.

> "I think Apple lost a lot in the Microsoft lawsuit. Apple should have sued them for not copying the Mac as closely as possible. Had we gone to Microsoft and said 'do anything the way we've already found is good, for 25 cents' the result might have been a commonality as beneficial to Apple as Microsoft. When you're comfortable with one OS because of all your skills, it's scary to change. Were the two platforms very similar, the comfort feeling wouldn't trap Mac users or PC users to their familiar machines."
>
> *Steve Wozniak*

After fighting the idea for years, Spindler reluctantly embraced licensing the Mac when he became CEO of Apple.

By the time Spindler took over from Sculley on June 18, 1993, he had had a change of heart and put licensing high on his list of priorities. He realized that Apple couldn't maintain its isolationist stance much longer. But when he raised the issue with his lieutenants, he got a dose of his own medicine. This time Ian W. Diery, executive VP, strongly opposed the idea, fearing it would siphon sales of Apple's Macs without expanding the market share. That August, the same month as the Newton introduction, IBM approached Apple and asked to license the Mac OS for use on a PowerPC-based Common Hardware Reference Platform computer that could be built using industry standard off-the-shelf parts rather than special, proprietary chips. As an added benefit, so-called CHRP (pronounced chirp) systems could run a variety of operating systems, including Apple's Mac OS, IBM's OS/2, Microsoft's Windows NT, and Unix-based AIX. IBM was already working on PowerPC-based workstations and wanted to offer CHRP as its personal computer. When Apple pushed to license its OS and forthcoming Power Mac hardware as a pair, IBM countered with a proposal to collaborate on the new CHRP specification. Apple wasn't interested, so IBM pursued a modification of the CHRP idea called the PowerPC Reference Platform (PReP)— which was essentially CHRP, except it wouldn't run the Mac OS. IBM unveiled its PReP plans at the Fall COMDEX 1993, and Spindler was upset that Apple had been left out. He demanded a high-level meeting the coming spring to resolve their differences, and IBM agreed.

At the shareholder meeting on January 26, 1994, Spindler announced that Apple expected to line up a major PC manufacturer to license the upcoming Power Macs by the end of the year. Spindler was hoping to snare a marquee company such as Compaq, Dell, Gateway, or IBM as Apple's first licensee. Indeed, by the time Apple and IBM returned to the negotiating tables, Spindler was willing to license the Mac OS if IBM was willing to push the Mac-inclusive CHRP, not the exclusionary PReP. IBM could live with that, but Apple insisted that the CHRP machines ship with Mac OS while IBM thought the operating system choice should be left to the consumers. Apple was proving so difficult to deal with that IBM contemplated just buying the company outright to get its way. When Spindler himself proposed merging, IBM was more than willing to talk, and by the fall it looked like it was going to happen, only to come undone at the last moment (see "From Diesel To Doctor," page 183).

On September 19, 1994, Apple announced it would initially sign up a maximum of six Mac licensees and would not restrict them in any way. Even with its wide-open proposal, Apple had difficulty signing even one licensee. Potential cloners questioned Apple's commitment to long-term licensing and wondered how they could compete effectively against Apple, which, by all rights, should have enjoyed massive economies of scale when it came to buying the many proprietary components required to build a Mac. If it was going to make licensing work, Apple realized it needed to change its thinking. It decided to license the existing Mac OS and hardware while working toward a day when the two wouldn't be so tightly integrated. To that end, on November 7, Apple, IBM, and Motorola announced intentions to jointly design the Common Hardware Reference Platform that Big Blue had proposed the previous year. Apple hoped hardware manufacturers would be more willing to license the Mac OS if they could build CHRP-compliant machines using industry-standard parts rather than rely on Apple for the Mac hardware as well as the operating system. IBM and Motorola hoped to encourage more vendors to build systems around their PowerPC chip so that they could reduce its costs with increased volume.

> "We believe that an openly licensed Mac OS running on top of an open, industry standard RISC hardware platform represents a broadside against the reigning Wintel platform, and will play a key role in our ongoing efforts to greatly increase the presence of Macintosh in all markets. Simply put, we believe today's announcement is good news for anyone who believes in innovation, competition, and responding to customer needs."
>
> *Apple CEO **Michael Spindler**, announcing the CHRP agreement*

Power Computing, a small startup lead by Stephen Kahng and staffed by former Apple engineers, was the first company to receive a Macintosh license.

Unable to interest any major players even after committing to CHRP, Apple granted the first Mac license to a startup called Power Computing. The company had been founded by Stephen S. "King" Kahng in November 1993 with backing from European PC vendor Ing. C. Olivetti & Compagnia SpA. Kahng—an engineer who in the 1980s designed the popular Leading Edge line of IBM PC clones—founded Power Computing with the express purpose of selling Mac clones via mail order. Formal talks with Apple began in April 1994, and it took until December 16 for Kahng to secure the first Mac license, which

Spindler's fears about licensing are best summarized in Apple's SEC filings: "There can be no assurance that the installed base will be broadened by the licensing of the operating system or that licensing will result in an increase in the number of application software titles or the rate at which vendors will bring to market application software based on the Mac OS. In addition, as a result of licensing its operating system, the Company is forced to compete with other companies producing Mac OS-based computer systems. The benefits to the Company from licensing the Mac OS to third parties may be more than offset by the disadvantages of being required to compete with them."

Courtesy of Power Computing

Power Computing aggressively attacked the Mac market with high-performance models using as many industry-standard parts as possible to compete on price. CEO Kahng, an avid golfer, vowed not to play a round of golf until he had shipped 30,000 Mac clones. He didn't have to wait long. Apple sold 4.5 million Macs in 1995, whereas Apple's clone partners—which had grown to include DayStar Digital, Pioneer Electronics, and Umax—sold only 200,000 units combined, but Power Computing accounted for a quarter of those sales.

he proudly announced to the world two days after Christmas. Apple was reluctant to start its licensing efforts with such small fry, but Spindler had promised to announce a licensee by year end, and Power Computing was the only company ready with a Mac clone. On January 5, 1995, Apple followed up by granting another license to long-time Mac monitor maker Radius. Both Radius and Power Computing were relatively small companies unable to build many computers, nonetheless Apple promised that a million clones would be sold by the end of 1995. Spindler's goal was to double Apple's market share from 10 percent to 20 percent by adding 1 percent each year for five years, and allowing the clone makers to match that. Apple's greatest concern was that the clone vendors wouldn't expand the market, but simply cannibalize sales at Apple's expense.

Seeing that Apple had finally committed to licensing in January 1995, Gateway 2000, a huge mail-order vendor of Wintel systems, called Spindler to inquire about obtaining a Mac license. It was willing to devote 200 people in the hopes of building a $300 million Mac business. By May, the contracts were waiting for signatures, but Apple got cold feet. In February, Power Computing had opened its manufacturing plant in Austin, Texas, and it had just shipped the first Mac clone that May with the help of many former Apple engineers who had developed the first Power Macs and had grown frustrated with Cupertino's corporate culture. Cheaper and faster than Apple's Macs, the Power clones found a ready market and received rave reviews. Power aggressively pursued the high end of the market where margins were fattest, and Apple felt Power was just stealing sales, not growing the Mac market. If an upstart like Power could cause Apple grief, who knew what sort of pain an established vendor like Gateway could inflict? Instead of worrying about the Mac's dwindling share of the overall PC market in the face of Wintel clones, Spindler remained focused on Apple's share of the Mac market in the face of Mac clones, and as a result, he nixed the Gateway deal.

A year after announcing CHRP, Apple, IBM, and Motorola released the specifications on November 13, 1995, at the Fall COMDEX in Las Vegas. At that time, CHRP was renamed the PowerPC Microprocessor Common Hardware Reference Platform, or simply the PowerPC Platform (PPCP). PowerPC alliance members hoped to ship PPCP systems in the second half of 1996. On January 31, 1996, shortly before Spindler's resignation, Apple gave the first public demonstration of the Mac OS running on PPCP at the Demo 96 trade show.

Spindler, a grudging supporter of Mac cloning, was replaced by Gilbert F. Amelio as chairman and CEO in February 1996. Within two

Gil Amelio strongly supported Mac licensing.

weeks, Apple announced that it had licensed System 7.5.X and its long-delayed Copland (see "The Copland Crisis," page 225) to the Motorola Computer Group. The deal allowed Motorola to distribute the Mac OS with its own computer systems (to be introduced in China in late 1996) and sublicense the operating system to other manufacturers who bought its motherboards. This was a big break with past policy. Now potential cloners could deal with a third party for all their needs rather than put up with Apple's arrogant and arbitrary demands, although Apple retained the right to certify all systems sold with the Mac OS to ensure compatibility. On May 6, Apple licensed the Mac OS to IBM in a deal similar to Motorola's, except that IBM planned to make its clones available worldwide. According to Jesse Parker, director of segment marketing in IBM's Microelectronics Division, "IBM at various times had discussed the possibility of licensing the Mac OS from Apple. However, it wasn't until Gil Amelio joined the company that discussions began to proceed more quickly. While Gil Amelio wasn't directly involved in the day-to-day negotiations, it was clear to me that his influence and direction helped move things along." For his part, Amelio said, "Our primary motivation is to expand the platform," and vowed, "We will be enthusiastic licensers."

> "We will aggressively license the Mac OS to serious players."
>
> *CEO **Gilbert Amelio**, speaking at Apple's WWDC in May 1996*

Courtesy of UMAX Data Systems Inc.

UMAX bought Radius' Mac license and began selling its revamped SuperMac line.

In late May, UMAX Data Systems Inc., a Taiwanese manufacturer of scanners, announced it had purchased Radius' Mac license after its clones failed to catch on with customers. By June, UMAX (www.umax.com) released its first low-cost SuperMac clones (originally the name of a manufacturer of Mac monitors acquired by Radius). Frank C. Huang, UMAX's chairman, said shipments were expected to hit between 150,000 and 200,000 units in the second half of the year, and he hoped to sell 400,000 to 500,000 clones in 1997.

Although Mac clone vendors had been only moderately successful so far, Apple remained worried about their effect on the bottom line. Apple earned a flat fee of $50 for every clone sold, but CFO Fred D. Anderson estimated that for each high-end sale that went to a cloner rather than Apple, the company lost ten times as much in profit. Apple's finances didn't allow it to subsidize cloners at that rate for long. In rereading the licensing agreements, Amelio saw a loophole that would allow him to address this problem. The license granted the cloners the right to System 7.5 and its updates. The update following System 7.6 was code-named Tempo and was expected to be called System 7.7 when released in July 1997. But if it were called Mac OS 8 instead, Apple could legally renegotiate the clone contracts for more favorable terms, and that's exactly what it set out to do. The clone community leaked word of the tactic to the press in hope of fostering a public outcry but eventually was willing to compromise to keep the business functioning.

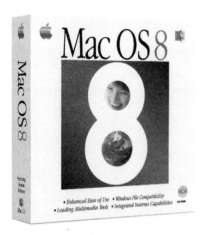

Apple renamed Tempo Mac OS 8, giving it an excuse to renegotiate license agreements.

In November 1996, Power Computing hired Joel J. Kocher as president and COO. Kocher had overseen Dell Computer's phenomenal growth in the early 1990s, and Kahng hoped he could do the same for Power. Kocher gave the go-ahead to begin construction of PowerTown, a long-planned 150-acre, $28 million headquarters in Georgetown, Texas. On December 27, Kocher signed a new agreement with Apple that increased the royalty rate and granted Power Computing a license to the upcoming Mac OS 8, or so he thought. Kocher also sought to reduce Power Computing's reliance on Apple and initiated the groundwork for producing Wintel clones by 1998. That would require additional funding, so an initial public offering was planned for the coming May.

Instead of basking in the glory of an oversubscribed IPO, Power Computing started to fear for its survival in the spring of 1997. Apple had just purchased NeXT Software to shore up its operating system plans, and had gotten the advisory services of founder Steve Jobs as part of the bargain. During a fireside chat at Apple's Worldwide Developers Conference (WWDC) on May 16, Jobs asserted his belief that clone vendors should pay more for the privilege of making Macs. Instead of a flat fee of $50 per unit, the price should be based on the volume and price of computers sold, he felt. He referred to cloners as "leeches" and chided them for going "ballistic" over renegotiating their licenses. It was clear that Jobs was no fan of licensing, but at least Amelio was still CEO.

On June 4, Power Computing's Kocher reached a basic agreement with Amelio on licensing terms for Mac OS 8, Rhapsody, and PPCP and two weeks later committed the terms to paper. With a signed license in hand, Power Computing filed an S-1 with the SEC on June 30, the first official step in an IPO that was likely to be a success. Power Computing was the fastest-growing PC company of the 1990s. It had grabbed almost 10 percent of the Mac market, generating $11 million in profit on sales of $246 million in 1996, and its revenues reached $84 million in the first quarter of 1997. Then everything was thrown into doubt with Amelio's July 9 surprise resignation and Jobs' assuming the role of strategic advisor at Apple.

On July 22, Apple shipped Mac OS 8 to consumers but refused to allow clone makers to include it on their systems, causing fits at Power Computing, which thought it had signed a deal for the new operating system. On the eve of the Macworld Expo in Boston on August 5, Kocher criticized Jobs and Apple for the new antagonistic stance toward cloners, warning, "If the platform goes closed, it is over. Total destruction. Closed is the kiss of death." He urged attendees to force Apple to address the licensing issue in public. To rally them to his cause, Kocher demonstrated a new 275MHz desktop clone based upon the latest generation PowerPC 750 chip (code-named Arthur and released by Apple as the G3), as well as a notebook based upon the same chip. When the audience burst into applause, Kocher snapped, "Don't clap, because I don't have the confidence that you will ever see this because Apple has yet to license the PowerBook design."

The week following Macworld Expo, in a 10-Q filing with the SEC, Apple hinted that the advantages of having opened its market to clone makers might be offset by the disadvantages inherent in competition. Days later Apple notified clone makers that it would not accept any PPCP machines for certification. In a classic Catch-22, Apple refused to ship Mac OS 8 to clone makers if their machines lacked certification. Guerrino De Luca, Apple executive VP of marketing, insisted, "We want to continue to license, but not under terms that would kill the platform." The current agreements called for separate fees for the Mac OS and hardware designs. If cloners moved to the PPCP machines, Apple would get paid only for the Mac OS. Motorola Computer Group indicated it would proceed with its PPCP plans with or without Apple's blessing. "We believe we have the license to ship our [PPCP] model, and we will ship it," said Jurgen Reinold, chief technologist and architect for Motorola's StarMax 6000. A furious Kocher tried to convince the Power Computing board to take Apple to court for breach of contract. When the board refused, Kocher resigned on August 19, followed by most of his executive staff.

Jobs, who had once called Mac cloners "leeches," didn't take long to put an end to licensing after he took over from Amelio.

Power Computing invigorated the Mac market with irreverent marketing campaigns reminiscent of the Mac's glory days. President Kocher wanted to fight Jobs, too, but his board refused to support him.

Power Computing had decided it was better to surrender than to continue fighting a losing battle. On September 2, Apple announced it would acquire Power Computing's customer database, its license to distribute the Mac OS, and certain key employees for $100 million in Apple stock and roughly $10 million to cover debts and closing costs. As part of the deal, Power Computing agreed not to sue Apple for breach of contract. "Power Computing has pioneered direct marketing and sales in the Macintosh market, successfully building a $400 [million] business," said Jobs. "We look forward to learning from their experience, and welcoming their customers back into the Apple family."

In a memo to Apple employees explaining the acquisition, Jobs wrote, "The primary reason is that the license fee Apple receives from the licensees does not begin to cover their share of the expenses to engineer and market the Mac OS platform. This means that, in essence, Apple is giving a several hundred dollar subsidy with each licensed copy of the Mac OS. Our Board is convinced that if Apple continues this practice the company will never return to profitability, no matter how well Apple performs, and the entire Macintosh 'ecosystem' will continue to decline, eventually killing both Apple and the clone manufacturers. This scenario has no winners." Jobs went on to say that Apple wouldn't acquire any other cloners and would continue to honor its current license agreements but wouldn't expand them to include a version of Mac OS for PPCP, nor would it renew them when they expired.

On September 8, 1997, Apple extended UMAX Data Systems' license through July 1998, allowing it to bundle Mac OS 8 with its clones, but not on PPCP systems. UMAX was spared Power's fate since it had aggressively pursued the low-end market where Apple had no offerings, rather than attack the fat margins at the high end.On September 11, Motorola discontinued its StarMax line and suspended future Mac clone efforts; IBM followed suit shortly thereafter. In May 1998, UMAX exited the Mac clone market after having lost roughly $36 million.

Power Computing was to retain its name and remain an independent company. It intended to sell Mac clones through the end of 1997, or as long as supplies lasted. Apple promised to provide Mac OS support for Power Computing customers, with Power Computing remaining responsible for hardware and warranty service. Power Computing reiterated its intention to expand its focus to include Wintel clones but was forced to halt production in December 1997 because of parts shortages. On January 29, 1998, an auction was held to sell the last of Power Computing's physical assets. Though he will never admit it openly, Jobs single-handedly pulled the plug on Power Computing and killed the clone issue once and for all at Apple.

"The show is over, the monkey is dead, and they've folded the tent."

Security guard, *on the day of Power Computing's asset auction*

Trademark Tiffs

Want to get rich? It's easy. Just think up a whole bunch of cool product names and create a few nifty logos, then secure the trademarks and sit tight. If you're lucky, eventually Apple will decide it just has to have the rights to your trademark. Now you're in the position to ask for whatever you think Apple will pay. If the following cases are any example, the sky's the limit, so think big and carry a hot-shot lawyer in your hip pocket.

Apple Battles Beatles

According to Steve Wozniak, it was Steve Jobs who thought up the name for their new computer company one afternoon in early 1976 as the two drove along Highway 85 between Palo Alto and Los Altos. "Steve was still half involved with a group of friends who ran the commune-type All-One Farm in Oregon. And he would go up and work there for a few months before returning to the Bay Area. He had just come back from one of his trips and we were driving along and he said 'I've got a great name: Apple Computer.' Maybe he worked in apple trees. I didn't even ask. Maybe it had some other meaning to him. Maybe the idea just occurred based upon Apple Records. He had been a musical person, like many technical people are. It might have sounded good partly because of that connotation. I thought instantly, 'We're going to have a lot of copyright problems.' But we didn't. Both of us tried to think of technical-sounding mixtures of words, like Executek and Matrix Electronics, but after ten minutes of trying, we both realized we weren't going to beat Apple Computer."

It briefly occurred to Woz that they might have some trouble with Apple Corps, the Beatles' recording company, but he dismissed the thought. Perhaps they should have done a little more brainstorming, because that name would end up costing them dearly. As it turned out, Apple Corps didn't take kindly to anyone infringing on their trademark, and in November 1981, Apple Computer and Apple Corps entered into a secret agreement that placed certain restrictions on the use and registration of their respective Apple trademarks. Essentially,

Apple's name recognition was so low in Japan during the early 1980s that workers there used refrigerated trucks to deliver shipments of Apple computers under the mistaken assumption that the boxes contained perishable fruit.

When Apple Corps sued Apple Computer in 1989, System 7 was still under development. One of the new features of System 7 was the ability to record your own system beeps in the Sound control panel using a microphone. An engineer had created a sound called Xylophone (described as a staccato E-flat diminished triad sound), which caused Apple's legal department to freak, since Apple Corps might take umbrage at the Mac's ability to record voice and music. Jim Reekes, the ultimate authority concerning system beeps, changed the name to Sosumi (pronounced *so-sue-me*) and informed the legal department that the word was Japanese for "the absence of all musicality" or "a light pleasing tone," depending on who is telling the story.

Apple Computer paid the British company an undisclosed sum for the worldwide rights to use the Apple name on computer products, but Apple Corps retained the rights in the music field.

In February 1989, Apple Corps filed suit against Apple Computer in London seeking unspecified damages, charging that Apple violated the terms of the trademark coexistence agreement by marketing products with music synthesizing capabilities. Specifically cited in the suit were the Mac Plus, SE, and II; the Apple IIGS and IIGS upgrade kit for the Apple IIe; the AppleCD SC drive; and Apple's MIDI (Musical Instrument Digital Interface) device. The Beatles' law firm suggested that Apple change its name to Banana or Peach if it wanted to continue making music products and estimated that Apple Corps would ultimately be paid $50 million to $200 million in royalties. Although Apple maintained that it had not broken the 1981 agreement, on October 9, 1991, it settled by paying Apple Corps $26.5 million.

Cold Cash for Classic

The Classic name cost a cool million.

As it prepared to make a serious push into the low end of the market with its October 1990 introduction of three new computers—the Macintosh Classic, LC, and IIsi—Apple got some unwelcome news. Someone else already owned the computer industry trademark rights to the Classic name: Modular Computer Systems Inc. (www.modcomp.com) of Fort Lauderdale, Florida. The company had been manufacturing the ModComp Classic, a series of real-time computer systems for the control and automation markets, since 1978. Apparently Apple was very much enamored of the Classic name because it entered into a five-year, renewable $1 million contract to acquire the rights to the name for use in the personal computer market. According to MODCOMP (the company changed its name in August 1997), Apple did not renew the contract when it expired. Apple last used the name on the Color Classic II, introduced on October 21, 1993.

What's the Big Idea?

In 1991, Alfred J. Mandel founded a Palo Alto-based marketing consulting firm called the Big Idea Group (www.bigideagroup.com) and produced a calligraphic logo of a lightbulb, the universal cartoon symbol for an idea. After Apple began promoting its Newton technology in 1992, Mandel received calls from friends asking if he had had anything to do with the personal digital assistant because the Newton logo Apple was using in its brochures and ads looked suspiciously like the BIG logo.

Mandel initially offered Apple a non-exclusive license to use his firm's logo on the Newton. After all, he had worked at Apple from 1982 to 1986—first on printer products for the Lisa and then as the event marketing manager for the Macintosh—and he bore no ill will toward his former employer. Uncomfortable with such an arrangement, Apple's legal department tried to establish that the BIG logo was based upon prior art. Anxious to avoid a protracted lawsuit, Mandel sold Apple the logo on July 29, 1993, with the provision that he could continue using it for one year. BIG switched to using a photorealistic representation of a lightbulb for its logo. Terms of the settlement remain confidential to this day.

Separated at birth? The Newton logo (left) bears an uncanny resemblance to BIG's logo.

Cosmos Carl

The November 29, 1993 issue of *MacWEEK* featured a cover story on three computers Apple would introduce on March 14, 1994, as the Power Macintosh 6100/60, 7100/66, and 8100/80. The story mentioned in passing that the computers went by the code names PDM, Carl Sagan, and Cold Fusion, respectively. Upon reading this, Carl Sagan, the astronomer, fired off the following letter, which appeared in the January 10, 1994 issue of *MacWEEK*:

Due to legal concerns, the code name for the Power Macintosh 7100/66 first changed from Carl Sagan to BHA and finally to LAW.

> I have been approached many times over the past two decades by individuals and corporations seeking to use my name and/or likeness for commercial purposes. I have always declined, no matter how lucrative the offer or how important the corporation. My endorsement is not for sale. For this reason, I was profoundly distressed to see your lead front-page story "Trio of PowerPC Macs spring toward March release date" proclaiming Apple's announcement of a new Mac bearing my name. That this was done without my authorization or knowledge is especially disturbing. Through my attorneys, I have repeatedly requested Apple to make a public clarification that I knew nothing of its intention to capitalize on my reputation in introducing this product, that I derived no benefit, financial or otherwise, from its doing so. Apple has refused. I would appreciate it if you would so apprise your readership.
>
> Carl Sagan
> Director, Laboratory for Planetary Studies
> Center for Radiophysics and Space Research
> Cornell University
> Ithaca, NY

Most Mac users felt Sagan should have been honored by the code name; it was never meant to be the final product name, so they thought he should lighten up. It has been suggested that what upset Sagan the most was being grouped with two discredited scientific "discoveries," Piltdown Man (PDM) and Cold Fusion.

In deference to the noted star-gazer, Apple changed the Power Macintosh 7100/66 code name to BHA. Relations between Apple and the astronomer were beginning to return to normal when Sagan learned that BHA supposedly stood for Butt-Head Astronomer. He put pressure on Apple's lawyers, who insisted the project engineers come up with a new name. They settled on LAW, which stands for Lawyers Are Wimps. Nonetheless, in the third week of April 1994, Sagan sued Apple in U.S. District Court in Los Angeles, charging it with defamation of character. He sought unspecified damages.

Judge Lourdes G. Baird found that the statement was mere opinion, thereby eliminating the libel claim. She also ruled that Sagan could not recover for infliction of emotional distress, noting that Sagan, as a public figure, could only recover for infliction of emotional distress by showing that a false statement of fact was made with actual malice. Baird's finding stated that "Plaintiff's libel action is based on the allegation that Defendant changed the 'code name' on its personal computer from 'Carl Sagan' to 'Butt-Head Astronomer' after Plaintiff had requested that Defendant cease use of Plaintiff's name ... There can be no question that the use of the figurative term 'Butt-Head' negates the impression that Defendant was seriously implying an assertion of fact. It strains reason to conclude that Defendant was attempting to criticize Plaintiff's reputation of competency as an astronomer. One does not seriously attack the expertise of a scientist using the undefined phrase 'Butt-Head.' Thus, the figurative language militates against implying an assertion of fact ... Furthermore, the tenor of any communication of the information, especially the phrase 'Butt-Head Astronomer' would negate the impression that Defendant was implying an assertion of fact."

Sagan appealed the decision to the Ninth Circuit Court of Appeals, and on November 15, 1995, the two parties reached "an amicable settlement," although the terms remain confidential to this day. Paul D. Carmichael, Apple's director of patents and trademarks, publicly stated, "Dr. Sagan has made great contributions in many areas of higher learning and in particular has made complex subject matter interesting and understandable to a wide audience. Apple has always had great respect for Dr. Sagan, and it was never Apple's intention to cause Dr. Sagan or his family any embarrassment or concern."

Carl Sagan died Friday, December 20, 1996, in Seattle at the age of 62, of complications arising from bone marrow cancer.

IBM Sings the Blues

Apple isn't the only company to experience trademark problems. Even its long-time rival, International Business Machines, has had its share of trouble. In 1984, entrepreneur Jeffrey G. Alnwick of Huntington, New York, established a family-owned computer wholesale company called Big Blue Products Incorporated (www.bigblue-usa.com) by reviving a defunct concern called Big Blue Corporation that had sold IBM System 23s. Things were going fine until May 1989, when $63 billion IBM (www.ibm.com) sent an intimidating letter to $2 million Big Blue Products, claiming "Big Blue is a trademark of the IBM Corporation," and giving Alnwick 30 days to cease using the name.

Alnwick decided to fight back. His trademark attorney discovered that IBM never properly registered the name Big Blue, so he put in his own application with the U.S. Patent and Trademark Office. When IBM got wind of this, it objected and filed its own application. While both sides' applications were wending their way though the trademark office, IBM's lawyers summoned Alnwick to their offices and told him to name his price, no matter how ridiculous. "$28 million," Alnwick blurted out. "That's ridiculous!" IBM protested, and negotiations collapsed. A few years later, IBM won a summary judgement to throw out Alnwick's "frivolous" trademark application, but he appealed and won, in part because IBM admitted that it didn't call itself Big Blue, others did.

In early November 1995, after spending over $50,000 in attorney's fees, Alnwick finally won the right to the Big Blue name from the trademark office. His first order of business was to turn around and send IBM a lightly reworded copy of its own 1989 "cease and desist" letter. "I don't know what the Big Blue name is worth, but IBM is going to regret this," promised Alnwick, claiming several computer companies are interested in marketing hardware and software under the Big Blue name that he now owns.

"It isn't clear how IBM got the nickname [Big Blue] in the first place: some say it's because IBM used to paint its enormous mainframes blue in the 1960s; others note its large, homogeneous sales force always wore blue suits. And, of course, there's the fact that the company logo is blue. IBM itself never used the name much, though for a brief time Big Blue appeared as a brand name on IBM typewriter ribbons."

The Wall Street Journal, *11/13/95*

The Clarion Call of Clerus

In 1985, electrical engineer Lloyd Douglas Clark founded a company to develop scientific instrumentation and specialized academia software for the Apple II and IBM PC. The firm was christened Clerus Laboratories because *clerus* is Latin for *clark*. On July 9, 1987, the phone starting ringing off the hook in his tiny San Francisco offices. That was the day Apple announced the name of its new software subsidiary: Claris Corporation. "We chose the name Claris for its inherent marketing appeal, reflecting clarity and distinctiveness, and to remind us that shaping the future requires a clear vision," said William V. Campbell, then president of Claris and formerly Apple's executive VP for U.S. sales and marketing.

Clark asked the federal Patent and Trademark Office to block Apple's registration of Claris, arguing that several years of active use of the Clerus name in the software field gave it trademark status. "Apple attorneys came out of the woodwork," recalls Clark. "There was a lot of shouting and yelling, but in the end we shook hands and they apologized." Apple acquired the rights to the Claris name, and Clark was given 90 days to stop using Clerus. Although terms of the agreement remain confidential to this day, Clark does allow that he offered to accept "a quarter or half of the settlement in memory chips," which were quite scarce and costly at the time, but Apple's lawyers scoffed at the proposal. A few months later the memory market was glutted and prices collapsed, so Clark enjoyed the last laugh after all.

In 1989, Clark renamed his scientific instrumentation company Paedia (www.paedia.com), derived from the Greek word meaning "the teaching of concepts in art and science." As luck would have it, Encyclopaedia Britannica tried to have Clark's registration for this name canceled in 1995, alleging it had been "abandoned." Faced with protracted litigation, he allowed the publisher to use the term in a very limited way in exchange for $3,500.

For its part, Claris went on to great success in the Macintosh and Windows markets, until Apple bewildered the software industry on January 27, 1998, by announcing that the subsidiary would be restructured to focus exclusively on its database product, FileMaker Pro (www.filemaker.com) and that the remaining best-selling Claris titles would be absorbed into Apple.

Blowin' Smoke in the Wind

In parallel with the Newton project (see "The Fallen Apple," page 143), engineers were also developing a programming language under the code name Ralph (after Ralph Ellison, author of *Invisible Man*). When the Newton team decided to pursue the Pocket Newt (code-named Junior) device, which lacked the power and memory Ralph required, the programming language was repurposed for use on the Macintosh. As the Mac version of Ralph neared completion, Apple decided to name the product Dylan, which stood for dynamic language. Beta versions were distributed on CDs at the Apple Worldwide Developers Conference in May 1994. On August 24, 1994, folk singer Bob Dylan sued Apple for trademark infringement in the U.S. Central District Court of California in Los Angeles.

Courtesy of Sony Music and Mark Seliger

It's ironic that Bob Dylan would sue Apple over the use of the name Dylan, considering he was born in Duluth, Minnesota, on May 24, 1941, as Robert Zimmerman and legally adopted the first name of early 20th-century Welsh poet Dylan Thomas in August 1962.

Bob Dylan took exception to Apple's use of his last name for a programming language.

Seeking unspecified damages, Dylan's lawyer, Joseph A. Yanny, requested a temporary restraining order barring Apple from using Bob Dylan's name in conjunction with any new software product. According to the lawsuit, "Apple is intentionally using, and intentionally has used, the names of famous individuals, including (Isaac) Newton, Carl Sagan and now Dylan, in conjunction with Apple's products in a deliberate attempt to capitalize on the goodwill associated with these famous individuals."

Shortly after the suit was filed, Apple reached a confidential out-of-court settlement and obtained the rights to trademark Dylan. In a December 14, 1994 FAQ distributed to developers, Apple explained, "It is our intention to license the Dylan trademark to any implementation which passes a standard test suite. The purpose of the trademark is to ensure quality and consistency among implementations." At that time, Apple was planning to release Dylan for 68000-based Macs in mid-1995.

Whatever problems Apple had previously with Dylan were swept aside in 1997 when Apple began using the singer's image in its *Think Different* advertising campaign, presumably with Dylan's approval.

Apple shipped Dylan in the fall of 1995, then abandonded the effort on November 17 during an overall reduction in research and development. Once Sun Microsystems' Java caught on in the Internet community, Apple reasoned that there really was no reason for it to continue developing Dylan. However, Harlequin Inc. of Cambridge, Massachusetts (www.harlequin.com), forged ahead with work on a version for Wintel clones. Harlequin's first implementation of Dylan targeted at Windows 95 and Windows NT shipped in mid-1998.

The Doctor's Strong Medicine

Courtesy of HarperBusiness and David Powers

Dr. Gil Amelio was given only 17 months to restore Apple to health before being booted.

Dr. Gilbert Frank Amelio's tenure as Apple's CEO was short and sour. When he took over the company, it was in the worst shape in its rocky history. He calmly surveyed the landscape, devised a no-frills recovery plan, and methodically went about its implementation. His efforts were often stymied by entrenched Apple executives, unforgiving market realities, and meddling outsiders. He probably could have overcome all of these obstacles had he not been blindsided by an advisor he himself brought back into the Apple fold with the gutsy purchase of NeXT: Steve Jobs.

> "Apple is a lot like Italy. It's a highly creative company, but with that comes chaos."
> *Marketing executive **Regis McKenna***

Amelio had earned a reputation as a "transformation manager" by helping reverse the fortunes of Rockwell International and National Semiconductor, the fourth-largest computer chip manufacturer. When he arrived at National Semiconductor on February 1, 1991, as chairman, president, and CEO, the firm was near bankruptcy, having suffered four consecutive years of losses totaling $320 million. In 1995, it reported its third straight year of profits, earning a record $264 million on sales of $2.4 billion. While it hadn't enjoyed the same growth as the overall booming chip market, National Semiconductor had clearly been pulled from the fire. Apple needed a man with Amelio's talents and so elected him to the board on November 9, 1994.

> "If [Apple's board] had called me, I would have recommended that Amelio was absolutely the wrong man for the job. He left National in a disaster."
> *Former National Semiconductor CEO*
> ***Charles Sporck***

The situation at Apple continued to deteriorate during 1995 under the leadership of CEO and chairman Michael H. Spindler. By December the rumor mill was operating around the clock, producing fresh reports of takeover and merger possibilities. Sensing that Spindler was mortally wounded, Jobs paid an unprecedented call to National Semiconductor and asked Amelio to back his bid to return to Apple as CEO, stating, "There's only one person who can rally the Apple troops, only one person who can straighten out the company. Apple is on its way out of business. The only thing that can save it is a strong leader, somebody who can rally employees, the press, users, and developers." Of course, Jobs considered himself that person, but when Amelio pressed him for details on his recovery plan, Jobs failed to provide any concrete solutions and left without Amelio's support. The significance of the meeting was lost on Amelio at the time, but Jobs wouldn't forget.

As Jobs had predicted, Apple's board was indeed dissatisfied with Spindler's performance. He had failed to find an acceptable merger partner for Apple and had presided over a series of quarterly losses and declining market share. During a January 31, 1996 emergency meeting of Apple's board at the New York law firm of Shearman and Sterling, Spindler was replaced by Amelio, who brought considerable managerial experience and technical knowledge to the position. He holds 16 patents and co-invented the world's first charge-coupled device (CCD), which is used in most video cameras produced today. Amelio earned a Ph.D. in physics from the Georgia Institute of Technology, entitling him to be addressed as "Doctor Amelio."

"It's nice to work for a CEO whose idea of technology is not how to put 64 ounces of sugar water in a plastic bottle."
*Apple Fellow **Guy Kawasaki**, praising Amelio while dissing Sculley*

Amelio stated he took the difficult job because, "I was frustrated by the deficiencies of the product and the organization behind it. I'm trying to help one of America's all-time great companies." To help convince him to take the position, the board agreed to a lucrative compensation package. Amelio negotiated a salary of $990,000, $296,000 more than he was earning at National Semiconductor. He was also to receive a two-part bonus. The first component was based on performance, with a range from $324,000 to $1,900,000 for 1996 (he got $1,134,000). By way of comparison, Spindler earned a total of $1.42 million in his last year at Apple. Amelio was also given a $200,000 signing bonus, a $5 million loan, an agreement to reimburse Aero Ventures for the business use of his Israeli Industries' twin-engine Astra Jet at a rate of $1,695 per hour, and a guaranteed payment of $10 million if the company was sold within a year and the acquiring company terminated his employment or he elected to quit within 30 days. In addition to all these goodies, he was to receive $1 million a year for five years to be credited against the loan, plus options on one million shares with an exercise price of $26.25, which would vest over five years based upon performance objectives. According to Pearl Meyer, a New York compensation consultant, Amelio's total compensation package was worth from $10 to $12 million a year, depending on performance. Angry shareholders initially filed a class action suit against Apple in March 1996, charging that Amelio's pay package was "wildly excessive," but it was never pursued seriously. Amelio defended his pay, saying, "Frankly, it was a very competitive package, in the 75th percentile of executive compensation."

When he arrived on the Apple campus on February 5, Amelio resolved "to build a business as great as our products," but it wouldn't be easy. As he recalls, "When I walked in the door, I was facing five crises: we were dangerously low on cash; the quality of our products was poor; the development of our next-generation [operating system] was behind schedule and in disarray; Apple's famously contrarian corporate culture was almost impossible to manage; and our product line and development efforts were fragmented to the point that the company was completely unfocused."

Despite its myriad problems, Amelio confidently stated, "We have ourselves in a little trouble now. The troubles are very fixable. I've been down this road before." Amelio asked the public to give him 100 days to study the company's problems and come up with answers. He predicted that Apple would return to profitability within nine months to a year and attain sustainable health within three years, but to get well Apple would have to swallow some powerful medicine. On March 27, Apple warned Wall Street of "an anticipated second fiscal quarter net after-tax loss of around $700 million," the biggest quarterly loss ever for a company based in Silicon Valley. When the final numbers were released April 17, Apple reported a $740 million net loss; $388 million went toward lowering the value of Apple's inventory of unsold Macs and components. Amelio explained, "The company had lost that money already. It just hadn't recognized it." About $130 million covered restructuring charges related to laying off 2,800 employees (up from the 1,300 job cuts Spindler announced in January). The remainder represented Apple's loss on operations. Following the huge loss, Amelio worked with newly hired CFO Fred D. Anderson to clean up the balance sheet by further writing off inventories, floating a new bond issue (crucial since the company had only $592 million in cash—enough to operate for just five weeks), and selling manufacturing sites around the globe.

Amelio's 100-day honeymoon ended on May 13, at Apple's Worldwide Developers Conference (WWDC) in San Jose. By all

> "I don't think anyone can manage Apple."
> *Former Apple CEO **John Sculley**,*
> *on the mess Amelio inherited*

> "The cure for Apple is not cost-cutting. The cure for Apple is to innovate its way out of its current predicament."
> *NeXT and Pixar CEO **Steve Jobs***

> "A year from now people will look back and wonder 'what was all the fuss about?'"
>
> *Apple CEO* **Gil Amelio**

In a move calculated to show that Apple had not given up on fine industrial design, Amelio announced that Apple would produce a limited run of a special Macintosh to celebrate the twentieth anniversary of Apple's incorporation. Little was revealed at WWDC, but when it shipped in June 1997, the Twentieth Anniversary Mac (code-named Spartacus) featured an active-matrix color LCD borrowed from the PowerBook line and an Alchemy logic board with a 250MHz PowerPC 603e from the Performa 6400. It came with an upright mounted 4x CD-ROM drive, 32MB RAM, Bose Acoustimass sound system, and in-home "concierge" set-up service. A Massachusetts factory produced only 11,601 units, initially priced at $7,500. With comparable Power Macs available for less than $2,000, the Twentieth Anniversary Mac wasn't a best-seller, even after Apple dropped the price by two thirds. One bright note: a shiny Twentieth Anniversary Mac could be seen in the corner of Jerry's living room during the final season of *Seinfeld*.

Apple was named the worst-run company of 1996 by investment giant CalPERS (California Public Employees' Retirement System).

accounts, Amelio seemed to have done his homework and offered a litany of solutions that appealed to the crowd and demonstrated that he understood the problems Apple was facing. "Number one is we've got to get back to basics and the fundamental business of how we design, how we develop, how we produce, and how we service," said Amelio. "And we have to do this far better than we've done it in the past. We need to simplify the product line. We need to simplify that a lot, because complexity costs money, and we've added costs unnecessarily as a consequence. We need to improve our time to market, get things out when we say we are, and stick to them." Acknowledging that Apple's clone effort had been half-hearted, Amelio vowed to "aggressively license the Mac OS to serious players." He also promised that Apple would no longer compete with developers, was in fact investing $18 million to produce the best development tools available, and had committed $20 million to get retail shelf space for Mac products. "Many people wonder if Apple will still be around in five years," acknowledged Amelio. "Hey, this is Apple, expect the impossible!"

With his crucial 100-day speech behind him, Amelio focused on getting Apple's operating system strategy back on track. He had promised to ship the long-delayed Copland in pieces beginning with the January 1997 release of Harmony (System 7.6) and followed by a release known as Tempo (Mac OS 8.0) six months later. To help him meet these goals, in July Amelio hired his National Semiconductor protégé Ellen M. Hancock as Apple's chief technology officer and executive VP, R&D. She soon came to the conclusion that Copland was a hopeless case and began shopping around outside the company for an alternative (see "The Copland Crisis," page 225).

After reporting a $32 million loss for the quarter ending June 28, Apple surprised everyone by announcing a small profit for its fourth fiscal quarter ending September 27. Revenues and unit shipments were both down compared to the same quarter a year ago, but up from the third quarter. Apple managed to post a profit of $25 million, largely as a result of reversed restructuring charges, a flurry of last-minute educational shipments, and some good old-fashioned channel stuffing. Still, it was the first sign of positive news from Cupertino in a long time. It was followed up by the December 20 announcement that Apple intended to buy NeXT Software in a friendly acquisition and bring Jobs back as an advisor. Although Apple agreed to pay $427 million for NeXT, it was hard to put a price on the public relations value of Jobs' return to the company he founded 20 years prior. Many applauded Amelio's grand gesture and willingness to overcome the "Not Invented Here" syndrome so commonplace in the high-technology industry, while wondering if he hadn't just signed his own termination agreement by bringing back Jobs.

The NeXT acquisition demonstrated that it wasn't business as usual at Apple anymore. The adults were finally in charge and willing to take bold, decisive actions. When Amelio walked onstage in the San Francisco Marriott ballroom to give the Macworld Expo keynote address on January 7, 1997, it should have been his finest hour, but instead, it was a disastrous three hours. He rambled on, discussing the $120 million loss in the previous quarter ended December 27, showing off prototypes of various projects in the works, introducing various celebrities, and unveiling the Twentieth Anniversary Macintosh. The only thing that kept the standing-room-only crowd of 2,000 awake was the hope that Jobs would make an appearance. Finally, after over two torturous hours, Amelio trotted out Jobs and the crowd went wild, celebrating his triumphant return after eleven years in exile. In a half hour, Jobs smoothly outlined how Apple would merge elements of Copland with NEXTSTEP to produce a new operating system named Rhapsody. Jobs' appearance was short and to the point, and it demonstrated that in the court of public opinion, Amelio didn't stand a chance against Apple's founder. Amelio had a trump card up his sleeve, but it didn't go as planned. After Jobs' presentation, Amelio announced that Apple's other founder was also returning in an advisory role. As he took to the podium, Steve Wozniak received a resounding ovation and Jobs walked off in a huff, denying Amelio the golden photo op he had so carefully orchestrated.

After the keynote, Jobs was quick to point out that he was only a part-time consultant and said of his new role, "I'll advise Gil as much as I can, until I think they don't want my help or I decide they're not listening." As for Woz, Amelio explained, "I do expect him along with Steve Jobs to wander the halls. It's sort of like the bumblebee that goes from flower to flower, puts a little pollen here and there."

The press roundly criticized Amelio's unfocused Macworld keynote, and the financial pressure mounted with another quarterly loss. It was becoming increasingly apparent to Amelio that he didn't have the luxury of turning Apple around over the course of three years, the length of time he thought necessary. Apple could very well be in the midst of what he termed a "death spiral" in his book, *Profit from Experience: The National Semiconductor Story of Transformation Management*. In a January 16 broadcast to employees, Amelio reviewed the disappointing first quarter results and announced the likelihood of still more layoffs, stopping at one point to stare into the camera and growl, "Don't put me in this position again, dammit." Amelio

> "Steve is going to fuck Gil so hard his eardrums will pop."
> **Anonymous Apple alumnus**, warning Ellen Hancock that bringing Jobs back to Apple would threaten Amelio's leadership

> "In *Jurassic Park* and the upcoming *Lost World*, I play Ian Malcolm, an expert on chaos theory, so I figure that qualifies me to speak at an Apple event."
> Actor **Jeff Goldblum**, introducing Amelio during the Macworld Expo keynote address

> "Working at Apple is like a ride at Disneyland. You know, you always feel as though the bar is down and you're not going to be flung out of the car. This time it's kind of like the ride without the bar. And you just don't know what's going to happen."
>
> *Former director of the Advanced Systems Group* **Frank Casanova**, *when asked if he was worried about Apple's future*

> "By the time this [article] comes out, I should be chairman of Apple."
>
> *Oracle CEO* **Larry Ellison**, *boasting in the June 1997 edition of* Vanity Fair

Ellison was elected to Apple's board, but not as chairman, in August 1997 following Amelio's resignation.

was frustrated at the marketing and sales people who continued to assure him they would meet their quotas right up to the eleventh hour. Apple had fostered a mutinous corporate culture where the CEO was viewed as a figurehead and his orders mere suggestions that would often go unheeded. Every division had its own agenda, and getting them to march to a single drummer was like herding cats.

Aware that the hemorrhaging of Apple's finances was continuing and would result in a second quarter loss of $708 million, on February 4, Amelio announced an executive shuffle that had Jobs' fingerprints all over it. Jobs often referred to Hancock as a bozo who lacked personal computer experience, so it came as little surprise that most of her charges would from then on report either to Avadis "Avie" Tevanian Jr., Ph.D, formerly NeXT's VP of engineering, or Jon Rubinstein, former executive VP and COO of FirePower Systems, who once headed up NeXT's hardware unit. COO Marco Landi was stripped of marketing and operations responsibilities but left in charge of worldwide sales; he quit Apple just two weeks later. Essentially, Amelio's lieutenants had been demoted and Jobs' buddies put into positions of power at Apple, but still Jobs denied having any designs on the CEO spot. "People keep trying to suck me in," said Jobs. "They want me to be some kind of Superman. But I have no desire to run Apple Computer. I deny it at every turn, but nobody believes me."

Perhaps he didn't want to officially run Apple, but behind the scenes he was happy to advise Amelio on which products to keep or kill as the company streamlined its efforts, though he didn't always prevail. For example, Jobs wanted to kill the Newton division, but Amelio tried to sell it and, by late May, decided to spin it off as an independent company (see "The Fallen Apple," page 143). The reorganization was followed on March 14 by the announcement that Apple was cutting another 2,700 positions. "This time, I'm going to use the two-by-four approach," stated a hardened Amelio. "I'm going to put this place through the most gut-wrenching change it's ever had."

Shortly after the consummation of the NeXT deal on February 4, 1997, Jobs' best friend and Oracle CEO Lawrence J. Ellison began boasting to the press that he was again considering making a run at Apple and indicated he had lined up a group of investors that would be willing to back him if he decided to go forward with the plan. Apple's investment bankers informed Amelio there was little they could do to prevent Ellison from taking over if he made a reasonable offer for Apple. The thing that didn't make sense was that most hostile takeover attempts are kept quiet; Amelio suspected that Ellison's true motive was to shake the board's confidence in the job he was doing as CEO.

On March 25, Amelio met with the board to beg for an increase in advertising spending to prop up sales, which were down drastically and showed no immediate signs of recovery. The board of directors began to feel that they had made a mistake in handing the company over to Amelio the previous year. To them, Amelio didn't seem to be attacking problems with the urgency that was needed, and he wasn't the marketing whiz they wanted.

In April, the Ellison takeover rumors gained credibility when Prince Alwaleed bin Talal bin Abdulaziz Alsaud, the 41-year-old nephew of Saudi Arabia's King Saud, purchased 5 percent of Apple's stock, 6.23 million shares, at an average price of $18.52, for a total of $115.4 million in late March 1997. The prince indicated he thought Apple was a strong brand that had potential to regain its former glory and he was interested in listening to Ellison's proposal. For his part, Ellison called off his bid on April 29, but refused to rule out a future takeover attempt. Then on June 26, someone sold a block of 1.5 million shares of Apple stock for roughly $15 apiece. Although many speculated that Jobs had disposed of the shares he acquired when NeXT was purchased, he wouldn't comment on the matter. If an insider like Jobs was dumping every share he owned, that was an ominous sign for Apple, and it further rattled the board.

Apple's board of directors began a 36-hour series of telephone meetings on Independence Day to discuss the situation. On the morning of July 6, board member Edgar S. Woolard Jr. called Amelio at Stonewood, his Lake Tahoe mansion, and broke the news to him. "We think you need to step down," said Woolard. "You've done a lot to help the company, but the sales haven't rebounded." Amelio tried explaining that sales were often the last thing to recover after other aspects of the business were set straight, but Woolard was intransigent. He kept insisting that what Apple needed was a great sales and marketing leader, an idea Jobs had reinforced when the board consulted with him on the matter. Jobs assured Amelio that he had nothing to do with his ouster, but Amelio remains suspicious. "He said he didn't," claims Amelio. "I would say that the data seems to suggest otherwise."

Including the $56 million loss the company would report for the third quarter ended June 27, Apple had suffered over $1.6 billion in losses during Amelio's watch, an amount that wiped out all the profits generated since fiscal year 1991. How much of that loss Amelio is responsible for is hard to say. There's no question he inherited a company in awful shape and made many difficult decisions that had been postponed by his predecessors. The company was manufacturing

Following Apple's announcement of its third consecutive profitable quarter in July 1998, the stock price jumped to a value not seen in over two and one-half years, doubling Prince Alwaleed's investment.

On August 11, Jobs finally admitted he had sold the block of shares in June. "I pretty much had given up hope that the Apple board was going to do anything. I didn't think the stock was going up," he told *Time*. "If that upsets employees," he huffed, "I'm perfectly happy to go home to Pixar."

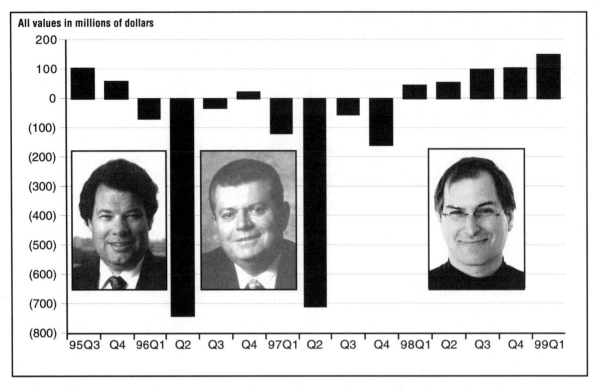

All values in millions of dollars

Spindler left Apple after it reported a loss in the first quarter of fiscal year 1996. Amelio then presided over a series of devastating quarterly losses. After taking control of Apple, Jobs delivered the first annual profit since 1995.

Ellen Hancock resigned from Apple the same day as Amelio. In March 1998, she was named president of an Internet startup company called Exodus Communications (www.exodus.com) and became CEO in September later that year.

the wrong products in the wrong quantities, and quality was abysmal. Inventories were high, cash was low, and executives were oblivious to these problems as they protected their fiefdoms and budgets to the detriment of Apple's well being. Amelio laid the groundwork for getting Apple back on its feet by replacing ineffectual executives, hoarding cash, simplifying the product line, releasing the world's fastest laptop and desktop computers, improving quality, spinning off Newton, and establishing a bold new operating system strategy. Nonetheless, after just 523 days in charge, Amelio resigned his positions as chairman and CEO of Apple. The company gave him a one-time lump sum cash payment of $6,731,870, less $1,500,000 as a partial repayment of the balance of a loan, plus 130,960 shares of stock and an additional bonus of $1,000,000. He used part of these proceeds to fund Parkside Group (www.parksidegroup.com), a strategic quality investment firm in San Francisco.

Gil Amelio's Resignation Letter

This is a verbatim copy of Gilbert F. Amelio's resignation letter sent via email to Apple employees everywhere on July 9, 1997:

Today, Apple announced my resignation as Chairman and CEO of Apple Computer effective immediately. I will remain an employee, but not an officer, until September 27, 1997, in order to effect a smooth transition.

I joined Apple on February 2, 1996, following a successful tenure as Chairman, President and CEO of National Semiconductor Corporation. I did so because as a Board member of Apple it had become increasingly clear that the company was entering a period of extreme crisis and the very survival of the company as an independent entity was in question. Someone had to take on the task of trying to bring Apple back to health.

As we came to discover, Apple actually faced five crises from the outset: (1) a shortage of cash and liquidity, (2) poor quality products, (3) a lack of a viable operating system strategy, (4) a corporate culture lacking in accountability and discipline, and (5) fragmentation—trying to do too much and in too many directions. These issues persisted notwithstanding a number of extremely talented contributors. Much of my time at Apple has been about confronting these and other matters. I am very confident that the decisions and actions taken have been the right ones. Today, these problems are either resolved or well on the way to being addressed. Today, Apple has the strongest product line-up in the history of the company. Today, we have an exciting operating system strategy and we are on the eve of announcing Mac OS 8 which has received very favorable reviews during beta testing. Rhapsody, our industrial strength operating system, is close behind and will establish a new paradigm in operating system architecture. Today, we have the strongest management team in recent history. And today, we have a cost structure more in line with achievable revenues.

It has been very difficult, but much has been accomplished in the last 17 months as I believe will become increasingly evident in the months and quarters ahead. Apple's next phase, and remaining challenge, is to follow through flawlessly on the programs we have launched and to rebuild the sales volume. I am confident that the team in place can handle this mission. On a personal note, I look forward to once again being able to spend a little more time with my family.

My time at Apple has been exciting and fulfilling. We have made great progress. It is now time to realize the value made possible by this work for all Apple stakeholders. Thank you for your unwavering support during my time here…it made the demands less formidable. I lovingly leave Apple in your care. Good luck, I'll be cheering from the sidelines!

Respectfully,
Gil

> "Give everyone a free bag of pot every day."
>
> *Former CEO **Gil Amelio**, when asked by Computerworld "If you were going to prescribe a medicine for Apple, what would it be?"*

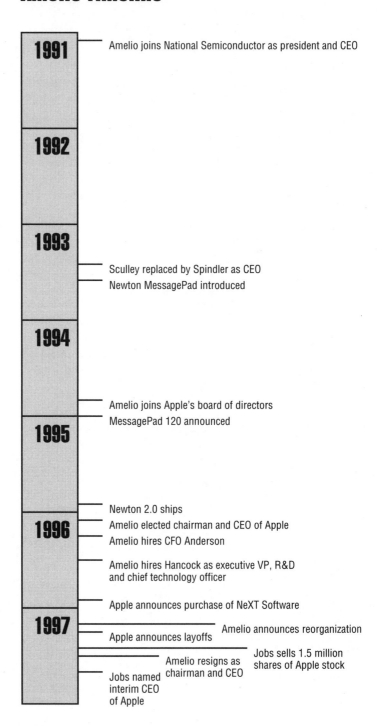

Amelio Timeline

1991 — Amelio joins National Semiconductor as president and CEO

1992

1993 — Sculley replaced by Spindler as CEO
Newton MessagePad introduced

1994

Amelio joins Apple's board of directors
MessagePad 120 announced

1995

Newton 2.0 ships

1996 — Amelio elected chairman and CEO of Apple
Amelio hires CFO Anderson

Amelio hires Hancock as executive VP, R&D
and chief technology officer

Apple announces purchase of NeXT Software

1997 — Amelio announces reorganization
Apple announces layoffs

Jobs sells 1.5 million
shares of Apple stock

Amelio resigns as
chairman and CEO

Jobs named
interim CEO
of Apple

For a while in early 1996, Apple's toll-free technical support number (1-800-SOS-APPL) was just a single misplaced digit away from an X-rated phone sex line. If you dialed the number zero instead of the letter O, you heard the following: "Hi sexy, you've just connected to the hottest cat line in America: 1-800-PUSSIES," before being asked for your credit card information.

The Copland Crisis

Even before the Mac celebrated its tenth anniversary in 1994, it was clear that its operating system was in need of a major overhaul if it was to remain ahead of Windows in terms of functionality, stability, and ease-of-use. That it continued to work so well a decade after its creation was testimony to its original elegance and the hard work of Apple's engineers in adding features without sacrificing backward compatibility. But there's just so much you can pile onto an old foundation before it starts cracking. Apple wanted a next generation OS to beat Windows 95 (code-named Chicago) to market in 1995 that would offer intelligent agents, a customizable interface, and a relational database engine for the Finder. Realizing that Taligent's Pink (see "The Strangest Bedfellow of All," page 45) was unlikely to ever see the light of day, a band of Apple engineers set about creating just such an advanced OS under the code name Copland (at the outset, the project was called V1, Faraday, and Maxwell), to be followed in 1996 by Gershwin (known internally as Edison), adding preemptive multitasking and memory protection. Nobody could have predicted then what a mess Copland would become, nor that a humbled Apple would one day find itself at the mercy of its two greatest visionaries in exile, both promising salvation with their own operating systems.

Copland was first announced publicly in March 1994 at the premiere of the Power Mac line and fell behind schedule almost immediately as managers responded to Microsoft's inroads by heaping new features onto the Copland specification. At the Macworld Expo held in Boston in early August 1995 just weeks before Microsoft unleashed Windows 95, David C. Nagel, senior VP and chief technologist, promised that Copland "would be in users' hands by mid-1996." On November 17, Apple celebrated the first beta release of Copland to some 50 Mac developers. At the time, Apple had announced its intention to ship a final version to consumers in 1996, but as a former engineer then confessed to *Business Week*, "There's no way in hell Copland ships next year. I just hope it ships in 1997." By the beginning

"I still have not met anyone at Apple who was working on Gershwin. Which gave me a clue that it's not soup yet."

Apple's chief technology officer
Ellen Hancock, *at the* MacWEEK *MVB conference on January 6, 1997*

of 1996, Apple had dedicated 500 engineers and a $250 million annual budget to the project. Then on April 26, Nagel bailed on Copland when he signed on as the first president of the new AT&T Laboratories. Apple product manager Peter Lowe promised that, even with Nagel's departure, Copland would ship in January 1997.

Apple had been touting Copland as a revolutionary new operating system that could thrust the company back into the forefront of the computer industry, so customers and developers were understandably disappointed when the project kept slipping. Coupled with the $740 million loss announced April 17, 1996, they began questioning if Apple had the wherewithal to ever get it out the door. At the Worldwide Developers Conference (WWDC) held in San Jose on May 13, after just 100 days as CEO, Gil Amelio announced that rather than ship a monolithic Copland as a single mega-release, pieces of its technology would ship continuously beginning with the January 1997 release of Harmony (System 7.6). That would be followed by a release known as Tempo (Mac OS 8.0) in July, which was supposed to add multitasking and multithreading, two features that improve performance by letting the operating system do multiple tasks at once.

"It's not like wine; it doesn't age very well."

*Apple CEO **Gil Amelio**, on Copland*

By August, Apple's new executive VP, R&D and chief technology officer, Ellen M. Hancock, recognized Copland for the bloated piece of inferior vaporware that it was (it didn't adequately address the Internet and lacked memory protection) and froze all aspects of its development not directly related to the Harmony and Tempo releases. The developer community, which had invested years of effort working on Copland and had stuck by Apple through tough times, freaked. Amelio promised to announce Apple's revised OS strategy at the upcoming Macworld Expo in San Francisco on January 7, 1997.

Apple executives began a frantic scramble to locate a technology partner. One of the first places they turned to was Be (www.be.com), a small Menlo Park, California, company started by Jean-Louis Gassée after he resigned as president of Apple Products on September 30, 1990. Gassée had tried to sell Be to Apple's then-CEO Michael Spindler in 1995. "I told Mike that Copland might develop a flat tire on the road to greatness and they might want to buy some insurance," claims Gassée.

As predicted, Copland started bogging down, and the nimble Be began generating very favorable press. On October 3, 1995, Be introduced the BeBox, a computer powered by two 66MHz PowerPC 603 processors and up to 256MB of RAM. It boasted a SCSI II bus, 16-bit CD-quality sound, three PCI slots, four MIDI, four serial ports, and five ISA slots. The BeBox ran a multithreaded, memory-protected, object-oriented, preemptively multitasking operating system. A bare-bones box cost only $1,600, and a moderately configured model would set you back just $3,000. No doubt, the system was impressive, but analysts wondered if Be wasn't making the same mistakes as Steve Jobs' NeXT, which had failed to find a market for its own advanced, proprietary OS and hardware. Gassée begged *Red Herring*, "For God's sake, don't compare us to NeXT. We want to be a better tool for developers, not to be tasteful. We don't cost $10,000. We have a floppy drive. We do not defecate on developers." It was speculated that Gassée never really wanted to be in the hardware business and had always hoped to one day sell the BeOS back to Apple for a tidy profit. Now it looked like that dream might become a reality.

In August 1996, Gassée presented Apple with seven different ways of using Be's technology. During her stint at IBM, Hancock saw the effect that Microsoft's OS licensing agreements had on Big Blue and insisted that Apple was only interested in buying Be outright, not licensing any of its technology. If Apple wanted to buy Be, that was fine by

Like NeXT, Be started off making its own proprietary hardware, but the real value of both firms was in their operating systems.

Although the BeOS excelled at many things, Apple felt it was missing several crucial features and would require considerable work to bring it up to Apple's standards.

Be CEO Jean-Louis Gassée knew he had Apple in a tight spot, but he asked for too much.

Gassée, but he overplayed his hand. In October, Gassée flew to Kauai, Hawaii, for a two-hour meeting with Amelio, who was giving a speech to Apple's Asia-Pacific sales force. Gassée proposed returning to Apple with his 50-person Be team. He would report to Hancock but wanted to oversee work on all future operating systems. While Gassée offered to work for one dollar a year, his backers demanded 15 percent of Apple and a seat on Apple's board of directors. Apple's due diligence placed the value of Be at about $50 million and in early November it responded with a cash bid "well south of $100 million," according to Gassée. Be felt that Apple desperately needed its technology and Gassée's expertise. Apple noted that only $20 million had been invested in Be so far, and its offer represented a windfall, especially in light of the fact that the BeOS still needed three years of additional expensive development before it could ship (it didn't have any printer drivers, didn't support file sharing, wasn't available in languages other than English, and didn't run existing Mac applications). Direct talks between Amelio and Gassée broke down over price just after the Fall Comdex trade show, when Apple offered $125 million. Be's investors were said to be holding out for no less than $200 million, a figure Amelio considered "outrageous."

> **"I've got them by the balls, and I'm going to squeeze until it hurts."**
> *Be CEO **Jean-Louis Gassée**, describing his negotiating tactics*

Apple was committed to revealing its OS strategy in January 1997, so Gassée knew Apple didn't have the luxury of time. One person close to the negotiations claims that Gassée quipped, "A man in the desert doesn't bargain on the price of water." To increase the pressure on Apple, Be signed up the preeminent Mac clone maker Power Computing (see "The Clone Quandary," page 193) as a licensee for its BeOS, and Gassée intentionally leaked progress of the negotiations to the press, which infuriated Apple executives.

With Be playing hard to get, Apple decided to play hardball and began investigating other options. Hancock ordered her staff to consider

Microsoft's Windows NT, Sun Microsystems' Solaris, and even the ill-fated Taligent, which Apple had handed off to partner IBM in December 1995. Hancock was partial to Unix-based Solaris, while COO Marco Landi preferred cutting a deal for Windows NT. To hedge her bets and assuage egos, on November 15, Hancock authorized Copland engineers to devise a plan to salvage their work by releasing a less-ambitious version.

Steve Jobs says he initially contacted Apple simply to warn it against buying Be, but he soon had Apple interested in NeXT.

Just before Thanksgiving, Steve Jobs called Amelio to discuss Apple's OS strategy, offer his advice, and urge him to steer clear of Be; he thought its software was wrong for Apple. On November 25, a mid-level manager at NeXT, Garrett L. Rice, contacted Hancock to discuss licensing the company's OPENSTEP operating system. Two days later, a couple of Apple engineers and a manager were meeting with some NeXT managers to see what they had to offer. OPENSTEP was technically elegant but had failed to make much of a dent in the market. Jobs had hired Goldman, Sachs & Company to take NeXT public earlier in the year, but the IPO never got off the ground since the firm's only profit came in 1994 when it earned $1.03 million on revenues of $49.6 million. Now it looked like maybe he could sell NeXT after all, to none other than the company he founded 20 years prior.

On December 2, Jobs met with Amelio, Hancock, and Douglas S. Solomon (senior VP of strategic planning and corporate development), in an eigth floor conference room next door to Amelio's office. It was the first time he had set foot on Apple's Cupertino campus since leaving in 1985. Jobs pitched NeXT as Apple's only hope at getting its OS back on track. It was a radical departure from the Copland project, but OPENSTEP was a proven technology, unlike BeOS. Apparently Jobs' reality distortion field was set to stun that day, because two days later Hancock informed Apple's board that they were seriously considering buying NeXT. On December 9 and 10, teams from NeXT and Be separately conferred with eight of Apple's senior managers,

In the late 1980s, Hancock's former employer, IBM, paid NeXT a reported $50 million for access to its technology but ultimately did nothing with it.

including Amelio, in a technology shootout at the upstairs meeting room of the Garden Court Hotel in Palo Alto.

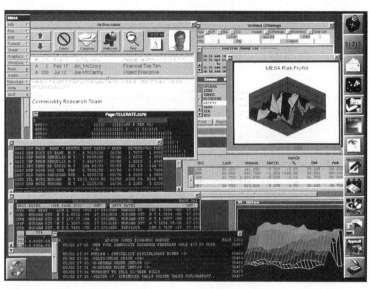

Jobs assured Apple that, although his OPENSTEP had been on the market for years and had failed to gain widespread acceptance, it was still ahead of its time.

Avadis "Avie" Tevanian Jr., Ph.D, NeXT's VP of engineering, gave the OPENSTEP demonstration, and Jobs boasted that their OS was still five to seven years ahead of its time and perfectly suited to Internet and multimedia creation, two of the Mac's few remaining strongholds. He turned over NeXT's financial papers, which showed that NeXT suffered net losses of nearly $50 million from 1993 through mid-1996, according to *The Wall Street Journal*. Privately, Jobs asked Amelio if he could be on the board of directors, but the board voted down that idea and Amelio instead asked him to stay on as an advisor. Gassée miscalculated, thinking that Be had the deal already wrapped up and that this meeting was a mere formality. He had nothing new to present to the Apple contingent, and they resented it.

> "The reality is that we live with System 7. Despite it being tarred and feathered, it will be around in some form for 10 years."
>
> **Gil Amelio**, *in a* San Francisco Chronicle *interview conducted just days before Apple bought NeXT*

On December 20, Apple announced its intention to purchase NeXT Software in a friendly acquisition. When the deal went through on February 4, 1997, the total purchase price, including the fair value of the net liabilities assumed, was $427 million, which comprised $319 million in cash, 1.5 million shares of Apple stock (valued at $25 million), options on 1.9 million shares (valued at $16 million), cash payments of $56 million to the NeXT debtholders, cash payments of $9 million for closing and related costs, and $2 million of net liabilities assumed. As the largest shareholder of NeXT (he owned 45 percent),

Jobs personally pocketed $100 million in cash and all 1.5 million shares of Apple stock, which he agreed not to sell for at least six months. All NeXT products, services, and technology research became part of Apple. Amelio now admits that Apple overpaid for NeXT, but it had little choice given the dire straits the company was in at the time.

Amelio told the world, "The next chapter in Apple's history begins today" with the merger of Apple and NeXT. In explaining the choice, Amelio wrote, "As we looked at various partners for our operating system development, we discovered that Apple and NeXT had surprisingly complementary products, technologies, and services. In fact, the more we looked at the two companies, the more we realized that we each were strong where the other faced challenges, and in many ways we filled in the blanks in each other's strategies. For example, Apple needed a truly modern operating system and NeXT had an exceptional operating system with modern services and APIs. At the same time, NeXT needed a high-volume installed base and Apple—one of the world's largest personal computer manufacturers—has sold more than 26 million Macintosh systems."

In a statement released the night Apple purchased NeXT, Jobs wrote, "Much of the industry has lived off the Macintosh for over ten years now, slowly copying the Mac's revolutionary user interface. Now the time has come for new innovation, and where better than Apple for this to spring from? Who else has consistently led this industry—first with the Apple II, then the Macintosh and LaserWriter? With this merger, the advanced software from NeXT will be married with Apple's very high-volume hardware platforms and marketing channels to create another breakthrough, leapfrogging existing platforms, and fueling Apple and the industry copy cats for the next ten years and beyond. I still have very deep feelings for Apple, and it gives me great joy to play a role in architecting Apple's future."

After the fanfare surrounding the acquisition of NeXT, Apple was surprisingly quiet about its plans for Rhapsody, the name it gave to its new NeXT-based high-end operating system. Instead of betting everything on Rhapsody, the plan called for a dual-OS strategy, with the venerable Mac OS aimed at the consumer desktop market and Rhapsody targeted at servers and enterprises, just as Microsoft has segmented the markets for Windows 98 and NT. Apple successfully released several Mac OS upgrades containing technologies originally developed for Copland, such as the multithreaded Finder and Appearance Manager that shipped in Mac OS 8. Apple was following a plan to continue improving the old warhorse as long as possible, using the periodic upgrades to fuel cash flow.

"We choose Plan A instead of Plan Be."

Gil Amelio, *taking a potshot at Gassée's spurned BeOS*

This early developer release of Rhapsody may look a lot like the old familiar Mac OS, but underneath the hood it's powered by the object-oriented OPENSTEP.

As for Rhapsody, Apple seeded outside programmers with Rhapsody Developer Release for Power Macintosh on October 13, 1997 and followed that up a month later with the Mac OS compatibility environment, code-named Blue Box. Developer release versions of Rhapsody for PC Compatibles and the advanced cross-platform development environment, Yellow Box for Windows, were also delivered to Apple developers.

On May 11, 1998, at Apple's WWDC, Jobs outlined a revised operating system software strategy for Apple that included shipping Mac OS 8.5 (code-named Allegro) and the first customer release of Rhapsody in the third quarter of 1998. Over the next few years, components from both products will transform into Mac OS X (ten), a new advanced version of the Mac OS that is scheduled to be available to developers in early 1999 and ship in the fall of 1999. Apple says that Mac OS X will feature preemptive multitasking, memory protection, and advanced virtual memory, all things Copland was originally intended to deliver. Mac OS X is designed to offer one thing Copland never promised: the ability to run almost all current Mac applications unaltered, ensuring a smooth transition to the operating system for both developers and customers.

Mac OS Timeline

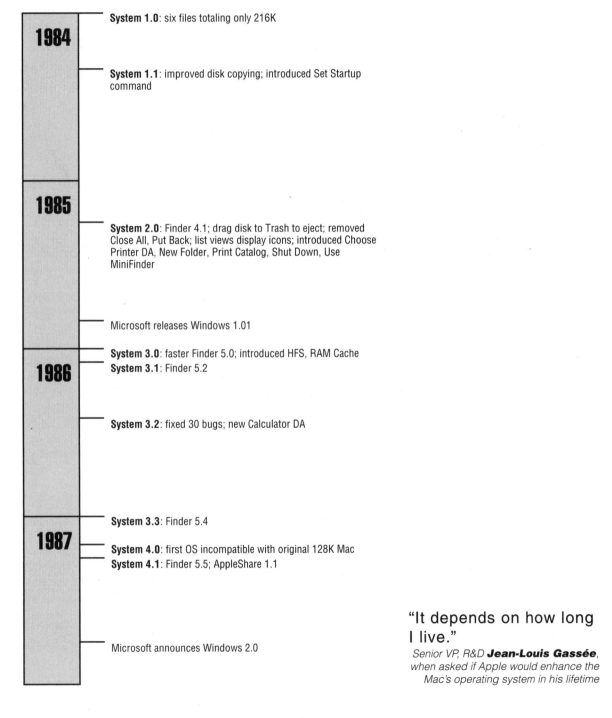

1984

System 1.0: six files totaling only 216K

System 1.1: improved disk copying; introduced Set Startup command

1985

System 2.0: Finder 4.1; drag disk to Trash to eject; removed Close All, Put Back; list views display icons; introduced Choose Printer DA, New Folder, Print Catalog, Shut Down, Use MiniFinder

Microsoft releases Windows 1.01

System 3.0: faster Finder 5.0; introduced HFS, RAM Cache
System 3.1: Finder 5.2

1986

System 3.2: fixed 30 bugs; new Calculator DA

System 3.3: Finder 5.4

1987

System 4.0: first OS incompatible with original 128K Mac
System 4.1: Finder 5.5; AppleShare 1.1

Microsoft announces Windows 2.0

"It depends on how long
I live."
*Senior VP, R&D **Jean-Louis Gassée**,*
when asked if Apple would enhance the
Mac's operating system in his lifetime

Mac OS Timeline (continued)

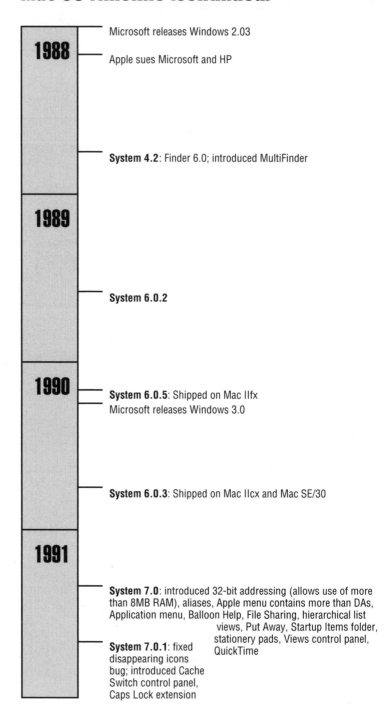

1988

Microsoft releases Windows 2.03

Apple sues Microsoft and HP

System 4.2: Finder 6.0; introduced MultiFinder

1989

System 6.0.2

1990

System 6.0.5: Shipped on Mac IIfx
Microsoft releases Windows 3.0

System 6.0.3: Shipped on Mac IIcx and Mac SE/30

1991

System 7.0: introduced 32-bit addressing (allows use of more than 8MB RAM), aliases, Apple menu contains more than DAs, Application menu, Balloon Help, File Sharing, hierarchical list views, Put Away, Startup Items folder, stationery pads, Views control panel, QuickTime

System 7.0.1: fixed disappearing icons bug; introduced Cache Switch control panel, Caps Lock extension

System 7 came with so much stuff that it was the first Mac OS to require a hard disk drive for installation.

Mac OS Timeline (continued)

1992

Microsoft releases Windows 3.1

System 7.1: introduced Date & Time control panel, enablers, Fonts folder, Numbers control panel, WorldScript

By August 4, 1992, System 7 was in use on more than 4 million Macs, nearly 50 percent of the total installed base.

1993

Microsoft releases Windows NT 3.1

System 7.1 Pro (System 7.1.1): introduced AppleScript, PowerTalk

1994

System 7.1.2: introduced Modern Memory Manager for Power Macs

System 7.1.3: introduced Control Strip for PowerBook 500

System 7.5: introduced Apple Guide, Apple Menu Options, drag and drop, menu clock, QuickDraw GX, WindowShade; bundled Mac Easy Open, PC Exchange

1995

System 7.5.1 (System 7.5 Update 1.0): fixed bugs; minor updates

Microsoft releases Windows 95

System 7.5.2: for new PowerBooks and PCI-based Power Macs; introduced Open Transport; increased max. volume to 2 terabytes

Macintosh
System 7.5

It's powerful, it's easy to use–it's the new operating system for your Macintosh.

Several "new" features in System 7.5, such as the menu clock and WindowShade, were merely revamped freeware items.

Mac OS Timeline (continued)

After an extremely limited release, System 7.5.4 was deemed too buggy and quickly replaced by System 7.5.5.

System 7.6 was the first Mac OS to require a 68030 processor or better.

Apple sold 1.2 million copies of Mac OS 8 in its first two weeks of availability and 3 million within six months.

Several Copland features, including the platinum appearance, tabbed windows, and multitasking Finder shown here in an early Copland screen shot, survived in Mac OS 8.

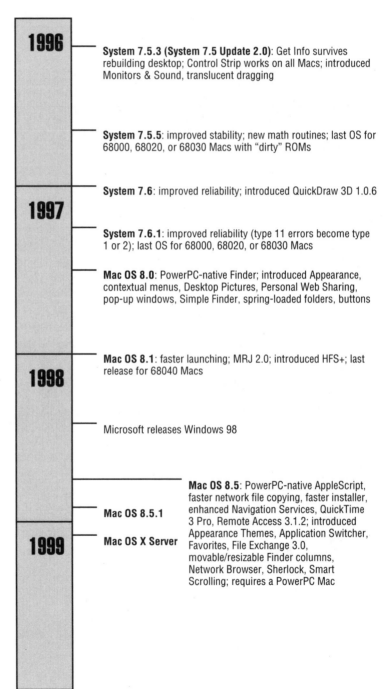

1996

System 7.5.3 (System 7.5 Update 2.0): Get Info survives rebuilding desktop; Control Strip works on all Macs; introduced Monitors & Sound, translucent dragging

System 7.5.5: improved stability; new math routines; last OS for 68000, 68020, or 68030 Macs with "dirty" ROMs

1997

System 7.6: improved reliability; introduced QuickDraw 3D 1.0.6

System 7.6.1: improved reliability (type 11 errors become type 1 or 2); last OS for 68000, 68020, or 68030 Macs

Mac OS 8.0: PowerPC-native Finder; introduced Appearance, contextual menus, Desktop Pictures, Personal Web Sharing, pop-up windows, Simple Finder, spring-loaded folders, buttons

1998

Mac OS 8.1: faster launching; MRJ 2.0; introduced HFS+; last release for 68040 Macs

Microsoft releases Windows 98

Mac OS 8.5.1

1999

Mac OS X Server

Mac OS 8.5: PowerPC-native AppleScript, faster network file copying, faster installer, enhanced Navigation Services, QuickTime 3 Pro, Remote Access 3.1.2; introduced Appearance Themes, Application Switcher, Favorites, File Exchange 3.0, movable/resizable Finder columns, Network Browser, Sherlock, Smart Scrolling; requires a PowerPC Mac

Happily Ever Apple?

After demanding Gilbert F. Amelio resign as CEO and chairman on July 5, 1997, Apple's board turned to part-time advisor Steve Jobs and asked him to take over as CEO. "I thought about it, but decided it wasn't what I wanted to do with my life," Jobs later revealed. "I declined, but agreed to step up my involvement with Apple for up to 90 days, helping them until they hire a new CEO." The board then asked Jobs to be chairman, which he also refused to accept. "I agreed to be a board member, and that's all I can give. I have another life now." Industry watchers felt Apple would have a tough time filling the vacant CEO position as long as Jobs remained on the board of directors, and they were right.

Steve Jobs refused to accept the board's request to take Gil Amelio's place as CEO and chairman of Apple, but he was happy to run the place for the time being.

Until Apple could find a permanent CEO, Jobs was the company's de facto leader. As he saw it, there was a ton of work to do. "It's like turning a big tanker. There were a lot of lousy deals that we're undoing," said Jobs. To boost morale, Jobs recommended the board reprice employee stock options to $13.25 so that they would be above water. When the directors resisted, he urged them to resign. On July 25, Delano E. Lewis, president and CEO of National Public Radio, did just that, citing pressing time demands at NPR. Apparently he felt it was better to jump than be pushed.

On August 6, at the Macworld Expo in Boston, Jobs announced some shocking news. First, Apple's board underwent a wholesale

> "Apple desperately needs a great day-to-day manager, visionary, leader and politician. The only person who's qualified to run this company was crucified 2,000 years ago."
>
> California Technology Stock Letter editor **Michael Murphy**

> "Right now the job is so difficult, it would require a bisexual, blond Japanese who is 25 years old and has 15 years' experience!"
>
> Be CEO **Jean-Louis Gassée**, describing the ideal CEO candidate and demonstrating why he's the most quotable executive in Silicon Valley

> "Apple is a company that still has opportunity written all over it. But you'd need to recruit God to get it done."
>
> Western Digital CEO **Charles Haggerty**

"If I were running Apple, I would milk the Macintosh for all it's worth … and get busy on the next great thing. The PC wars are over. Done. Microsoft won a long time ago."

Steve Jobs, *in a February 1996* Fortune *interview*

"Thank you for your support of this company. I think the world's a better place for it."

Steve Jobs, *to Bill Gates*

Almost immediately upon assuming control of Apple, Amelio had tried to patch up relations with Microsoft. One stumbling block was Apple's insistence that Windows 95 violated some of its patent rights, despite having lost its look-and-feel lawsuit on August 24, 1993. The two firms attempted to put that dispute behind them with a settlement that would allow them to go from combatants to collaborators, but Gates refused to grant Amelio the one concession he desperately wanted: a commitment to develop Microsoft Office for Rhapsody.

reorganization. Gone were all but two former directors: Gareth C. Chang (president of Hughes International) and Edgar S. Woolard, Jr. (retired chairman of E.I. DuPont de Nemours & Company), who had been instrumental in removing Amelio. Resigning from the board were Bernard Goldstein, Katherine M. Hudson, and Mike Markkula. Throughout Apple's history, the only constant had been Markkula. At various times Markkula held the positions of president, chairman, and CEO, and even though he shunned the spotlight, behind the scenes he orchestrated the ouster of every Apple leader: Mike Scott, Steve Jobs, John Sculley, Mike Spindler, and Gil Amelio. Now it was Markkula's time to go, along with most of the rest of the board that had sat back and dithered as Apple withered on the vine. Jobs hand-picked the new board members: William V. Campbell (president and CEO of Intuit), Lawrence J. Ellison (chairman and CEO of Oracle), and Jerome B. York (vice chairman of Tracinda Corporation and former CFO of IBM and Chrysler). The new board decided not to name a chairman until a new CEO was selected, but clearly Jobs was now firmly in control of Apple. Less than two years before, Jobs and Ellison considered a hostile takeover of Apple, and now they were running the show. Best of all, instead of having to spend billions, Apple had actually paid Jobs millions to return by buying out NeXT Software.

Microsoft More shocking than the board shakeup was the announcement that Apple had entered into patent cross-licensing and technology agreements with Microsoft. The finished agreement was faxed from Seattle to Boston just three hours before Jobs announced it to the public. For its part, Microsoft agreed to continue making Mac versions of its Microsoft Office and Internet Explorer products for five years. In turn, Apple would bundle Internet Explorer with the Mac OS as the default browser. In addition to giving its word to continue development for the Mac, Microsoft gave Apple an undisclosed amount (rumored to be $100 million) to settle patent infringement claims and paid $150 million for 150,000 shares of Apple series A, non-voting, convertible preferred stock that could not be sold for at least three years. Apple's board of directors can grant a dividend of $30 for each share of the preferred stock, payable in common stock.

When Bill Gates' face appeared on screen during the keynote address, the crowd erupted in boos and hisses. Jobs berated the crowd for its childish behavior, saying that "Apple has to move beyond the point of view that for Apple to win, Microsoft has to lose." Apparently Wall Street agreed. Within hours of the announcement, Apple's stock jumped 33 percent to $26.31. When the euphoria died down weeks

When the smiling face of Bill Gates appeared before them during the keynote at the Macworld Expo in Boston (left), many in the crowd voiced their displeasure by booing, as if the Microsoft CEO personified Big Brother from the famous *1984* commercial.

later, however, the stock settled back to its pre-announcement level. Microsoft's $150 million investment in Apple was a pittance for a company with $9.1 billion in cash, but it was a wonderful public relations stunt. It showed that the world's largest software publisher was committed to the Macintosh platform, making it much safer to consider buying a Mac. Of course Microsoft is nothing if not shrewd. It earns roughly $300 million a year from Mac sales alone, so it is in its best interest to keep that market alive. In addition, it's likely that the move was calculated to make Microsoft look good in the eyes of the Department of Justice, which was in the midst of an investigation into alleged anti-competitive practices at Microsoft.

Chiat/Day's ad promoted the speed of Apple's G3 by likening Intel's Pentium II to a snail.

Following the Macworld news, Apple announced on August 8 that it had canned its long-time advertising agency, BBDO, and awarded its account to Omnicom Group's TBWA Chiat/Day (www.tbwachiat.com), the firm responsible for the *1984* commercial that introduced the Mac (see "The Greatest Commercial That Almost Never Aired," page 87). Chiat/Day quickly devised Apple's *Think Different* campaign, originally derided by critics as a soft lifestyle campaign. It soon turned into a hard-hitting product benefit series with ads such as *Snail* and *Toasted Bunny*, which drove home the point that the Mac's G3 processors were up to twice as fast as Intel's Pentiums.

On May 27, 1986, after Apple shifted its $50 million account from Chiat/Day to Batten, Barton, Durstine & Osborne (BBDO)—John Sculley's advertising agency of choice at Pepsi—the deposed Steve Jobs took out a full-page ad in *The Wall Street Journal*'s western edition that read, "Congratulations, Chiat/Day. Seriously. Congratulations on seven years of consistently outstanding work. You helped build Apple and were an integral part of the marketing team. You took risks, sometimes failed, never compromised. The personal computer industry is now being handed over from the 'builders' to the 'caretakers;' that is, from the individuals who created and grew a multi-billion dollar American industry to those who will maintain the industry as it is and work to achieve marginal future growth. It is inevitable that in this turbulent transition many faces will change. You created some truly great work—the kind that gives advertising a good name. The kind people will remember for years. The kind people remain proud to have been associated with. I'm expecting some new, 'insanely great' advertising from you soon. Because I can guarantee you: there is life after Apple. Thanks for the memories." The ad copy was signed Steven P. Jobs.

> "Apple has some tremendous assets, but I believe without some attention, the company could, could, could ... I'm searching for the right word—could, could die."
>
> ***Steve Jobs***

The board reorganization and Microsoft deals weren't the only topics discussed at Macworld Expo that August. Clone maker Power Computing made a public stink about Apple's new combative stance toward Mac OS licensees (see "The Clone Quandary," page 193). Jobs had never been a fan of cloning—at the Worldwide Developers Conference the previous May, he referred to cloners as "leeches"—so it came as little surprise when Apple announced on September 2 that it would acquire Power Computing's core assets and essentially put an end to the licensing program at Apple. The move was immensely unpopular in the Mac community, but the board of directors had no qualms; it anointed Jobs interim CEO on September 16.

One of the first actions Jobs had to take as interim CEO was to announce a $161 million loss for the fourth fiscal quarter ended September 26, which included a $75 million writeoff related to the purchase of the Mac OS license from Power Computing. For the fiscal year, revenues were down 28 percent to $7.1 billion. "The July introduction of Mac OS 8 has resulted in record sales, covering two million seats to date," stated CFO Fred Anderson. "Our U.S. education business contributed over half a billion dollars in revenues during the quarter, and we saw sequential improvement in both business and consumer sales in the U.S. However, we were disappointed by sluggish demand outside the U.S., particularly in Japan. We remain focused on our primary goal of returning Apple to sustainable profitability. Our goal for fiscal 1998 is to continue to reduce Apple's break-even point through a combination of further expense reductions and gross margin improvements."

Apple's "store within a store" concept boosted Mac sales significantly at CompUSA.

To help prop up flagging sales, on November 4, Apple announced it had struck a deal with CompUSA (www.compusa.com), one of the nation's leading computer resellers, to launch a new "store within a store" featuring Macintosh products in every one of its 148 retail locations. Then on November 10, Apple unveiled high-end Power Mac computers based on the third-generation PowerPC G3 processor from IBM and Motorola, and it simultaneously opened The Apple Store (www.apple.com/store), an Internet site powered by former NeXT product WebObjects, where customers could order customized Macs direct from Apple. Both the CompUSA "store within a store" and The Apple Store programs were immediate successes. The Apple Store generated over $12 million of orders in its first 30 days of operation, and in those CompUSA locations featuring an Apple "store within a store," Apple claims Mac sales soared from 3 percent of CompUSA's overall PC business to 14 percent.

So successful was the experiment that on February 2, 1998, Apple made CompUSA its exclusive national retailer.

As 1997 wound to a close, Apple was still searching for a CEO. Michael Murdock—a 36-year-old Burlingame, California-based computer consultant and former Pixar employee—had been campaigning for Apple's top spot in a series of emails sent to the executive staff. Two days before Christmas, Jobs and board member Ellison finally replied to Murdock, in jest agreeing to let him take over. "OK. You can have the job," Ellison wrote first. Then came Jobs' email: "Yep, Mike, it's all yours. When can you start?" Murdock answered that he would report for duty on January 5, 1998, prompting Jobs to get serious and reply, "Please do not come to Apple. You will be asked to leave, and if you don't, you will be arrested." Jobs and Ellison had sent Murdock the emails as a little joke between billionaires, but they wouldn't be laughing long. A month later an email attributed to Jobs circulated throughout the offices of Pixar, accurately divulging the positions and salaries of Pixar's 400 employees. Jobs denied sending the email, and many at Pixar suspected it was the work of Murdock. For his part, Murdock denied having anything to do with the email.

At the keynote address for the Macworld Expo held in San Francisco on January 6, 1998, Apple showed off Mac OS 8.1 and QuickTime 3.0, Microsoft announced Office 98, and Jobs surprised the audience by casually mentioning at the very end of his speech that Apple expected to report a profit for the first fiscal quarter of 1998. "We are thrilled that our new plans are beginning to work," gushed Jobs. "While there is still lots of work to do, Apple is clearly coming back as a major player." When the final numbers were tallied, Apple managed to earn $47 million on the strength of selling 133,000 G3-based Power Macintosh systems with increased gross margins.

 Just as Apple was starting to garner some positive press with news of a potential turnaround, it made a pair of moves that left many scratching their heads trying to figure out its true motives. First, on January 27, Apple laid off 300 Claris employees when it renamed its profitable software subsidiary FileMaker, Inc. to focus exclusively on the database package of the same name. Most other Claris products, including the tremendously popular ClarisWorks, were folded back into Apple, but the company made no real commitment to the continued development of any Claris titles. Exactly a month later, Apple announced that it was discontinuing further development of the Newton operating system and Newton

"We've reviewed the road map of new products and axed more than 70 percent of them, keeping the 30 percent that were gems. The product teams at Apple are very excited. There's so much low-hanging fruit, it's easy to turn around."

Steve Jobs

OS-based products, including the well-received MessagePad 2100 and eMate 300. The move came less than six months after Jobs had nixed the spin-off of Newton Inc. as an independent company and brought it back inside Apple (see "The Fallen Apple," page 143). "This decision is consistent with our strategy to focus all of our software development resources on extending the Macintosh operating system," said Jobs. "To realize our ambitious plans we must focus all of our efforts in one direction."

> "Some people worry about the word 'interim,' but they weren't worried about the last CEO, and he wasn't interim."
>
> **Steve Jobs**

> "Nobody has tried to swallow us since I've been here. I think they are afraid how we would taste."
>
> **Steve Jobs**, *discussing Apple as an acquisition target during the shareholders meeting on April 22, 1998*

Although industry observers had a hard time figuring out why Apple closed down Claris and Newton, they rejoiced on April 15 when Apple announced a $55 million profit, its second quarterly profit in a row. Revenues remained down, but gross margins had increased to 25 percent. "Apple had a great quarter, no question about it," said Jobs. "We are very pleased with the strong demand for our Power Macintosh G3 computers, which accounted for 51 percent of all units sold." So pleased were Apple's directors that they asked Jobs to drop the interim label from his title and offered him options for up to six million shares of common stock plus a million shares of restricted stock. Jobs declined, insisting, "This is not about money. That's not why I'm there. I have more money than I've ever wanted in my life." What, then, does Jobs really want? In a meeting with some prospective engineers in the fall of 1997, Jobs was asked how long he planned to stay at Apple, to which he replied, "I'm either going to be CEO or chairman of the company forever. I turned Apple over to a bozo once." When asked the same question in mid-1998, Jobs replied, "Several months ago, I woke up and decided that … I will do as best as I can for as long as I can and not worry about what other people think. My focus is on my family, Apple, and Pixar, in that order."

On July 15, 1998, Apple reported its third consecutive profitable quarter under Jobs. Even though sales slipped 19 percent, Apple earned $101 million for the quarter, thanks to continued strong demand for the profitable Power Mac G3 series (750,000 sold since introduction), the $33 million it earned by selling some of its stake in chip manufacturer ARM Holdings Plc on April 16, and despite a $7 million charge to buy digital video technology from Macromedia. "Steve [Jobs] is like the cleanup hitter who drove in the men that Gil [Amelio] put on base for him," said financial analyst Lou Mazzucchelli Jr. of Gerard Klauer Mattison & Co. Inc. "Some of what you see—the operational cuts and efficiency in Apple's organization—was started under Gil's watch and carried out by [CFO] Fred Anderson."

One project for which Jobs can take full credit is the iMac. Begun almost immediately upon his return to power at Apple, the iMac project was a throw-back to the creation of the original Mac. Jobs insisted on doing something radically different, with a small group of dedicated, talented employees, in almost total secrecy. So successful was Jobs at keeping a lid on the project that when the iMac was unveiled along with a revised PowerBook G3 series (code-named Wall Street) on May 6, 1998—during a press event held in the same auditorium where the original Mac was unveiled in 1984—most Apple employees had never even heard of the new computer. That would soon change.

Apple took its advertising slogan "Think Different" to heart with the radical industrial design of the iMac, which marked the firm's reentry into the consumer marketplace.

According to Apple, the iMac represents "the Internet-age computer for the rest of us," but initially critics couldn't see past the curious decision to leave out a floppy drive. What they failed to notice was all the other stuff Apple had crammed into that stunning translucent Bondi blue (named after a famous beach in Sydney, Australia) plastic case: 233MHz PowerPC G3, 32MB of RAM, 15" display, 4GB hard drive, 24X CD-ROM drive, V.90 modem, and 10/100Base-T Ethernet. Essentially Apple included everything a consumer could possibly need, all for just $1,299, and the marketplace responded appropriately. Between the time Apple announced the iMac and actually released it on August 15, the company booked an unprecedented 150,000 orders. In the first six weeks of availability in North America, Japan, and Europe, Apple sold a total of 278,000 iMacs, making it the fastest-selling Macintosh model ever. Almost as important as the sheer number of iMacs being sold was who bought the computers. In exit

> "The launch of the iMac was the largest-selling day of any given computer we've ever had."
>
> *CompUSA executive VP of merchandising* **Larry Mondry**

> "We designed iMac to deliver the things consumers care about most—the excitement of the Internet and the simplicity of the Mac. iMac is next year's computer for $1,299, not last year's computer for $999."
>
> **Steve Jobs**

> "Sometimes what Apple is doing may have an electrifying effect on the rest of us. [The iMac] is nothing we couldn't have done, but Apple went ahead and did it."
>
> *Intel chairman* **Andrew Grove**

interviews of 1,900 iMac buyers conducted by the research firm Audits and Surveys, it was revealed that 29.4 percent had never owned a computer before, and 12.5 percent previously owned a Wintel clone but not a Macintosh. Of the remaining iMac buyers, roughly half were replacing an old Mac, and half intended to keep their old Mac in addition to the new iMac. That meant that approximately 70 percent of all iMac sales were adding to the total number of Macs in use. Research firm IDC, in Framingham, Massachusetts, projected that as many as 800,000 iMacs would be sold by the end of 1998, helping Apple double its worldwide market share to 6 percent.

As it turns out, Apple indeed sold 800,000 iMacs in 1998, a rate of one iMac sold "every 15 seconds of every minute of every hour of every day of every week," according to Steve Jobs, iCEO.

On October 14, 1998, Apple made the unusual move of announcing its annual financial results in the middle of the day, rather than wait until after the stock market had closed, as is the customary practice. In addition to demonstrating Mac OS 8.5 (code-named Allegro), which would be released three days later, and announcing that Apple was broadening its national distribution to include 300 Best Buy stores across the United States, Jobs delivered the good news the Mac faithful had gathered to hear. With demand running high for its entire product line (unit shipments rose dramatically to 834,000), Jobs announced a $106 million profit on revenues of $1.56 billion for the company's fiscal fourth quarter, which ended September 30, marking the company's fourth straight profitable quarter. Under Jobs' control, Apple recorded an annual profit of $309 million—not much compared to the $1.6 billion in losses incurred under Amelio's 17 months at the helm, but it represented Apple's first profitable year since Spindler ran the ship aground in 1995.

And the new year brought even more new good news from Cupertino. Apple received critical acclaim for its introduction of iMacs in five different colors and a revised Power Mac G3 minitower at the Macworld Expo in San Francisco on January 5, 1999. The following week, Apple announced a net profit of $152 million on revenues of $1.7 billion and gross margins of 28.2 percent for the fiscal quarter which ended December 26, 1998. Users and analysts alike rejoiced at the fact that profits, revenues, gross margins, and unit growth all increased over the prior year. "Unit growth year-over-year was three to four times higher than the industry average," said Jobs. "In addition, Apple ended the quarter with only two days of inventory, besting industry-leading Dell's seven days of inventory." Furthermore, Apple had a cushion of nearly $2.6 billion in cash and short-term investments.

Whether the company can remain profitable in the long term remains to be seen, but if the past is any guide, you can be sure that Apple's future will be anything but dull.

Bibliography

Amelio, Gil and William L. Simon. *On The Firing Line: My 500 Days At Apple*. New York, NY: Harper Collins Publishers, Inc., 1998.

Butcher, Lee. *Accidental Millionaire: The Rise and Fall of Steve Jobs at Apple Computer*. New York, NY: Paragon House Publishers, 1988.

Cringely, Robert X. *Accidental Empires: How the Boys of Silicon Valley Make Their Millions, Battle Foreign Competition, and Still Can't Get a Date*. Reading, MA: Addison-Wesley Publishing Co., 1992.

Dvorak, John C. *Dvorak Predicts: An Insider's Look at the Computer Industry*. Berkeley, CA: Osborne/McGraw-Hill, 1994.

Freiberger, Paul and Michael Swaine. *Fire in the Valley*. New York, NY: Osborne/McGraw-Hill, 1984.

Gassée, Jean-Louis. *The Third Apple: Personal Computers & the Cultural Revolution*. Orlando, FL: Harcourt Brace Jovanovich, Publishers, 1985.

Goldberg, Adele. *A History of Personal Workstations*. New York, NY: ACM Press, 1988.

Hyman, Michael. *PC Roadkill*. Foster City, CA: IDG Books Worldwide, Inc., 1995.

Kawasaki, Guy. *The Macintosh Way: The Art of Guerrilla Management*. New York: HarperPerennial, 1990.

Kawasaki, Guy. *Selling the Dream: How to Promote Your Product, Company, or Ideas—and Make a Difference—Using Everyday Evangelism*. New York, NY: HarperCollins Publishers, 1991.

Kounalakis, Markos and Doug Menuez. *Defying Gravity: The Making of Newton*. Hillsboro, OR: Beyond Words Publishing, Inc., 1993.

Kunkel, Paul. *AppleDesign: The Work of the Apple Industrial Design Group*. New York, NY: Graphis Inc., 1997.

LeVitus, Bob and Michael Fraase. *Guide to the Macintosh Underground: Mac Culture from the Inside*. Indianapolis, IN: Hayden Books, 1993.

Levy, Steven. *Insanely Great: The Life and Times of Macintosh, The Computer That Changed Everything*. New York, NY: Penguin Books USA Inc., 1994.

Malone, Michael S. *The Big Score*. Garden City, NY: Doubleday & Co., Inc., 1985.

Manes, Stephen and Paul Andrews. *Gates: How Microsoft's Mogul Reinvented an Industry—And Made Himself the Richest Man in America*. New York, NY: Doubleday, 1993.

McGrath, Michael E. *Product Strategy for High-Technology Companies*. Burr Ridge, IL: Irwin Professional Publishing.

Moritz, Michael. *The Little Kingdom: The Private Story of Apple Computer*. New York, NY: William Morrow and Company, Inc., 1984.

Price, Rob. *So Far: The First Ten Years of a Vision*. Cupertino, CA: Apple Computer, Inc., 1987.

Rose, Frank. *West of Eden: The End of Innocence at Apple Computer*. New York, NY: Viking Penguin Inc., 1989.

Sculley, John C. and John A. Byrne. *Odyssey: Pepsi to Apple...A journey of adventure, ideas and the future*. New York, NY: Harper & Row, Publishers, 1987.

Stross, Randall E. *Steve Jobs & the NeXT Big Thing*. New York, NY: Atheneum Macmillan Publishing Co., 1993.

Thygeson, Gordon. *Apple T-Shirts: A Yearbook Of History At Apple Computer*. Scotts Valley, CA: Pomo Publishing, 1998.

Various. *Maclopedia*. Indianapolis, IN: Hayden Books, 1996.

Wallace, James and Jim Erickson. *Hard Drive: Bill Gates and the Making of the Microsoft Empire*. New York, NY: John Wiley & Sons, Inc., 1992.

Young, Jeffrey S. *Steve Jobs: The Journey Is the Reward*. Glenview, IL: Scott, Foresman and Company, 1988.

Index

About the Author

Apple Confidential was written by Owen W. Linzmayer, a San Francisco-based freelance writer who has been covering Apple Computer and its products for industry magazines since 1980. He is the author of four Macintosh-related books, has contributed to every major Mac publication, and currently writes the monthly "Ask Us" column for *MacAddict* magazine.

About the Cover Photographs

The picture of Stephen Gary Wozniak which appears on the front cover was taken in 1995 by Anne Knudsen, who worked for nine years as a staff photographer for the *Los Angeles Herald-Examiner* photographing assignments such as the 1984 Olympics, World Series, Presidential Elections, Academy Awards, Grammys, celebrity portraits, and visiting heads of state. Anne now runs a freelance business photographing people for Silicon Valley clients including Apple, Cisco Systems, Hewlett-Packard, and Silicon Graphics. For additional information, call Anne at (650) 326-2201 or send email to anneknudsen@earthlink.net.

The picture of Steven Paul Jobs which appears on the front cover was taken in 1998 and was provided courtesy of AP/Wide World Photos.

The picture of Jobs and Wozniak which appears on the back cover was taken in 1976 by Woz's mother and was provided courtesy of Margaret Wozniak.